Winner and Waster and its Contexts

Winner and Waster and its Contexts

Chivalry, Law and Economics in
Fourteenth-Century England

† W. Mark Ormrod

D. S. BREWER

© The Estate of W. Mark Ormrod 2021

All Rights Reserved. Except as permitted under current legislation
no part of this work may be photocopied, stored in a retrieval system,
published, performed in public, adapted, broadcast,
transmitted, recorded or reproduced in any form or by any means,
without the prior permission of the copyright owner

The right of W. Mark Ormrod to be identified as
the author of this work has been asserted in accordance with
sections 77 and 78 of the Copyright, Designs and Patents Act 1988

First published 2021
Paperback edition 2024
D. S. Brewer, Cambridge

ISBN 978-1-84384-581-2 (Hardback)

ISBN 978-1-84384-709-0 (Paperback)

D. S. Brewer is an imprint of Boydell & Brewer Ltd
PO Box 9, Woodbridge, Suffolk IP12 3DF, UK
and of Boydell & Brewer Inc.
668 Mount Hope Ave, Rochester, NY 14620–2731, USA
website: www.boydellandbrewer.com

A catalogue record for this book is available
from the British Library

The publisher has no responsibility for the continued existence
or accuracy of URLs for external or third-party internet websites
referred to in this book, and does not guarantee that any content on
such websites is, or will remain, accurate or appropriate

Contents

Acknowledgements		vii
Note on Editions		ix
List of Abbreviations		xi
	Introduction: *Winner and Waster*: A Poem on the Times	1
1	Chivalry and Internationalism: The Garter Feast of 1358 and English Diplomacy during the 1350s and 1360s	15
2	Treason, Public Order and Dispute Settlement: The Statute of Treasons of 1352 and Royal Arbitration	39
3	Landed Society, Conspicuous Consumption and the Political Economy: The Sumptuary Laws of 1363	61
4	The Private and the Public Spheres: The Royal Household and State Finance under Edward III	83
5	Satire, Complaint and Authorship: *Winner and Waster* and the Alliterative Revival of the Fourteenth Century	105
6	*Winner and Waster*: Timeliness and Timelessness	131
	Appendix 1: Timeline, 1337–70	137
	Appendix 2: A Modern English Version of Winner and Waster	139
	Bibliography	157
	Index	185
	Publisher's Note	189

Acknowledgements

This study began life as a set of comments in a research seminar, developed into a potential journal article, and ended up being re-organised in the early stage of my retirement to form a short book. I am grateful to my current and former colleagues in the Centre for Medieval Studies, University of York, and especially to Jeremy Goldberg, Nicholas Havely, Nicola McDonald, Sarah Rees Jones, Felicity Riddy, Craig Taylor and Jocelyn Wogan-Browne, for their encouragement of my efforts at literary history. I owe thanks to the staff of the University Library at York, the British Library at Boston Spa and the National Archives of the United Kingdom at Kew for assistance with my researches. I am also indebted to Michael Bennett and Sebastian Sobecki for reading sections of the book in draft and offering stimulating comments on its contents. The publisher's anonymous reader provided a number of constructive criticisms, including a suggestion for the re-ordering of some of the material, and I have aimed to follow that advice throughout. At Boydell & Brewer, Caroline Palmer, Elizabeth McDonald and the whole team have been a constant source of encouragement, advice and good sense; to all of them, I offer my warm thanks.

Permission to reproduce passages from *Wynnere and Wastoure*, ed. Stephanie Trigg, EETS OS 297 (Oxford, 1990), is granted by the Council of the Early English Text Society. Permission to reproduce passages from *The Complete Harley 2253 Manuscript*, ed. and trans. Susanna Fein with David Raybin and Jan Ziolkowski, 3 vols (Kalamazoo, 2015) and *The Simonie*, ed. James M. Dean (Kalamazoo, 1996), is granted by the editor of the Middle English Texts section of the Teaching Association for Medieval Studies. Permission to reproduce a passage of *Knighton's Chronicle, 1337–1396*, ed. and trans. Geoffrey H. Martin (Oxford, 1995), is granted by Oxford University Press. I express particular thanks to Bella Millett for allowing me, in a great expression of scholarly generosity, to draw extensively on her own online modernised version of *Wynnere and Wastoure*.

W. Mark Ormrod
York, July 2020

Note on Editions

Winner and Waster has been edited a number of times. The default text used here is *Wynnere and Wastoure*, ed. Stephanie Trigg, EETS OS 297 (Oxford, 1990) (hereafter Trigg) (although I render thorns and yoghs in modern orthography). This study also draws on the texts in *A Good Short Debate between Winner and Waster: An Alliterative Poem on Social and Economic Problems in England in the Year 1352, with Modern English Rendering*, ed. Sir Israel Gollancz (London, 1920; repr. Cambridge, 1974) (hereafter Gollancz); 'An Anthology of Medieval Poems and Drama', ed. Thorlac Turville-Petre, in *Medieval Literature: Chaucer and the Alliterative Tradition*, ed. Brian Ford, rev. edn. (Harmondsworth, 1982), 387–602, at 398–415 (hereafter Turville-Petre); and *Wynnere and Wastoure and The Parlement of the Thre Ages*, ed. Warren Ginsberg (Kalamazoo, 1992), 13–42 (hereafter Ginsberg). For other critical editions produced as PhD dissertations and in anthologized editions, see Trigg, p. liii, and 'The Digital Index of Middle English Verse', https://www.dimev.net, DIMEV 4918. In addition to Gollancz's modern English version, see the translation by Bella Millett, 'Winner and Waster: Translation' in 'Wessex Parallel WebTexts', www.soton.ac.uk/~wpwt/trans/winner/wintrans.htm (hereafter Millett).

List of Abbreviations

EETS	Early English Text Society
	OS original series
ELH	*English Literary History*
Ginsberg	Warren Ginsberg (ed.), *Wynnere and Wastoure and The Parlement of the Thre Ages* (Kalamazoo, 1992).
Gollancz	Sir Israel Gollancz (ed. and trans.), *A Good Short Debate between Winner and Waster: An Alliterative Poem on Social and Economic Problems in England in the Year 1352, with Modern English Rendering* (London, 1920; repr. Cambridge, 1974).
Millett	Bella Millett (trans.), 'Winner and Waster: Translation', in 'Wessex Parallel WebTexts', www.soton.ac.uk/~wpwt/trans/winner/wintrans.htm.
PMLA	Publications of the Modern Language Association of America.
PROME	Paul Brand, Seymour Phillips, W. Mark Ormrod, Geoffrey Martin, Chris Given-Wilson, Anne Curry and Rosemary Horrox (eds and trans.), *The Parliament Rolls of Medieval England* (16 vols, Woodbridge, 2005).
SR	*Statutes of the Realm*, ed. A. Luders *et al.* (11 vols, London, 1810–28).
TNA	Kew, The National Archives of the United Kingdom.
Trigg	Stephanie Trigg (ed.), *Wynnere and Wastoure*, EETS OS 297 (Oxford, 1990).
Turville-Petre	Thorlac Turville-Petre (ed.), 'An Anthology of Medieval Poems and Drama', in *Medieval Literature: Chaucer and the Alliterative Tradition*, ed. Brian Ford, rev. edn. (Harmondsworth, 1982), pp. 387–602.
W&W	*Winner and Waster*

Introduction

Winner and Waster: A Poem on the Times

Winner and Waster (*W&W*) is a Middle English poem written, most likely, during the third quarter of the fourteenth century.[1] It survives in a single manuscript, London, British Library Additional MS 31042, one of the two miscellanies of texts made in the mid-fifteenth century by Robert Thornton, a gentleman of East Newton in the North Riding of Yorkshire.[2] The extant text is divided into a prologue and three 'fitts', or sections, divided at suitable points where the performer (assuming it to be a social reading) might refill his wine-cup (lines 216–17, 366–7). Thornton's text of *W&W* is, however, incomplete. The poem breaks off after 503 lines at a hiatus in the manuscript; supposing that the original was longer (and it remains possible that Thornton was also working with an incomplete version), it is unclear what proportion is now lost. The text is also corrupt in places, and the final extant folio is badly damaged; the level of intervention in modern editions has varied greatly and the precise meaning of some passages remains uncertain.

The prologue to the poem represents a general complaint upon the unsettled times, in which the services of artful poets are no longer recognised as they once had been. In the first fitt, the narrator then tells of his journey into 'the West' where, in a delightful woodland setting, he fell asleep and dreamed the dream that follows. The scene is an opening within the woods, surrounded by earthworks. Armed men and others are gathered in the groves to either side, and at the crest of the earthworks sits a pavilion adorned with the imagery of the Order of the Garter. A wild man (sometimes referred to as the first knight) stands nearby, bedecked in the heraldry of King Edward III. The king himself is revealed, seated in state within the pavilion and clothed in fantastic robes which themselves also bear the emblem of the garter. The king calls forth the finest knight (some-

---

[1] For the existing critical editions and translations, see above, p. ix.
[2] John J. Thompson (ed.), *Robert Thornton and the London Thornton Manuscript: British Library MS Additional 31042* (Cambridge, 1987). See also Karen Stern, 'The London Thornton Miscellany: A New Description of BM Addit. MS. 31042', *Scriptorium*, 30 (1976), 26–37, 210–18. For Thornton, see also below, pp. 134–5.

times referred to as the second knight, or herald) in his own entourage and instructs him to go amongst the assembled forces to find out the nature of the quarrel reported there, so that it can be brought to peaceful resolution. This messenger accordingly sets out, and the poem provides an extended account of the various elements that make up the accompanying onlookers, with particular emphasis on the presence of men of religion gathered under the banners of their orders. The first fitt concludes with the messenger's speech commanding the protagonists in the reported quarrel to come forward; when they arrive at the pavilion, the king greets them as long-serving members of his own household.

In the second and third fitts, the two lead characters are introduced as Wynnere and Wastoure, and each makes four extended speeches outlining the faults in the other's way of life – faults that they both see as fundamentally undermining the stability of society. The rubric in the Thornton manuscript describes these speeches as a *refrayte*, or debate, and each man certainly tries to refute the arguments of the other in extended passages that caricature the lifestyle of the opponent. Wynnere represents the careful (but often avaricious) stewardship of resources so as to store up money against an uncertain future. The problem with his approach to wealth, as Wastoure puts it, is that saving is futile: at Wynnere's death, his great stores of money will be scattered and, for his sin of avarice, he will be taken by the Devil as one of his own. Wastoure exemplifies the pleasures and benefits of generosity and, at their extreme, of gluttony and prodigality. Wynnere casts his competitor as heedless of the risks of high expenditure, and unable to understand the fickleness of the world: simply laying on lavish feasts does not guarantee the loyalty of one's friends and followers. The eight speeches contain extended reconstructions of the lifestyle of the opponent: of particular note are Wynnere's second and third speeches, in which he imagines Wastoure first at the ale-house and then at a sumptuous banquet laid on for his followers and friends.

At the end of his fourth speech, Wastoure calls upon the king to draw the debate to a conclusion, since neither argument appears to be holding sway. The judgment is a peculiar one, seemingly designed to reflect the fact that the successful functioning of society requires some elements both of acquisitiveness and of liberality. Wynnere is despatched by the king to Rome to live among the princes of the Church, who are deemed just as rapacious as him. Wastoure, by contrast, is sent to London to sate himself on the pleasures of the city. The existing text ends with a prophetic note in which the regal figure warns Wynnere to hold himself in readiness for the king's return, in order that he might follow the monarch to the 'church of Cologne where the Kings lie': a reference to the shrine of the Three Kings at Cologne Cathedral, which was a major centre of pilgrimage.

The characteristic metre of *W&W* is the so-called alliterative 'long line': a four-stress line, broken halfway by a caesura, in which the first three of the stresses alliterate: thus *aa/ax*.³ Scholars are divided as to whether this metre was already in regular usage before the middle of the fourteenth century or whether it was part of a conscious revival of older forms at a time when English (rather than French) was becoming more widely used in works of imaginative literature. The conventional dating of *W&W*, which sets it as composed in 1352–3, makes it one of the first, if not *the* first, extant poem in this alliterative long-line tradition. The other works of the later fourteenth century that follow the alliterative form, notably *Piers Plowman*, the *Alliterative Morte Arthure*, and the four poems of the so-called *Pearl* (or *Gawain*) Poet – *Pearl*; *Sir Gawain and the Green Knight*; *Cleanness*; and *Patience* – all have a West Midlands provenance, and it has long been posited that alliterative verse (both rhymed and, in the case of *W&W* and others, unrhymed) was a characteristic form of the Midlands, spreading east and north but never gaining popularity in the South of England. It is therefore often argued that alliterative verse was self-consciously 'provincial' and exhibited certain old-fashioned interests and values, in stark comparison with the new forms of 'metropolitan' literature developing in the South, and specifically around the royal court and the London bourgeoisie, in the time of Geoffrey Chaucer.

This is not to deny, however, the sophistication and imaginative reach of the alliterative poets, or indeed of those who heard their work. The four poems associated with the *Pearl* Poet represent a huge range and diversity of influences, particularly *Pearl* itself, which is a veritable *tour de force* of fourteenth-century intellectual thought and artistic practice. In his 1976 survey of medieval dream-poetry, A. C. Spearing pronounced *Pearl* 'one of the greatest single works of medieval English literature'.⁴ The complex world of signs and symbols presented in *Sir Gawain and the Green Knight* has prompted numerous modern interpretations, some frankly bizarre, but all demonstrating the sheer evocative richness of the text. In comparison with the *Pearl* Poet's poems, *W&W* has tended to be neglected by recent generations of critics, their silence indicating a general agreement that the poem falls into a second, lesser league of texts, interesting for its unusual content but inferior to the 'greats' in its poetic ambition and accomplishment. On the other hand, those who have bothered to read and critique

---

³ For the remainder of this paragraph, see Thorlac Turville-Petre, *The Alliterative Revival* (Cambridge, 1977); Trigg, pp. xxvii–xxix, xxxi–xxxvi; Ian Cornelius, *Reconstructing Alliterative Verse: The Pursuit of a Medieval Metre* (Cambridge, 2011); Eric Weiskott, *English Alliterative Verse: Poetic Tradition and Literary History* (Cambridge, 2016); and further discussion below, pp. 118–20.
⁴ A. C. Spearing, *Medieval Dream-Poetry* (Cambridge, 1976), p. 113.

the poem find it as having clear elements of genius.[5] The same point about sophistication applies to the audience. As John Speirs put it in 1971, the central theme of W&W 'is presented with such masterly ease and vigour in the traditional alliterative mode that we feel the poet could have had no doubt that this mode was still simply the accepted and natural contemporary one both for himself and his audience'.[6]

These points are important to bear in mind when considering the implications of linguistic dialects in W&W. It is usually assumed that the poet came from the extreme North-West Midlands, perhaps South Lancashire. At the same time, the poem also betrays dialectal forms unique to the North-East Midlands, and especially the area where Nottinghamshire, Lincolnshire and Yorkshire meet.[7] From these points we can develop a number of propositions. The references to 'the weste' (line 32) ('the West') and to a *westren wy* (line 7) ('western man') (the latter sometimes being taken as the narrator himself) have tended to strengthen arguments that the ur-text of W&W was written in, or at least by a man from, the North-West. On the other hand, the W&W poet had sufficient knowledge of London as to include a long passage describing the abundance of buying and selling on the (named) streets of the capital (lines 472–95). And as argued in Chapter 1, he was also confident enough of places and events in the South as to evoke events that took place at the royal park of Windsor.[8] The presence of forms unique either to the North-West or to the North-East Midlands does not therefore imply a limit on the poet's geographical range of experience: indeed, it remains possible that they were interventions made during the copying of an imperfect text by Thornton and his scribal workshop in the North Riding of Yorkshire during the fifteenth century.[9]

[5] See, for example, John W. Conlee, *Middle English Debate Poetry: A Critical Anthology* (East Lansing, Michigan, 1991), p. xxi.

[6] John Speirs, *Medieval English Poetry: The Non-Chaucerian Tradition*, 2nd edn (London, 1971), p. 263.

[7] Angus McIntosh, 'The Textual Transmission of the Alliterative *Morte Arthure*', in Norman Davies and C. L. Wrenn (eds), *English and Medieval Studies Presented to J. R. R. Tolkien on his Seventieth Birthday* (London, 1962), pp. 231–40, at pp. 231–2; and see the detailed summary of arguments by Trigg, pp. xviii–xxi. Angus McIntosh, M. L. Samuels and Michael Benskin (eds), *A Linguistic Atlas of Late Medieval English* (4 vols, Aberdeen, 1986), vol. 1, p. 101, ascribes the linguistics of parts of Thornton's miscellany in BL Additional MS 31042 to the North Riding of Yorkshire, and some to the far North-East Midlands, but without clarifying which texts belong to which categories.

[8] See below, pp. 16–19.

[9] For the importance of accounting for the dialect of the copyist, see, for example, Simon Horobin, '"In London and *opeland*": The Dialect and Circulation of the C Version of *Piers Plowman*', *Medium Aevum*, 74 (2005), 248–69.

W&W is a poem 'on the times' in at least two senses: it references recognisable historical personages and phenomena; and it concerns itself with a range of public debates that were timely and relevant to English society at particular moments in the later Middle Ages. Literary scholars have given much attention to the historical allusions in the poem, partly as a means of dating it but also in order to elucidate what they have seen as its multiple messages. Many commentaries on the poem continue to rely on the historical interpretations offered by Sir Israel Gollancz in his second edition of the poem, published in 1920. The *wodewyse* or wild man (first knight) acts as the king's supporter, bearing the royal arms of France and England quartered (lines 76–80).[10] This refers to the assumption, by King Edward III of England, of the title of 'king of France' in January 1340; Edward and his successors used the quartered arms of France and England for most of the rest of the fourteenth century and long beyond.[11] Both the wild man and the *caban* (pavilion, or viewing gallery) in which the king sits are bedecked with the imagery and the motto of the Order of the Garter, founded by Edward III in the summer of 1348, and which held its first formal meeting on St George's Day (23 April) 1349 (lines 59–68).[12] When the protagonists in the debate accept the arbitration of the king, they note that they have both been in his service 'this fyve and twenty wyntere' ('twenty-five years'; line 206); while this certainly need not be taken literally, scholars have duly noted that Edward III's twenty-fifth regnal year in England ended in late January 1352.[13] 'Scharshull', whom Wastoure con-

[10] For the tradition of the wild man, see Richard Bernheimer, *Wild Men in the Middle Ages* (Cambridge, Massachusetts, 1952); and Timothy Husband, *The Wild Man: Medieval Myth and Symbolism* (New York, 1980).

[11] The critical literature on *W&W* often mistakenly claims that the royal arms were quartered in 1337; Edward III only did this in 1340. For details, see W. Mark Ormrod, 'A Problem of Precedence: Edward III, the Double Monarchy and the Royal Style', in James Bothwell (ed.), *The Age of Edward III* (York, 2000), pp. 133–54; W. Mark Ormrod, *Edward III* (London, 2011), pp. 604–8.

[12] For the modern orthodoxy on the chronology of the foundation, now linked to the Windsor tournament of June 1348, see Juliet Vale, *Edward III and Chivalry: Chivalric Society and its Contexts, 1270–1350* (Woodbridge, 1982), pp. 76–91; D'Arcy Jonathan D'Acre Boulton, *The Knights of the Crown: The Monarchical Orders of Knighthood in Later Medieval Europe, 1325–1520* (Woodbridge, 1987), pp. 96–166; Richard Barber, *Edward III and the Triumph of England: The Battle of Crécy and the Company of the Garter* (London, 2013), pp. 259–339.

[13] For details, see C. R. Cheney, *A Handbook of Dates for Students of British History*, new edn, rev. M. Jones (Cambridge, 2000), pp. 34–5. Thorlac Turville-Petre, '*Wynnere and Wastoure*: When and Where?', in L. A. J. R. Houwen and A. A. McDonald (eds), *Loyal Letters: Studies on Medieval Alliterative Poetry & Prose*

demns as one of those who had earlier dared to suggest that he had ridden in warlike fashion and broken the king's peace (lines 317–18), is clearly Sir William Shareshull, the chief justice of the court of king's bench from 1350 to 1361 and the drafter and chief enforcer of a major programme of social and economic legislation put into effect in the parliaments of the early 1350s.[14] More speculatively, the speech delivered by the second knight to the main protagonists has been seen by several generations of critics as directly referencing the Statute of Treasons, which was promulgated in the parliament of 1352 (lines 130–4).[15]

Other less direct and more elusive historical references have also been detected. Juliet Vale has argued on the basis of the provision of costumes for teams of Dominican friars and merchants at Edward III's Christmas *ludi* of 1352 that *W&W* effectively has its origins in a court entertainment of that year.[16] The dialect evidence, together with the possibility that the unnamed second knight might be read as Edward of Woodstock (later known as the Black Prince), the eldest son of Edward III (lines 108–23), has led several generations of scholars to see the poem's concern with law and order as specifically referencing the special eyre (judicial visitation) that the Black Prince's administration launched, under Shareshull's presidency, in the prince's palatine jurisdiction of Cheshire (that is, in the North-West)

(Groningen, 1994), pp. 155–66, at pp. 156–7, insists that the reference is to be taken literally to mean the regnal year 25 Edward III.

[14] Bertha H. Putnam, *The Place in Legal History of Sir William Shareshull, Chief Justice of the King's Bench* (Cambridge, 1950), esp. pp. 59–78. Both the parliaments of February–March 1351 and of January–February 1352 opened within the regnal year 25 Edward III (January 1351–January 1352), with the result that the statutes arising are formally classified as a single group within that year: *SR*, vol. 1, pp. 310–28. This has led to some confusion on the date of the Statute of Treasons both in the literary scholarship and, indeed, in historical works: for example, J. H. Baker, *An Introduction to English Legal History*, 4th edn (Oxford, 2007), p. 527, refers to the statute as dating from 1351. Vale, *Edward III and Chivalry*, p. 73, incorrectly refers to the calendar year 1352 as the regnal year 25 Edward III.

[15] For the statute, see *PROME*, vol. 5, pp. 35–6, 44–5; *SR*, vol. 1, pp. 319–20. For the status of the second knight, see below, pp. 44–5, 57–8, 125–8.

[16] Vale, *Edward III and Chivalry*, pp. 73–5, followed by Richard W. Kaeuper, *War, Justice, and Public Order: England and France in the Later Middle Ages* (Oxford, 1988), p. 339. For the likelihood of the poem being written for staged performance, see Speirs, *Medieval English Poetry*, pp. 268–71. There are certainly indications in the text that it was intended for oral delivery: the wild man who appears towards the beginning of the poem, for example, has no subsequent function in the plot, and may be thought of as a mute performer to whom the audience would look for a certain amount of physical 'business' during a reading.

in 1353.¹⁷ All of this feeds into a remarkably enduring argument, enshrined as orthodoxy in the *Manual of the Writings in Middle English* in 1975, that the poem referenced, and was written during or shortly after, a very precise series of events that occurred in 1352 and 1353.¹⁸

Not all scholarship has agreed with this position. During the round of discussion prompted by the publication of Gollancz's second edition of *W&W*, J. R. Hulbert argued that, even supposing that the poem refers to events in the early 1350s, there is no need to presume that it was necessarily written (or completed in its present form) at that point. In particular, given the fact that William Shareshull remained active in the administration of justice after his resignation as chief justice in 1361, the *terminus ante quem* for composition could be stretched to *c.*1367, which Hulbert took as the point of Shareshull's final retirement from public life.¹⁹ Later, David Lawton and Elizabeth Salter extended this thinking further in independently researched articles published in 1977 and 1978 respectively. Lawton worked his way systematically through Gollancz's arguments and found that none of them precluded a date of composition in the later 1350s or 1360s.²⁰ His

---

17 Jesse May Anderson, 'A Note on the Date of *Winnere and Wastere*', *Modern Language Notes*, 43 (1928), 47–9; Michael J. Bennett, *Community, Class and Careerism: Cheshire and Lancashire Society in the Age of* Sir Gawain and the Green Knight (Cambridge, 1983), pp. 231–5; Turville-Petre, '*Wynnere and Wastoure*: When and Where?', pp. 164–6. For historical studies of the eyre of Cheshire, see Putnam, *Shareshull*, p. 39; P. H. W. Booth, 'Taxation and Public Order: Cheshire in 1353', *Northern History*, 12 (1976), 16–31; P. H. W. Booth, *The Financial Administration of the Lordship and County of Chester, 1272–1377*, Chetham Society, 3rd ser., 28 (Manchester, 1981), pp. 120–1.

18 Rossell Hope Robbins, 'Poems Dealing with Contemporary Conditions', in E. Burke Severs and Albert E. Hartung (eds), *A Manual of the Writings in Middle English, 1050–1500* (8 vols, New Haven, 1967–89), vol. 5, pp. 1385–1536, at pp. 1500–1. Especially influential in establishing this orthodoxy were: J. R. Hulbert, 'The Problems of Authorship and the Date of *Wynnere and Wastoure*', *Modern Philology*, 18 (1920), 31–40; J. M. Steadman, 'The Date of *Winnere and Wastoure*', *Modern Philology*, 19 (1921), 211–19; and D. V. Moran, '*Wynnere and Wastoure*: An Extended Footnote', *Neuphilologische Mitteilungen*, 73 (1972), 683–5. For the legacy of these works, see (*inter alia*) Speirs, *Medieval English Poetry*, pp. 263–89; Thomas H. Bestul, *Satire and Allegory in* Wynnere and Wastoure (Lincoln, Nebraska, 1974), pp. 1–2; Turville-Petre, *The Alliterative Revival*, pp. 1–4, 32; Conlee, *Middle English Debate Poetry*, p. 63. For a convenient summary of the wider debates on dating from the 1890s to the 1980s, see Trigg, pp. xlviii–li.

19 Hulbert, 'Problems of Authorship', pp. 34–7. Hulbert's work is widely cited but his conclusions are generally marginalized: see, for example, Bestul, *Satire and Allegory*, p. 1 n. 1.

20 David A. Lawton, 'Literary History and Scholarly Fancy: the Date of Two Middle

contribution is particularly important in terms of his observation that the poet chose the number of twenty-five to represent the length of Wynnere and Wastoure's service at line 206 simply because 'fyve' matched the alliteration of the line and the 'and twenty wyntere' that follows conveniently completed the metre of the line. Any idea that the number should be taken literally is, Lawton urged, invalid: the quarter-century is meant simply as a signifier of 'a long time'.

Meanwhile, Salter concentrated on the heraldic details of the second knight described at lines 108–23 and argued that the 'thre wynges ... umbygon with a gold wire' ('three wings ... surrounded by gold thread') at lines 117–18 indicate a reference not to the Black Prince but to Sir John Wingfield (d.1361), who had moved from an earlier career in the service of Edward III's great friend, William Montagu, earl of Salisbury (d.1344), to prominence in the military and administrative establishments of the king and his eldest son during the 1350s.[21] Salter went on to argue that the shackling of *W&W* to the events in 1352–3 was unnecessary, and made the bold suggestion that the poem was written significantly later than the events and people that it appears to describe – perhaps, indeed, as late as the 1380s or 1390s – and that it was composed in response to a commission from one of a number of possible members of the Wingfield family. Even if we are cautious about accepting Salter's specific line of argument about the Wingfield connection, her study was of fundamental significance in demonstrating that there is no particularly definitive *terminus ante quem* for the poem's composition.

Lawton's 1977 essay was published in a journal with narrow circulation and is now very difficult to access; had it been more widely read, subsequent scholarship might have paid more attention to the possibility of freeing *W&W* from the chronological confines imposed by Gollancz. As it is, the reception of Salter's more celebrated article has tended to be cautious, if not actively hostile, and a clear majority of critics – notably John Scattergood and Thorlac Turville-Petre – have continued to argue for a composition date in the early 1350s.[22] Stephanie Trigg, however, has

---

English Alliterative Poems', *Parergon*, orig. ser., 18 (1977), 17–25. I am grateful to Amanda McVitee for supplying me with a copy of this article. See also David Lawton, 'The Unity of Middle English Alliterative Poetry', *Speculum*, 58 (1983), 72–94, at 80–1.

[21] Elizabeth Salter, 'The Timeliness of *Wynnere and Wastoure*', *Medium Aevum*, 47 (1978), 40–65, repr. in Elizabeth Salter, *English and International: Studies in the Literature, Art and Patronage of Medieval England*, ed. Derek Pearsall and Nicolette Zeeman (Cambridge, 1988), pp. 180–98. Subsequent citations of this article are given by page reference in Salter, *English and International*. For further discussion of the Wingfield connection, see below, pp. 125–6.

[22] John Scattergood, '*Winner and Waster* and the Mid-Fourteenth-Century Econo-

shown that several of the other supposed historical references in the poem not covered by Lawton and Salter are also spurious, not least because they are the consequence of defective or even wilful modern editing.²³ Most notoriously, Gollancz read 'Yis lorde' at line 108 as *Y serve*; in his over-eagerness to see the second knight as a representation of Edward of Woodstock, the Black Prince, he then claimed that *Y serve* was an Englishing of the prince's personal motto, *Ich dene*.²⁴ Similarly, Trigg shows that the inclination of other early critics to identify the 'colde' ('cold') (line 293) and the 'droghte' ('drought') (line 312) as references to particular climatic conditions in the winter of 1352–3 was highly subjective and, in all probability, a serious misreading of words and phrases meant to have allegorical, rather than literal, meaning. Finally, Trigg has pointed to the reductive nature of much of the scholarship intent on tying the date of composition to the early 1350s, which assumes far too readily that all of the political and economic issues addressed in the poem can be related directly to the Statute of Labourers of 1351 and the debate on law and order in the parliament of 1352.²⁵ Trigg therefore concludes, like Salter, that there is no definitive *terminus ante quem* for the composition of the poem, although she ultimately rejects Salter's distant dating of the 1380s

---

my', in Tom Dunne (ed.), *The Writer as Witness: Literature as Historical Evidence*, Historical Studies, 16 (Cork, 1987), pp. 39–57; Turville-Petre, '*Wynnere and Wastoure*: When and Where?', pp. 155–66. See also, for example, Joyce Coleman, 'The Complaint of the Makers: *Wynnere and Wastoure* and the "Misperformance Topos" in Medieval England', in Evelyn Birge Vitz, Nancy Freeman Regalado and Marilyn Lawrence (eds), *Performing Medieval Narrative* (Cambridge, 2005), pp. 27–40, at pp. 35–6; J. A. Burrow, 'Winning and Wasting in *Wynnere and Wastoure* and *Piers Plowman*', in Carol M. Meale and Derek Pearsall (eds), *Makers and Users of Medieval Books: Essays in Honour of A. S. G. Edwards* (Cambridge, 2014), pp. 1–12. Like most literary scholars commenting on *W&W*, Agnès Blandeau, '*Wynnere and Wastoure*, a 14th-Century Alliterative Poem at the Crossroads of Fact and Fiction', *Caliban: French Journal of English Studies*, 33 (2013), 133–52, is content to leave open the question of the precise dating of the poem, in favour of more general discussions of the (supposed) later fourteenth-century social and political *zeitgeist*.

²³ For what follows see Stephanie Trigg, 'Israel Gollancz's "Wynnere and Wastoure": Political Satire or Editorial Politics?', in Gregory Kratzmann and James Simpson (eds), *Medieval English Religious and Ethical Literature: Essays in Honour of G. H. Russell* (Cambridge, 1986), pp. 115–27; and Trigg's detailed summary of her arguments in her critical edition, pp. xxii–xxvii.

²⁴ For the detailed arguments about the text of line 108, see Gollancz, n. to line 108; Trigg, p. 23. See also Lawton, 'Literary History', p. 21; Salter, *English and International*, pp. 193–4.

²⁵ See also Lawton, 'Literary History', p. 20.

and argues instead for a reinstatement of the argument that the poem was written some time before the death of William Shareshull in 1370. Most recently, in 2016, Eric Weiskott has followed Trigg in suggesting that *W&W* may not date much before *c.*1370.[26]

The logic of Lawton, Salter, Trigg and Weiskott provides an important starting point for the present analysis by demonstrating beyond reasonable doubt that there is nothing within the poem to suggest that it could not have been written *after* 1353 – and, potentially at least, quite significantly later. *W&W* may well imagine and aim to recreate a moment or moments in the past. The prologue to the poem (like that of *Sir Gawain and the Green Knight*) self-consciously follows what Weiskott has called the 'olde-tyme' topos of reference back to the mythological English past of Brutus of Troy.[27] In this way, *W&W* imagines events and situations that may hark back to the recent historical past: the image of Edward III in his prime (the 'comliche kynge' ['comely king'] [line 86]) and head of a household where Wynnere and Wastoure had served for a generation (lines 205–6) is certainly evocative, in a general sense, of a phase of his reign in the late 1340s and 1350s when the king stood at the very height of his popularity following the spectacular military successes at the battles of Crécy and Neville's Cross (1346), the siege of Calais (1347), and the battle of Poitiers (1356).[28] Indeed, the earlier sections of the poem may even seek in some way to commemorate both the foundation of the Order of the Garter in 1348–9 and the great campaign for the enforcement of law in the 1350s that was especially closely associated with William Shareshull's term as chief justice of the king's bench.

Even if all this is the case, however, there is nothing to prevent us from arguing that the poet used such referents in a self-consciously historical mode while writing in the 1360s, or later: as he himself tells us in the prelude, the events that he is about to unfold came to him in a dream that happened in the past ('I schall tell yow a tale that me bytyde ones' ['I shall tell you a tale of a time in my past'] [line 31]). More particularly, the poet employs such events to reflect upon a critical debate emerging in his own time, concerning the economic challenges of Edward III's campaign of courtly magnificence, with the figures of Wynnere and Wastoure being

[26] Weiskott, *English Alliterative Verse*, p. 111 and p. 202 n. 25.

[27] *Ibid.*, pp. 109, 112–13. For the medieval myth of the foundation of Britain by Brutus, grandson of Aeneas, see H. David Brumble, *Classical Myths and Legends in the Middle Ages and Renaissance: A Dictionary of Allegorical Meanings* (London, 1998), pp. 57, 107, 328.

[28] For Edward III as 'comly kynge' in other fourteenth-century texts (though omitting the reference in *W&W*), and an attempt to link this motif with the Robin Hood ballads of the fifteenth century, see Thomas Ohlgren, '*Edwardus redivivus* in *A Gest of Robyn Hode*', *Journal of English and Germanic Philology*, 15 (2000), 1–28, at 3–4.

used to represent economic and financial issues current in thinking at court and in parliament. It is the purpose of this study to demonstrate that there are additional, hitherto unnoticed, historical references in W&W that may allow us to alter the *terminus a quo* of the poem from the foundation of the Garter (1348) or the Statute of Treasons (1352) to the occasion of the great Garter feast of 1358, and to fix the *terminus ante quem* around a series of public debates on aspects of the political economy that took place in the parliaments of 1362, 1363 and 1365. The net effect is to move the date of composition forward from the previously held orthodoxy of 1352–3 to some time in the mid- or even late 1360s.

If the sole purpose of this exercise were simply to adjust the possible date of composition of W&W by a decade or so, then its interest and significance would inevitably be rather narrow. But the analysis that follows has two wider purposes. The first is to re-imagine the place of W&W in the flourishing of alliterative verse during the second half of the fourteenth century and its relationship to certain other texts, including *Piers Plowman*.[29] The second and more pervasive purpose is to demonstrate that a re-dating of W&W helps us to clarify the underlying (and sometimes rather unstable) purpose and message of the poem. The enduring conviction that W&W in some way addresses the contents of the Statute of Treasons of 1352 and the events that led up to the Black Prince's visitation of Cheshire in 1353 has led many scholars, consciously or unconsciously, to view one of the poem's primary functions as providing a critique of the lawless behaviour of landed society and the threat that this posed to the stability of the realm. Similarly, the inexhaustible greed of Wynnere and the ruinous overspending of Wastoure have long been read as epitomising the strains of taxation and credit finance during the Hundred Years War, with the result that the poem is sometimes read primarily as an attack on the fiscal policies of Edward III. The argument that W&W effectively concertinas a series of events and issues beginning around 1350 and ending in the mid-1360s helps us to re-assess some of these themes and to understand the tensions that exist in the poem between those parts that are adulatory of Edward III and those that take an apparently more critical stance of the king and his achievements. Most importantly, however, a fresh investigation of the chronological context of the poem serves to highlight its principal didactic purpose: namely the requirement, in an uncertain world knocked out of kilter by plague, famine and war, for the crown and the landed elite to join together in guaranteeing effective stewardship of the political economy and thus to uphold traditional notions of a well-ordered society.

---

[29] See esp. the discussion below, pp. 118–21.

W&W is not in any simple sense a *roman à clef*: it was not written with the primary intention of disguising, and then uncovering, a series of real historical events. While the references to the Order of the Garter in the first fitt, for example, may conceivably be taken to suggest an initial target audience of the poem, the subject matter that follows is in certain important senses timeless and universal: the fact that the poet can cite the authorities of Aristotle and Augustine (line 316) reminds us that his own search for the Aristotelian golden mean between avarice and generosity is a theme that redounds across the medieval centuries and beyond. The poem is no more restricted by a specific set of historical events than it is by issues of genre: one of the things that makes *W&W* so interesting to scholars of literature is its pressing of the bounds, containing as it does various elements of what critics have defined as the dream poem, the *chanson de geste*, debate, allegory, satire and complaint.[30] The author is at once embedded in his social milieu and free of its restraints: alongside the referential elements in the debate on frugality and prodigality are substantial passages that explore these themes in an altogether original manner and tone.[31]

It is no part of this study, then, to suppose that *W&W* either can or should be reduced to a simple set of comments on a discrete series of events in mid-fourteenth-century England. Rather, what provides the basis (and opportunity) for the historicist reading that follows is the unusual specificity of some of the historical references within the poem and the susceptibility of other passages to interpretation as being prompted by debates that we know from other sources to have taken place in the third quarter of the fourteenth century. In particular, a reading of *W&W* in the context of the chronicles of the period and certain political sources (especially the records of parliament) can enrich understandings of the issues raised by the poem and of the social milieu for which it was intended.

This study therefore takes a traditionally historicist approach towards the poem, while aiming to differentiate between the sometimes reductive process of 'finding' history in literary texts and the wider and more productive purpose of infusing such texts with meaning derived from contemporary ethical and political culture. Students of Geoffrey Chaucer have long had to address

---

[30] Spearing, *Medieval Dream-Poetry*, pp. 129–34; Nicolas Jacobs, 'The Typology of Debate and the Interpretation of *Wynnere and Wastoure*', *Review of English Studies*, NS, 36 (1985), 481–500; Bestul, *Satire and Allegory*, pp. 24–45; Britton J. Harwood, 'The Displacement of Labor in *Winner and Waster*', in Kellie Robertson and Michael Uebel (eds), *The Middle Ages and Work: Practicing Labor in Late Medieval England* (New York, 2004), pp. 157–77; Britton J. Harwood, 'Anxious over Peasants: Textual Disorder in *Winner and Waster*', *Journal of Medieval and Early Modern Studies*, 36 (2006), 291–319. See also below, pp. 105–14.

[31] Jerry D. James, 'The Undercutting of Conventions in *Wynnere and Wastoure*', *Modern Language Quarterly*, 25 (1964), 243–58.

the issue of whether the ample life records available for this self-identifying poet provide evidence of the constraints acting upon his writing or simply help us to understand the initial mindset of a writer with an exceptionally rich poetic imagination.[32] In the case of *W&W*, the very anonymity of the author effectively destabilises any modern efforts at an assertively positivist historicism: there is simply too little evidence from which to construct either a precise identity for its author or a catalogue of the direct influences that acted upon his sense of choice and judgment.[33] The poet cannot speak on his own behalf; and so *W&W* must, in all senses, speak for itself.

In what follows, then, I shall employ various arguments for the re-dating of *W&W* as the starting point for a reconsideration and re-ascription of the possible wider meanings of the poem. In so doing, I should make explicit an important preliminary point about the unknown author. This study is predicated on the idea that the person who wrote *W&W* was well aware of the practices of the royal court and its delight in arcane ceremonial, as well as being well versed in the high politics of the royal council and of parliament. This does not necessarily mean that the poet was himself a member of the royal household (or, as one might conceivably venture, a Member of Parliament): it might simply denote that he lived and worked close to a key source of information for events at the centre of politics. Several such contexts lend themselves as possibilities in this respect, and are discussed in detail in Chapter 5.[34] Whichever way we interpret the circle of patronage of *W&W*, however, it is taken as read here that any element of 'provincialism' evident in the poet's dialect was no bar either to his understanding of courtly chivalric culture or indeed to the comprehension and applicability of the poem by people born in and living in the South. Not only is the dialect of the poem such as to suggest the poet's possible 'reach' across multiple aristocratic households; its confident style is also such as to assert an implied audience in a wide span of fourteenth-century political society. The themes are ones that apply to landed society as a whole, whether great or small; and they are ones that were germane to people from all parts of England, whether in the alliterative 'zone' of the North-West or outside it. Lois Roney has emphasised that the self-conscious 'Englishness' of the poem owes much to the fact that its main message is one applicable to the nation at large.[35] *W&W* therefore takes its place alongside a wider body of

---

[32] For a recent analysis that addresses issues of balance between history and literature, see Marion Turner, *Chaucer: A European Life* (Princeton, 2019).

[33] For further discussion of the question of authorship, see pp. 120–5.

[34] See below, pp. 122–4.

[35] Lois Roney, '*Winner and Waster*'s "Wyse Wordes": Teaching Economics and Nationalism in Fourteenth-Century England', *Speculum*, 69 (1994), 1070–1100, at 1086–8.

literature of the fourteenth century that constructed and debated the 'idea of England'.[36] As the arguments develop, I aim to demonstrate how this characterisation of the poet's social and political milieu also allows us to re-assess his presentation of the issues of frugality and prodigality, as well as his possible relationship with other writers of the period.

The following four chapters therefore focus on particular historical events with which it is possible to associate sections of *W&W*. Chapter 1 examines the poet's interest in chivalry and the tournament, and proposes that the poem references the great feast associated with the ceremonies of the Order of the Garter in 1358, when Edward III was joined in the celebrations by not one but two captive kings: David II of Scotland and John II of France. Chapter 2 explores the themes of public order and dispute settlement in the poem, arguing that claims about the supposed allusions to the Statute of Treasons of 1352 are incorrect and that the poem reflects much more immediately on the unruly nature of aristocratic society in general, and of the knightly members of the king's household in particular. In Chapter 3, we turn to the sections of *W&W* that comment on the political economy, and link these with the debates that resulted in the promulgation – and swift annulment – of the famous sumptuary laws of 1363. Chapter 4 picks up points from the previous chapters to make a concerted examination of the nature of public debate on the royal household of Edward III and its management during the 1350s and 1360s. Finally, in Chapter 5, we consider how *W&W* fits into the wider tradition of complaint literature in fourteenth-century England before drawing together, in Chapter 6, some comment on the political relevance of the poem in the lifetime of its collector, Robert Thornton. The book concludes with a modern rendering of the extant text of *W&W*.

---

[36] Among a very large bibliography on the topic, see: Thorlac Turville-Petre, *England the Nation: Language, Literature, and National Identity, 1290–1340* (Oxford, 1996); Ardis Butterfield, *The Familiar Enemy: Chaucer, Language, and Nation in the Hundred Years War* (Oxford, 2009); Andrea Ruddick, *English Identity and Political Culture in the Fourteenth Century* (Cambridge, 2013); and Joanna Bellis, *The Hundred Years War in Literature, 1337–1600* (Cambridge, 2016).

= 1 =

Chivalry and Internationalism: The Garter Feast of 1358 and English Diplomacy during the 1350s and 1360s

Although *W&W* is often represented in the critical literature as a debate between the chivalric and the mercantile elements in fourteenth-century society, it is the contention of the present study that the poem is much more preoccupied with the activities, values and attitudes of the landed classes in general, and particularly that large portion of the lay elite that participated actively in the early stages of the Hundred Years War.¹ This chapter argues that *W&W* references the special tournaments and feast of the Order of the Garter organised by Edward III in 1358, as well as the diplomatic manoeuvres that went on during the later 1350s and the first half of the 1360s around the attempts (many of them sponsored by the papacy) to promote an agenda of lasting peace between England and France. In so doing, we take the *terminus ante quem* for the composition of the poem into the mid-1360s where, as Chapter 3 argues, we can also best locate the opinions about the political economy that dominate the formal debate between Wynnere and Wastoure. This chapter focuses more on the opening and concluding sections of the poem which, it argues, provide clear evidence of the poet's detailed knowledge not only about the form and nature of the activities of the Order of the Garter but also about the contemporary controversies, articulated in parliament, about unwelcome papal influence in the kingdom.

---

[1] For the critical literature that represents Wynnere as a merchant and thus a member of the urban bourgeoisie, see below, pp. 61–5. For high levels of participation by the armigerous classes in the wars of Edward III, see Andrew Ayton, *Knights and Warhorses: Military Service and the English Aristocracy under Edward III* (Woodbridge, 1994); Andrew Ayton, 'Edward III and the English Aristocracy at the Beginning of the Hundred Years War', in Matthew Strickland (ed.), *Armies, Chivalry and Warfare in Medieval Britain and France* (Stamford, 1998), pp. 173–206; Andrew Ayton, 'Armies and Military Communities in Fourteenth-Century England', in Peter R. Coss and Christopher Tyerman (eds), *Soldiers, Nobles and Gentlemen: Essays in Honour of Maurice Keen* (Woodbridge, 2009), pp. 215–39.

An important starting point is the inferred location in which the events of the poem unfold. Previous critics of *W&W* have commented extensively on its description of the setting in which the debate between Wynnere and Wastoure is called forth and takes place. Yet this location has almost always been seen solely as representing a type – the outdoor theatre or the tournament arena – rather than a specific, 'real' place.[2] The poet finds himself, in his dream, in 'a loveliche lande that was ylike grene,/ That laye loken by a lawe the lengthe of a myle' ('a lovely laund of an even green/That lay encircled by earthworks extending a mile') (lines 48–9), and from there espies armed men gathered 'In aythere holte' ('In either grove') (line 50) at the sides of the laund. The king sits away from the crowd, his 'caban' (pavilion) being situated 'At the creste of a clyffe' ('At the crest of a cliff') (line 59); subsequently we find that the disputants can walk from the 'lande' to the 'clyffe' (lines 209–10), so the locations are presumably part of a linked sequence of natural and man-made features.

All of this may be so much imaginative detail, and there is no reason to suppose that any or every topographical feature found in the poem relates to a specific space. Nevertheless, this is not the only study to suggest that the poet's description was prompted by a real place and/or event. Britton J. Harwood has suggested that the king's presence on the 'clyffe' set over an implied valley below provides a rebus for Vale Royal, the Cistercian abbey in Cheshire founded by Edward I and patronised by the Black Prince.[3] The present analysis depends much more on the implications of the 'lande', which is arguably far more than a mere valley bottom. *La[u]nde* (Old French), still surviving in English usage as 'laund', has both the general sense of a glade within a forest and the more technical meaning of a managed clearing within an emparked area of woodland suitable as a space for hunting (as later in *W&W*, at line 405) and for tournaments.[4] The fact that the 'lande'

---

[2] Ralph W. V. Elliott, 'The Topography of *Wynnere and Wastoure*', *English Studies*, 48 (1967), 134–40; Thomas H. Bestul, *Satire and Allegory in* Wynnere and Wastoure (Lincoln, Nebraska, 1974), pp. 102–3; Maura B. Nolan, '"With tresone within": *Wynnere and Wastoure*, Chivalric Self-Representation, and the Law', *Journal of Medieval and Early Modern Studies*, 26 (1996), 1–28, at 11–13. D. Vance Smith, *Arts of Possession: The Middle English Household Imaginary* (Minneapolis, 2003), pp. 87–8, recognises the strong features of the tournament in the setting of *W&W*.

[3] Britton J. Harwood, 'Anxious over Peasants: Textual Disorder in *Winner and Waster*', *Journal of Medieval and Early Modern Studies*, 36 (2006), 291–319, at 302–3, 307, 309–10.

[4] Oliver Rackham, *Ancient Woodland: Its History, Vegetation and Uses in England* (London, 1980), p. 195; Stephen Moorhouse, 'The Medieval Parks of Yorkshire: Function, Contents and Chronology', in Robert Liddiard (ed.), *The Medieval Park: New Perspectives* (Macclesfield, 2007), pp. 99–127, at p. 111. Elliott, 'Topography', p. 137, misses this meaning.

in *W&W* is surrounded by a mile of earthworks (line 49) strongly suggests that it, and the 'clyffe', are part of a single, man-made area of open land such as was found in royal and other seigniorial forests and parks and used specifically for sport and leisure.[5] Thus, for example, at the English royal palace of Clarendon (Wiltshire), the space known in the thirteenth century as the 'king's park' and today as the 'tilting field' was marked out in the late Middle Ages by ditches, fences and hedges and had an elaborate series of earthen terraces along its south side likely used as viewing platforms.[6]

The fact that the insignia and arms of the Order of the Garter appear with such prominence in the decoration of the royal pavilion is a strong indicator that *W&W* was intended to be understood as set not simply in a royal hunting ground-cum-tournament site but specifically in the Great Park of Windsor, the large area of royal forest around the royal residence of Windsor Castle.[7] To suggest that this was the space evoked by the poet of *W&W* is not to argue that the latter necessarily knew the topography of the Great Park first-hand, but that he was undoubtedly confident about describing the kind of events over which the real-life king presided. The evocation of Windsor relies specifically on the detailed imagery of the Order of the Garter found in the description of the king's *caban*:

> At the creste of a cliffe a caban was rerede
> Alle reylede with rede the rofe and the sydes
> With Ynglysse besantes full brighte betyn of golde
> And ichone gaily vmbygone with garters of inde
> And iche a gartere of golde gerede full riche.
> Then were th[er] wordes in the webbe warped of he[u],
> Payntted of plunket and poyntes bytwene
> That were fourmed full fayre appon fresche letters
> And alle was it one sawe appon Ynglysse tonge,
> 'Hethyng haue the hathell that any harme thynkes.'
>   (lines 59–68)

---

[5] See, in general, S. A. Mileson, *Parks in Medieval England* (Oxford, 2009), pp. 15–44, 82–98.

[6] Amanda Richardson, *The Forest, Park and Palace of Clarendon, c.1200–c.1650*, British Archaeological Reports British Series, 387 (Oxford, 2005), pp. 62–3 and fig. 29. Note also the use of woodlands and waterways to mark out rural tournament sites: Juliet Vale, 'Violence and the Tournament', in Richard W. Kaeuper (ed.), *Violence in Medieval Society* (Woodbridge, 2000), pp. 143–58, at pp. 154–5.

[7] For the Great Park, see Grenville Astill, 'Windsor in the Context of Medieval Berkshire', in Laurence Keen and Eileen Scarff (eds), *Windsor: Medieval Archaeology, Art and Architecture of the Thames Valley*, British Archaeological Association Conference Transactions, 25 (Leeds, 2002), pp. 1–14, at pp. 10–12.

(At the crest of a cliff was set a pavilion,
The roof and the sides all arrayed with red,
Adorned with English bezants embossed with gold
Girdled about with garters of dark blue;
And every garter glittered richly with gold.
Then there were coloured words in the weave of cloth,
Painted in light blue, with points in between,
That were well designed, with well-formed letters,
And all stating one motto, in English words,
'Shamed be the knight who thinks ill of it.')

Edward III, who had been born at Windsor and held the place in particular affection, hosted what is now generally regarded as the founding meeting of the Order of the Garter at the castle in June 1348.[8] Thereafter, the king and the other members of the order gathered annually at Windsor on the feast of St George (23 April) for several days of religious ceremony and feasting. The descriptions of the materials that were distributed to members of the order to prepare their robes for these occasions, found in the 'particulars' or itemised royal household accounts (which only survive for certain years), indicate that the essential iconography of the order, focused on the blue garters distributed to each of the knights of the order to adorn their robes, was well established from the outset. Gollancz's efforts to link *W&W* specifically to the garter badges worn at the feast of April 1351 are therefore, as Trigg remarks, part of his reductive strategy of assigning to the early 1350s phenomena and events that were actually of much more general application later in the decade and beyond.[9] It is, however, most important for the present analysis that there is no certain evidence from the second half of Edward III's reign that the insignia and motto of the Order, which are the essential reference points in *W&W*, were ever displayed other than during the Garter feast at Windsor in April each year.[10] The main significance of

---

[8] See the summary of modern scholarship on the chronology of the foundation by W. Mark Ormrod, 'For Arthur and St George: Edward III, Windsor Castle and the Order of the Garter', in Nigel Saul (ed.), *St George's Chapel, Windsor, in the Fourteenth Century* (Woodbridge, 2005), pp. 13–34.

[9] Trigg, p. 22. For viable summaries of most of the available household accounts and other financial records relating to the Garter under Edward III, see George Frederick Beltz, *Memorials of the Most Noble Order of the Garter* (London, 1841), pp. 2–11.

[10] It is just possible that the garter emblem (most likely intended to represent a miniature sword belt) had been deployed very briefly on the streamers of the royal ship that took Edward III to and from his great campaign in France in 1346–7 and as a royal badge at a tournament held at Eltham in 1348. But it is noticeable that such references cease after the first St George's Day meeting of the order in April 1349;

the prominent place accorded to the Order of the Garter early in the poem is therefore that it directs an audience with any knowledge of Edward III's chivalric order and its practices unequivocally to the royal seat of Windsor.

This is not to say that tournaments were a regular element in the proceedings at early meetings of the Order of the Garter. Juliet Vale's persuasive argument that the order's uncharacteristically small membership – the king, his eldest son, and twenty-four knights – owes itself to the tournament teams put together by Edward III and the Black Prince at the first Garter feast in June 1348 leads to a too easy assumption that tournaments, either as individual combats or as general mêlées, were a regular feature of the ensuing St George's Day meetings of the Order of the Garter.[11] As Richard Barber has recently emphasised, the annual feast day of the Garter was, in fact, much more occupied in religious rites than it was in tournaments, reflecting the concern of the king with the duties owed to God in return for military victory and the urgent need, following the Black Death, of honouring and commemorating deceased members of the order's confraternity.[12]

This emphasis on the religious elements of the order helps set some distance between the objectives of the Garter and Edward III's earlier attempt to establish an Arthurian Round Table in 1344. The latter plan had involved the partial construction of a circular arena, surrounded by a roofed structure to provide seating for onlookers, within the upper ward of Windsor Castle. This building had been quickly abandoned following the king's decision not to pursue the accompanying chivalric order of three hundred knights, and the partially constructed arena seems to have been levelled to make way for the significant building works that ensued during the later 1350s and early 1360s on the royal and state apartments in the vicinity.[13]

---

thereafter the device was purely associated with the order and its ceremonies. See Juliet Vale, *Edward III and Chivalry: Chivalric Society and its Contexts, 1270–1350* (Woodbridge, 1982), p. 149 n. 36; W. Mark Ormrod, *Edward III* (London, 2011), p. 303 and n. 20; Richard Barber, *Edward III and the Triumph of England: The Battle of Crécy and the Company of the Garter* (London, 2013), p. 272 and p. 592 n. 51.

[11] Vale, *Edward III and Chivalry*, pp. 76–91.

[12] Barber, *Edward III and the Triumph of England*, pp. 178–339. See also Richard Barber, *Magnificence and Princely Splendour in the Middle Ages* (Woodbridge, 2020), p. 116.

[13] Julian Munby, Richard Barber and Richard Brown, *Edward III's Round Table at Windsor: The House of the Round Table and the Windsor Festival of 1344* (Woodbridge, 2007), pp. 38–65. For reliable chronicle accounts of the scheme of 1344, see Edmund Maunde Thompson (ed.), *Adae Murimuth, Continuatio chronicarum. Robertus de Avesbury, De gestis mirabilibus Regis Edwardi Tertii*, Rolls Series, 93 (London, 1889), pp. 155–6, 231–2; and J. Viard and E. Déprez (eds), *Chronique de Jean le Bel* (2 vols, Paris, 1904–5), vol. 2, pp. 34–5. See also Christopher Berard, 'Edward III's Abandoned Order of the Round Table', in Elizabeth Archibald and David F. Johnson (eds), *Arthurian Literature XXIX* (Cambridge, 2012), pp. 1–40. For the building

Even had it survived, the purpose-built architectural space within the upper ward would only ever have provided a venue for individual jousting. The sort of event initially contemplated in *W&W* is, by contrast, a general mêlée, in which entire tournament teams or even whole armies might participate, and which under certain circumstances could be fought not merely as forms of entertainment (*à plaisance*) but to the death (*à outrance*).[14] These larger-scale encounters were fought not in confined arenas but on open ground, and sometimes indeed over significant swathes of land. No archaeological work has yet been undertaken in the Great Park at Windsor to locate possible areas where general mêlées may have taken place. In any case, it is unnecessary to imagine that the author of *W&W* had Windsor in mind in any other sense than its place as the setting for the Garter feast.

These associations with Edward III's palace and park of Windsor raise important questions about the precise nature and extent of the intended or potential audience of the poem. Did the author of *W&W* content himself with providing incidental references to specific phenomena and events with the general intention that those 'in the know' about the rituals of courtly life could identify with the more general social messages of the poem? Or did he write with the specific intention of honouring one or more members of the Order of the Garter, thereby deliberately restricting his audience to the highly privileged group of twenty-six knights of the order and making a new genre of heraldic literature into an elaborately coded set of musings on the preoccupations of the landed and political elite?

A poem that dwells on the moral dilemma of magnificence might well have rung true with at least some of the high nobility who were members of the Order of the Garter. In particular, Henry of Grosmont's account of his spiritual anxieties, the *Livre de seynts medicines*, written in the 1350s, exposes the way in which contemporary aristocrats contrasted their privileged and lavish lifestyles with the sense of revulsion about their own base corporeality, and were increasingly preoccupied with the virtues of humility and poverty which they believed were prerequisites for entry to the kingdom of Heaven.[15] Unsurprisingly, perhaps, *W&W* embraces this penitential trope. Each side claims that the other will go to Hell and the Devil (lines 236, 260–2,

---

scheme of the later 1350s and early 1360s see below, p. 92.

[14] See the convenient summary of these complex categories by Will McLean, 'Outrance and Plaisance', *Journal of Medieval Military History*, 8 (2010), 155–70.

[15] [Henry of Grosmont, First Duke of Lancaster,] *Le livre de seyntz medicines*, ed. E. J. Arnould, Anglo-Norman Text Society, 2 (Oxford, 1940); Henry of Grosmont, First Duke of Lancaster, *The Book of Holy Medicines*, trans. C. J. Batt, The French of England Translation Series, 8 (Tempe, Arizona, 2014). For the penitential framework of aristocratic piety, see Jeremy Catto, 'Religion and the English Nobility in the Later Fourteenth Century', in Hugh Lloyd-Jones, Valerie Pearl and Blair Worden (eds), *History and Imagination: Essays in Honour of H. R. Trevor-Roper* (London, 1981), pp. 43–55.

291, 441, 444). While Wastoure's speeches are infused with the implications of Wynnere's avarice (lines 246–62, 294–323), Wynnere repeatedly accuses Wastoure of two of the other cardinal sins: pride and gluttony (lines 230, 267, 277–85, 326–63, 415–22). In return, Wastoure devotes a sustained passage to the hopelessness of Wynnere's attempts to ensure his passage to Heaven in the form of post-mortem acts of charity (lines 294–307). And yet it would be inappropriate to describe *W&W* as a penitential poem responding to the specific spiritual agenda of the high nobility: the mood of the text, after all, is prevailingly secular rather than religious, mocking rather than contrite. The chapters that follow assume a rather wider potential audience for the poem among landed society in general, including not only the great magnates who came to dominate the ranks of the Garter but also – and perhaps more particularly – the gentry, great and small, of provincial England. It does well, however, at least to keep open the possibility that *W&W* was first conceived as a moral entertainment provided at a feast laid on by an early member of the Order of the Garter for the benefit of his gentry retainers, in the same manner that Turville-Petre imagines the circulation of another early poem of the Alliterative Revival, *William of Palerne*.[16]

The question as to the understanding that both the poet and the original readership took from the detailed referencing of the Order of the Garter and its iconography also raises some important questions about the likely date of *W&W*. The foundation and early meetings of the order down to the mid-1350s were 'closed' events, with attendance apparently confined to the immediate members of the Garter. As a consequence, the St George's Day festivities held before 1358 were of little public note.[17] In fact, the only English chronicler to provide any details of the Order's emblem of the garter is Geoffrey le Baker, who wrote at some point after 1350 and possibly as late as 1357.[18] *W&W*, by contrast, provides a detailed description of the insignia and motto of the order, the latter (*Honi soit qui mal y pense*) rendered 'appon Ynglysse tonge' ('in English words') as 'Hethyng haue the hathell that any harme thynkes' ('Shamed be the knight who thinks ill of it') (lines 59–69, with quotations at lines 67, 68).[19] As Hugh Collins has pointed out, dating

---

[16] Thorlac Turville-Petre, 'Humphrey de Bohun and *William of Palerne*', *Neuphilologische Mitteilungen*, 75 (1974), 250–2.

[17] Hugh E. L. Collins, *The Order of the Garter, 1348–1461: Chivalry and Politics in Late Medieval England* (Oxford, 2000), pp. 234–78, *passim*.

[18] Edward Maunde Thompson (ed.), *Chronicon Galfridi le Baker de Swynebroke* (Oxford, 1889), pp. 108–9; David Preest (trans.), *The Chronicle of Geoffrey le Baker of Swinbrook* (Woodbridge, 2012), pp. 94–5; Barber, *Edward III and the Triumph of England*, p. 275.

[19] For discussion of the translation of the motto, see Smith, *Arts of Possession*, pp. 56–7, 89; and Stephanie Trigg, *Shame and Honor: A Vulgar History of the Order of the Garter* (Philadelphia, 2012), pp. 55–6.

W&W specifically to 1352–3 has the effect of making the poet uniquely privileged in terms of his detailed knowledge both of the symbol and of the motto chosen by Edward III for the new confraternity.[20]

The only other English literary work that includes references to the Order of the Garter and could date from this early in the order's existence is *Sir Gawain and the Green Knight*, which some critics believe to have been written in the 1350s, and again within the context of the Order of the Garter.[21] Certainly, *Sir Gawain*'s preoccupations with the delicate balance between the chivalric themes of honour and shame and its delight in the esoteric meanings of associated signs and symbols make it a more obviously courtly poem than *W&W*. In the case of *Sir Gawain*, however, the Garter motto (in a variant spelling of its Anglo-French form, as *Honi soyt qui mal pence*) is simply inserted as an otherwise unexplained gloss to the poem at its end (and possibly written into the unique manuscript at a later stage).[22] Although some recent critics have reopened the argument that *Sir Gawain and the Green Knight* was influenced by the foundation myths that developed around the Garter, this poem shows nothing of the direct referencing found in *W&W*. That *W&W* exhibits such detailed awareness of an emblem and motto that had, as yet, no part in the public insignia of the English crown certainly does not prevent us from dating it as early as 1352–3. There are other historical reasons, however, for supposing that the inclusion of the emblem and motto of the Garter points the way to a slightly later meeting of the Order at Windsor, and specifically to that of 1358.

The capture of King John II of France at the battle of Poitiers in September 1356 and his transfer to confinement in England in the spring of 1357 led Edward III to plan a spectacular sequence of festivities culminating in the Garter ceremonies of April 1358.[23] For the first time, systematic

---

[20] Collins, *Order of the Garter*, pp. 256–7.

[21] For arguments reviving the suggestion that *Sir Gawain and the Green Knight* was written in the 1350s, see W. G. Cooke, '*Sir Gawain and the Green Knight*: A Restored Dating', *Medium Aevum*, 58 (1989), 34–48; W. G. Cooke and D'A. J. D. Boulton, '*Sir Gawain and the Green Knight*: A Poem for Henry of Grosmont?', *Medium Aevum*, 68 (1999), 42–54; and Francis Ingledew, Sir Gawain and the Green Knight *and the Order of the Garter* (Notre Dame, 2006), pp. 133–57.

[22] For the older debate on whether or not Gawain's robes (as described in *Sir Gawain and the Green Knight*, ed. J. R. R. Tolkien and E. V. Gordon [Oxford, 1967], lines 1928–31) could reference the livery of the Garter, see Collins, *Order of the Garter*, pp. 256–7.

[23] W. Mark Ormrod, 'The Foundation and Early Development of the Order of the Garter in England, 1348–1399', *Frühmittelalterliche Studien*, 50 (2016), 361–92, at 375–6. For the public performances en route from Plymouth to London and in the city of London itself in 1357, see Barber, *Magnificence and Princely Splendour*,

efforts were put in place to draw great crowds to the feast, to include within it a specific programme of tournaments, and to make it part of the wider public relations machine of an image-conscious monarch. We know from the royal financial records that heralds were despatched to France, the Low Countries and Germany announcing the forthcoming event at Windsor as a tournament open to all comers.[24] Among those who answered the call, reported the chronicler Henry Knighton, were Wenceslaus, duke of Luxembourg and Brabant (brother of the Emperor Charles IV), and a large contingent of Gascon knights; other foreign nobles who likely attended the event appear on this occasion as recipients of gifts from the Black Prince.[25] The Westminster chronicler, John of Reading, also specifies that Henry of Grosmont, duke of Lancaster, and his followers excelled themselves in feats of arms at this event.[26] The king later gave the sum of £3 6s 8d to William Volaunt, 'king of heralds', for his good services there.[27] For the first time, moreover, there is direct evidence of English lords and ladies beyond the immediate membership of the Garter being invited to Windsor for the St George's Day feast.[28] Furthermore, the 1358 feast is the first (and, indeed, during the reign of Edward III, the only) occasion on which we have documented evidence of the king providing resource – in this case the very considerable sum of £500 – for his consort, Philippa of Hainault, to adorn herself for the occasion.[29] The decision to have both John II of France and, indeed, the captive David II of Scotland (who had been in English custody since 1346) present was a significant security risk, but

pp. 181–3. The first critic to point to the possibility that *W&W* references the Garter feast of 1358 was George Neilson, 'A Note on *Wynnere and Wastoure*', *The Athenaeum*, 118, no. 3853 (7 September 1901), 319.

[24] TNA, E 403/388, 9 March, 12 March 1358; E 403/392, 13 April, 4 May 1358.

[25] Geoffrey H. Martin (ed. and trans.), *Knighton's Chronicle, 1337–1396* (Oxford, 1995), pp. 158–9; *Register of Edward the Black Prince* (4 vols, London, 1930–3), vol. 4, pp. 252, 323. The duke of Luxembourg was then in the process of complicated diplomatic negotiations with the English crown: Fritz Trautz, *Die Könige von England und das Reich, 1272–1377* (Heidelberg, 1961), pp. 376–80. The Gascon presence can be rationalised in terms of the number of Gascon lords who had taken prisoners at Poitiers and sold them on, through later negotiations, to Edward III: Chris Given-Wilson and Françoise Bériac, 'Edward III's Prisoners of War: The Battle of Poitiers and its Context', *English Historical Review*, 116 (2001), 802–33, at 814–20, 830–3.

[26] James Tait (ed.), *Chronica Johannis de Reading et Anonymi Cantuariensis* (Manchester, 1914), p. 130.

[27] Beltz, *Memorials*, p. 5. For Volaunt, see also below, pp. 127–8.

[28] See the entries from the issue rolls of the exchequer summarised by Beltz, *Memorials*, p. 5.

[29] Collins, *Order of the Garter*, p. 79 n. 185.

one evidently considered worth taking for its diplomatic value. As Neil Murphy has recently asserted, 'The St George's Day festivities of 1358 must surely rank amongst the most successful displays of English royal propaganda in the fourteenth century.'[30]

It would no doubt be reductive to argue that the *mise en scène* of *W&W* was simply a replication of the Garter feast of 1358. But it is worth stressing how extraordinary this event was in its programming, its scale of sumptuousness and its international reach. There were other ceremonial events at Windsor within another few years that approached the magnificence of 1358. In particular, we might note the celebrations organised for the marriages of Edward III's two eldest children: the wedding of Prince Edward to his cousin, Joan of Kent, in October 1361; and the nuptials of Princess Isabella and the French nobleman Enguerrand de Coucy, in July 1365.[31] On the other hand, there is no substantive evidence that the Garter iconography was used on these occasions. The exceptional affinity between the Garter feast of 1358 and the anticipated tournament in *W&W* becomes further evident when we note that the annual gatherings of the Garter actually reverted after 1358 to quite restricted events with 'closed' invitation lists: only at the very last meeting of Edward III's reign are there signs of a larger-scale event with a wider political purpose, when the royal family sought to use the Garter feast of April 1377 as a means of advertising the reconciliation of factions that had opened up within its ranks over the previous year.[32] Finally, the expectation of a major tournament aroused by the sending of heralds to the near Continent serves to highlight the unusual range of activity on this occasion: for one moment in time, Edward III sought to extend the 1358 meeting of the Garter beyond the normal religious rites in order to open up the event as a general gathering of European knighthood. The anonymous Canterbury chronicler saw this as the holding of an Arthurian round table; while other commentators did not draw a connection with Arthur, it is clear from the general accounts of the event that it was seen as a celebration of Edwardian chivalry.[33]

---

[30] Neil Murphy, *The Captivity of John II, 1356–60: The Royal Image in Later Medieval England and France* (Basingstoke, 2016), chap. 2 (unpaginated e-book).

[31] Ormrod, *Edward III*, pp. 448–51.

[32] *Ibid.*, pp. 450, 532–3, 548, 573–4.

[33] Charity Scott-Stokes and Chris Given-Wilson (eds and trans.), *Chronicon Anonymi Cantuariensis: The Chronicle of Anonymous of Canterbury, 1346–1365* (Oxford, 2008), pp. 42–3. For other contemporary or near-contemporary notices in the chronicles, see Frank S. Heydon (ed.), *Eulogium historiarum*, Rolls Series 9 (3 vols, London, 1858–63), vol. 3, p. 227; Sir Thomas Gray, *Scalacronica*, ed. and trans. Andy King, Surtees Society, 209 (Durham, 2005), pp. 150–1.

If we therefore engage with the possibility that the very unusual nature of the Garter feast held at Windsor in 1358 may have provided some direct inspiration to the author of W&W, then a number of possible resonances within the poem follow. First, there is the question of the nature of the 'armies' of Wynnere and Wastoure. There is an initial short description of these two forces early in the poem:

> In aythere holte was ayne here in hawberkes full brighte,
> Harde hattes apon hedes and helmys with crestys;
> Brayden owte thaire baners bown for the mete;
> Schowen owte of the schawes in schiltrons thay felle.
> (lines 50–3)
>
> (In either grove were two armies in bright hauberks,
> Hard hats on their heads, and helmets with crests;
> Their banners were unfurled and lowered ready to meet;
> Rushing out of the woods, they formed up in phalanxes.)

When the knight-messenger goes out into the crowd to call forth the chief protagonists, however, he provides a detailed description of other social elements present upon the laund – principally the order of knighthood and the four orders of friars, but also lawyers, merchants and men-at-arms. The argument here is that the various groups most obviously prepared for war do not all come to the meeting in pursuit of a private quarrel between their leaders. The knight-messenger's description of the second of the three classic medieval estates, the *bellatores* or warriors, technically stands free of a description of one or other army, seemingly transcending both:

> 'Full wyde hafe I walked amonges thies wyes one,
> Bot sawe I never siche a syghte, segge, with myn eghne;
> For here es all the folke of Fraunce ferdede besyde,
> Of Lorreyne, of Lumbardye, and of Lawe Spayne;
> Wyes of Westwale, that in were duellen;
> Of Ynglonde, of Yrlonde, Estirlynges full many,
> That are stuffede in stele, strokes to dele.'
> (lines 136–42)
>
> ('I have travelled far and wide through foreign lands,
> But never saw I such a sight, I tell you;
> For here are all the men of France in fighting array,
> Of Lorraine, of Lombardy, and of lowland Spain,
> Men from Westphalia, that live in a state of war,

From England and Ireland, and many Easterlings,[34]
All armed in steel, ready to deal strokes.')

If we think of the occasion for the gathering as a tournament, then this passage can be read as describing a group of high-status lords and knights who had come together as participants and spectators at the feats of arms that would follow, rather than *sensu stricto* as the military followers of Wynnere and Wastoure.

Such a reading also helps to resolve the otherwise distinctly odd disparity between the long and detailed description of the supposed supporters of Wynnere (the pope, the lawyers, the four orders of friars, and the merchants at lines 143–92) and the brief few lines given over to Wastoure's supposed forces (at lines 193–6).[35] By referring back to the serious military purpose of the two armies described at lines 50–3, we can argue that the element described as being 'one that other syde' ('on the other side') at line 193 is not the army of one or other protagonist but rather a description of the types of fighting men from which both sides drew their essential support ('one that other syde' here having the more general sense of 'over there'):

---

[34] Britton J. Harwood, 'The Displacement of Labor in *Winner and Waster*', in Kellie Robertson and Michael Uebel (eds), *The Middle Ages at Work: Practicing Labor in Late Medieval England* (New York, 2004), pp. 157–77, at p. 163, uses the inclusion of men of *Ynglonde* (line 141) in this otherwise 'foreign' group to argue that the poem is set in Cheshire, which, as a palatine county, was formally outside the normal direct jurisdiction of the English crown. My own stress is on the internationalism of the tournament, which largely removes the apparent anomaly between denizens and foreigners, and places much more emphasis on the rank of knighthood. A too ready assumption by commentators that the 'Estirlynges' at line 141 have to be identified as Hanseatic merchants tends to weaken and obscure the force of this passage, which is again read much more straightforwardly and specifically as referring to the estate of knighthood. Merchants have their own, later coverage at lines 188–92; and 'Easterling' was a geographical and linguistic signifier, not a social one, that denoted a speaker of Low German from the Baltic and Prussia. (I owe this point to Sebastian Sobecki.) The assumption of a mercantile context is explicit, for example, in Bestul, *Satire and Allegory*, p. 4; Turville-Petre, p. 403 n. 5; Trigg, p. xxxvii; and Ginsberg, p. 17 (marginal n. to line 141).

[35] Lois Roney, '*Winner and Waster*'s "Wyse Wordes": Teaching Economics and Nationalism in Fourteenth-Century England', *Speculum*, 69 (1994), 1070–1100, at 1093–6, argues that the apparently truncated description of Wastoure's army arises because a section of text has been lost, hypothesising that this would have originally included a range of craftspeople and retailers. For further discussion of this issue, see Helen Barr, *Socioliterary Practice in Late Medieval England* (Oxford, 2001), pp. 12–13; and Katharine Breen, 'The Need for Allegory: *Wynnere and Wastoure* as an *Ars poetica*', *Yearbook of Langland Studies*, 26 (2012), 187–229, at 209–10.

And sekere one that other side are sadde men of armes,
Bolde sqwyeres of blode, bowmen many,
That if thay strike one stroke stynt thay ne thynken
Till owthir here appon hethe be hewen to dethe.
(lines 193–6)

(And strong, over there, are simple men at arms,
Bold well-born squires and many bowmen
Who, if they strike one stroke, will not think of stopping
Till either army is hewn to death upon the heath.)

This accurately describes the composition of English armies in this period, when men at arms (knights, as heavy cavalry) were joined on the field by two increasingly prominent groups: light cavalry (esquires); and archers, who frequently travelled to the field on horseback but dismounted for the fight.[36] Most importantly, this reading suggests that there are two levels of description going on within the poem: the one relating to the elite of international chivalry drawn together for a tournament, as at the St George's Day celebrations of 1358; and the other accounting for the presence of two much smaller contingents of modest fighters who have appeared on the laund in support of the chief protagonists to a private vendetta.

Reading W&W in such a way also allows the opportunity to reconsider the prominence that the poet ascribes to the ecclesiastical orders within his text (lines 143–8, 156–87). Banners bearing imaginary heraldic devices are only mentioned once in the poem in relation to the very social order with which heraldry was most closely associated: nobility and knighthood. This comes in the initial description of the armies of Wynnere and Wastoure at lines 50–3. By contrast, the later mention of banners, in the knight-messenger's description of the people arrayed on the laund, is dominated by the fictitious heraldry ascribed to the clerical orders. The first is the banner of the pope, decorated with images of the formal authority of his office, the bull or papal seal (lines 143–8). The second banner, emblazoned with their characteristic headgear, belongs to the lawyers (lines 149–55). The third, fourth, fifth and sixth banners return to the clergy and are each linked to the four orders of friars, with long descriptive passages on each one (lines 156–87). There was a lively debate at the beginning of the twentieth century over the significance of the heraldic arms that the author of W&W chose to ascribe to the mendicant orders.[37] This technical discussion, however, largely

[36] For the structure of English armies in the first phase of the Hundred Years War, see Ayton, *Knights and Warhorses*; and Adrian Bell, Anne Curry, Andy King and David Simpkin, *The Soldier in Later Medieval England* (Oxford, 2013).

[37] For the early debate on the heraldry of the banners in W&W, see Henry Bradley, 'Wynnere and Wastoure', *The Athenaeum*, 120, no. 3943 (23 May 1903), 657–8;

missed the point as to why friars needed to be represented in such elaborate form in the kind of context where they appear in the poem. Assuming that W&W was written after 1358, however, allows us to see the particular prominence accorded to the mendicant orders as a direct consequence of a cluster of public controversies that arose in England in the later 1350s.[38]

The first such controversy was aroused by the sensational series of vernacular, anti-mendicant sermons preached at St Paul's churchyard in London by Richard FitzRalph, archbishop of Armagh, in 1356–7. FitzRalph was vehemently opposed to the insistence of the friars (and especially the Franciscans) on the pursuit of evangelical poverty, and stoutly defended the rights of the secular clergy by arguing the legitimacy of the holding of property and wealth by the Church. In this instance, Edward III leapt to the defence of the friars, who were known to provide him with important personal and political services. For acting in defiance of a royal injunction, FitzRalph was forced to flee the realm and to refer his dispute to the papal curia; he died at Avignon in 1360.[39]

The second affair, which caused a particularly significant stir among the political and ecclesiastical elites, was the acrimonious quarrel between Blanche, Lady Wake, cousin of Edward III, and the Dominican Thomas de Lisle, bishop of Ely, over the murder of one of Blanche's servants by the bishop's henchmen in 1355. Edward III publicly declared himself Blanche's champion in the parliament of 1355 and set about destroying the uppity bishop, whose own status as a friar made him rather isolated within the wider episcopate. Found guilty of felony in 1356, Lisle had no option but to flee to Avignon where, in direct contravention of the recent Statute of

---

George Neilson, '"Wynnere and Wastoure" and the "Awntyres"', *The Athenaeum*, 120, no. 3946 (13 June 1903), 754–5; George Neilson, '"Wynnere and Wastoure"', *The Athenaeum*, 120, no. 3955 (15 August 1903), 221; Henry Bradley, '"Wynnere and Wastoure"', *The Athenaeum*, 120, no. 3948 (27 June 1903), 816–17. See also N. R. Havely, 'The Dominicans and their Banner in *Wynnere and Wastoure*', *Notes & Queries*, 30:3 (June 1983), 207–9.

[38] The point was made by George Neilson, 'A Note on "Wynnere and Wastoure"', *The Athenaeum*, 118, no. 3849 (3 August 1901), 157, but subsequently ignored. See also the debate prompted by this note: Israel Gollancz, 'A Note on "Wynnere and Wastoure"', *The Athenaeum*, 118, no. 3852 (24 August 1901), 254–5; George Neilson, 'A Note on "Wynnere and Wastoure"', *The Athenaeum*, 118, no. 3854 (7 September 1901), 319; and Israel Gollancz, 'A Note on "Wynnere and Wastoure"', *The Athenaeum*, 118, no. 3855 (14 September 1901), 351.

[39] Katherine Walsh, *A Fourteenth-Century Scholar and Primate: Richard FitzRalph in Oxford, Avignon and Armagh* (Oxford, 1981), pp. 239–78, 349–451; James Doyne Dawson, 'Richard FitzRalph and the Fourteenth-Century Poverty Controversies', *Journal of Ecclesiastical History*, 34 (1983), 315–44, at 341–3; Tim Rayborn, *Against the Friars: Antifraternalism in Medieval France and England* (Jefferson, North Carolina, 2014), pp. 134–61.

Praemunire (1353), he sought to appeal the judgment of the secular courts before Pope Innocent VI. Later in 1356, Innocent went so far as to excommunicate the two royal justices who had pronounced the sentence of felony, William Shareshull and Robert Thorpe. Such indeed were the sensitivities over the king's vendetta against Lisle and the resulting breaches of clerical privilege that John Thoresby, archbishop of York, resigned as chancellor of England in November 1356.[40]

There is nothing in the text of *W&W* to suggest that its author intended particularly to attack the Franciscans and the Dominicans for their quarrels with FitzRalph and with the crown. Where these events do become significant to the text, however, comes in their implications for Anglo-papal relations. Both the FitzRalph and the Lisle cases were interpreted in England as clear evidence of Pope Innocent VI's bias against Edward III, and can therefore also be used to explain the particular place accorded to the figure of the pope within *W&W*. The poet thinks he may espy the pope himself under the first of the banners, embroidered with emblems of papal bulls and with a sealed cord hanging down: 'That hede es of holy kirke I hope he be there' ('The head of Holy Church, I believe he is here') (lines 143–8, with quote at line 147). While no pope visited England in the Middle Ages, cardinals appointed by the curia to undertake a range of ecclesiastical and political duties did so reasonably regularly, not least in connection with the role that the papacy asserted during the Hundred Years War as arbiter between the competing powers of England and France.[41] The author of *W&W* appears to share the common English assumption of the time that, despite its claims of neutrality, the papacy, which was settled at Avignon between 1309 and 1378, was institutionally biased against England. He characterises both the Franciscans and the Dominicans as fighting men whose intellectual resourcefulness ('witt'; meaning 'wit', 'reason', or in less complimentary form 'guile') is greater than that of all the lords of the land (lines 169–73). After the subsequent description of the third order of mendicants, the Carmelites, the poet turns this 'witt' into the threat of real force:

[40] John Aberth, *Criminal Churchmen in the Reign of Edward III: The Case of Bishop Thomas de Lisle* (University Park, Pennsylvania, 1996), pp. 117–85, 240–50; Ormrod, *Edward III*, pp. 381–3.

[41] Karsten Plöger, *England and the Avignon Popes: The Practice of Diplomacy in Late Medieval Europe* (London, 2005), *passim*. For the activities and reputations of Clement VI (1342–52) and Innocent VI (1352–62) as peacemakers, see Guy Mollat, 'Innocent VI et les tentatives de paix entre la France et l'Angleterre (1353–1355)', *Revue d'histoire ecclésiastique*, 10 (1909), 729–43; Diana Wood, *Clement VI: The Pontificate and Ideas of an Avignon Pope* (Cambridge, 1989), *passim*; and, more generally, Françoise Autrand, 'The Peacemakers and the State: Pontifical Diplomacy and the Anglo-French Conflict in the Fourteenth Century', in Philippe Contamine (ed.), *War and Competition between States* (Oxford, 2000), pp. 249–77.

if I may, he says, it seems clear that the friars themselves, along with others, will win the day in the impending quarrel (lines 178–9). The poet's main concern, however, appears to be that the friars are under the special protection and jurisdiction of the pope, so that their own presence in England is in some senses representative of an unwelcome papal influence (line 169). In this sense, too, his satire chimes with some elements of the debates on the mendicants prompted by FitzRalph's polemic and the king's vendetta against Thomas de Lisle.

The main preoccupation of contemporary lay society in England in the mid-fourteenth century, however, lay not with the influence of the mendicants but with what was perceived as the gradual and insidious takeover of the wealth of the English Church by the practice of papal provision, by which Italian and French cardinals and other high-ranking members of the curia came to be granted some of the most profitable benefices in England. Papal provisions to English ecclesiastical titles increased significantly during the pontificate of Clement VI (1342–52).[42] The debate in England tended to be particularly forceful when cardinals, acting as papal envoys, were known to be playing a prominent part in Anglo-French diplomatic talks. At the parliament of 1343, the Commons made the following protest:

> Pur ce qe les aliens tiegnet tantz de beneficz en ceste terre … et le tresore de ceste terre est molt apportez pardela, en meyntenance de voz enemys, et les privetez de ceste terre descovertz … Et sur ce ore de novel plusours cardinalx sont faitz dont le pape par ses bulles ad grantez as deux de eux beneficz en ceste terre, a la montance de vi m. mars au tax, sure un si generale et coverte manere qe la somme passera x m. mars avant qe le doun soit accepte, si la chose soit ensi soeffert; et la commune ad entenduz qe l'un des deux cardinalx avantditz, c'est a dire le cardinal de Peragortz, si est le plus fere enemye qe soit en la courte, et plus contraire a les busoignes nostre seigneur le roi.

> (Since aliens hold so many benefices in this land … and much of the treasure of this land is exported overseas in maintenance of your [i.e., the king's] enemies, and the secrets of this land are disclosed … And many cardinals were recently made, wherefore the pope by his bulls has granted benefices in this land to two of them, to the amount of 6,000 marks in tax, in so general and secretive a manner that the amount will exceed 10,000 marks before the gift is accepted, if the thing is allowed. And the Commons have understood that one of the two aforesaid cardinals, that is to say the cardinal of Périgord, is the most bitter enemy that is in the curia, and the most hostile to the business of our lord the king.)[43]

---

[42] For papal provisions, see Katherine Harvey, *Episcopal Appointments in England, c.1214–1344: From Episcopal Election to Papal Provision* (Abingdon, 2016).

[43] *PROME*, vol. 4, p. 349.

The named man here, Hélie de Talleyrand, cardinal of Périgord, was well known to be one of those leading Pope Clement VI's efforts at a round of peace talks that led to an ultimately unsuccessful conference at Avignon in 1344.[44] Edward III found it convenient at this moment to sympathise with the Commons and issued a brief-lived Ordinance of Provisors, which prefigured the more famous Statute of Provisors of 1351 by banning (at least in theory) the holders of papal provisions from taking up their benefices in England.[45] Edward's sympathies were also demonstrated by his deliberately provocative behaviour at a tournament held in London in June 1343, at which he and his team dressed up as the pope and twelve cardinals.[46]

Much the same background is evident in 1353, when a peace conference was held at Guînes under the presidency of Guy de Boulogne, cardinal bishop of Porto, who had close family links with the court of France and equally close intellectual connections with the Dominicans.[47] After reporting the unsatisfactory terms offered by the French to a great council in September of that year, the crown responded to a common petition by issuing the Statute of Praemunire, which forbade appeals to the curia against cases brought in English courts on rights to ecclesiastical benefices within the kingdom of England.[48]

During the time of the Windsor Garter feast of 1358, cardinals were again at work on a papal mission for peace not just at conferences on the continent, but in England too.[49] The transfer of John II to England in 1357

---

[44] E. Déprez, 'La conference d'Avignon, 1344: L'arbitrage pontifical entre la France et l'Angleterre', in A. G. Little and F. M. Powicke (eds), *Essays in Medieval History Presented to Thomas Frederick Tout* (Manchester, 1925), pp. 301–20.

[45] *PROME*, vol. 4, pp. 351–2; A. D. M. Barrell, 'The Ordinance of Provisors of 1343', *Historical Research*, 63 (1991), 264–77.

[46] Juliet Barker, *The Tournament in England, 1100–1400* (Woodbridge, 1986), pp. 95–6; Vale, *Edward III and Chivalry*, p. 67.

[47] Ormrod, *Edward III*, 336.

[48] *PROME*, vol. 5, pp. 82, 83; *SR*, vol. 1, p. 329. For the real impact of the anti-papal statutes and their successors in the second half of the fourteenth century, see E. B. Graves, 'The Legal Significance of the Statute of Praemunire', in Charles H. Taylor (ed.), *Anniversary Essays Presented to C. H. Haskins* (New York, 1929), pp. 57–80; F. Cheyette, 'Kings, Courts, Cures, and Sinecures: The Statute of Provisors and the Common Law', *Traditio*, 19 (1963), 295–349; W. R. Jones, 'Relations of the Two Jurisdictions: Conflict and Cooperation in England during the Thirteenth and Fourteenth Centuries', *Studies in Medieval and Renaissance History*, orig. ser., 7 (1979), 102–32; Diane Martin, 'Prosecutions of the Statutes of Provisors and Praemunire in the King's Bench, 1377–1394', in Jeffrey Hamilton (ed.), *Fourteenth Century England VI* (Woodbridge, 2006), pp. 109–23.

[49] For the complex diplomacy of the period 1356–60, see John Le Patourel, *Feudal Empires: Norman and Plantagenet* (London, 1984), chaps XII, XIII; Jonathan

meant that diplomatic discussions between England and France became focused, for a few years, on London. The principal papal envoys to these talks were Cardinals Talleyrand and Capocci. Hélie de Talleyrand had been a conspicuous figure in the war before and after the battle of Poitiers, when he had attempted to avoid open conflict and, after the battle became inevitable, had begun the process of treating for John II's release. Some of his own men had, however, fought on the French side in 1356, and there was widespread distrust of Hélie and his like in England.[50] The chronicler Henry Knighton reports that Edward III met Talleyrand and Capocci 'arrayed in his imperial state, and with the face of a lion' (*quasi in apparatu imperiali et fero uultu tanquam leonis*).[51] The peace settlement that emerged in the so-called first Treaty of London was put before parliament in February 1358. Unfortunately, the official record of this assembly is lost; but two chroniclers, Sir Thomas Gray and Thomas Walsingham, provide what seem like credible accounts of the discussion that ensued.[52] The draft treaty was controversial: despite offering a very high ransom for the release of John II and promising English control of a significant swathe of territory in northern and western France, the text was silent on the matter of whether Edward III might reserve, or have to relinquish, his title to the throne of France. The Commons smelled a rat and declared that Pope Innocent's protection of Thomas de Lisle was clear evidence of his hostility to the English. They also demanded that Innocent desist from his recent attempts to re-activate the payment of Peter's Pence, the customary tribute paid by England in return for King John's acceptance of the suzerainty of Innocent III in 1213. In fine, the accustomed English suspicion both of the papacy and of its representatives, the cardinals, was notably heightened as a consequence of the diplomatic operations of Cardinals Talleyrand and Capocci, and reached something of a climax in the hyperbole of the parliamentary Commons in 1358.

To give credence to this frame of reference is also to allow the opportunity for a new reading of the closing lines of *W&W* in which, following his exiling of Wynnere to Paris and Rome (lines 460–71), the king predicts that he will, at some point in the future, lead an army to 'the proude pales of Parys the riche' ('the proud walls of great Paris') and thence to Cologne

---

Sumption, *The Hundred Years War* (4 vols, London, 1990–2015), vol. 2, pp. 289–91; Ormrod, *Edward III*, pp. 385–413.

[50] For full details, see Barbara Bombi, *Anglo-Papal Relations in the Early Fourteenth Century: A Study in Medieval Diplomacy* (Oxford, 2019), pp. 205–24.

[51] Martin (ed. and trans.), *Knighton's Chronicle*, pp. 152–3. See also Scott-Stokes and Given-Wilson (eds and trans.), *Chronicon Anonymi Cantuariensis*, pp. 38–43; Thomas Walsingham, *Historia Anglicana*, ed. Henry T. Riley, Rolls Series, 28 (2 vols, London, 1863–4), vol. 1, pp. 283–4.

[52] For what follows, see Gray, *Scalacronica*, pp. 150–3; Walsingham, *Historia Anglicana*, vol. 1, p. 285; *PROME*, vol. 5, p. 131; Ormrod, *Edward III*, p. 393.

Cathedral, where lie the remains of the Magi (lines 496–503). Until Victoria Flood's 2015 article, critical analysis had failed to note in any other than a very general sense the way in which this passage chimes with the text known to modern scholarship as *The Prophecy of the Six Kings*, which emerged as a new variant upon the Merlin tradition around the start of Edward III's reign and became embedded in a number of insular manuscript traditions, first in Anglo-Norman French and later in Middle English and Welsh.[53] The prophecy told of how the 'boar of Windsor' (clearly identifiable as Edward III) 'will whet his tusks on the gates of Paris' (*anguisera ses dentz sur les portes de Paris*) and conquer France; after taking the Holy Land, he will be buried at the shrine of the Three Kings at Cologne.[54] In this tradition, Paris and Cologne are taken as exemplifying Edward III's claims to the throne of France and to the office of Emperor.

When Edward, on his visit to Cologne in 1338, had declared an intention to be buried there, he had done so within the context of his election, a few weeks later, as vicar general of the Emperor Ludwig IV.[55] Although Edward subsequently declined nomination as Ludwig's successor in 1348, people in England had taken this simply as a sign of the king's firmness of purpose in following his other destiny, in France.[56] With the collapse of the Anglo-French peace negotiations of 1358–9, Edward prepared and led a major invasion of

[53] Victoria Flood, '*Wynnere and Wastoure* and the Influence of Political Prophecy', *Chaucer Review*, 49 (2015), 427–48. For the textual history of the prophecy, see T. M. Smallwood, 'The Prophecy of the Six Kings', *Speculum*, 60 (1985), 571–92; Lesley A. Coote, *Prophecy and Public Affairs in Later Medieval England* (York, 2000), pp. 83–119; Victoria Flood, *Prophecy, Politics and Place in Medieval England: From Geoffrey of Monmouth to Thomas of Erceldoune* (Cambridge, 2016), pp. 87–102. For earlier discussion of the wider influence of prophecy on *Wynnere and Wastoure*, see, for example, Bestul, *Satire and Allegory*, pp. 59–65; Geoffrey Shepherd, 'The Nature of Alliterative Poetry in Late Medieval England', in J. A. Burrow (ed.), *Middle English Literature: British Academy Gollancz Lectures* (Oxford, 1989), pp. 141–60, at pp. 151–2.

[54] See the reconstruction of the original Anglo-Norman prose version of the prophecy in Flood, *Prophecy, Politics and Place*, p. 89 n. 92 and p. 97. Compare the later fourteenth-century English prose translation in F. W. D. Brie (ed.), *The Brut, or, The Chronicles of England*, EETS OS 131, 136 (2 vols, London, 1906–8), vol. 1, pp. 74–6. For other texts written around the time of the Crécy-Calais campaign of 1346–7 that imagine Edward's final victory in France specifically in terms of the conquest of Paris, see Flood, *Prophecy, Politics and Place*, pp. 98–9.

[55] Tait (ed.), *Chronica Johannis de Reading et Anonymi Cantuariensis*, pp. 132–3; H. S. Offler, 'England and Germany at the Beginning of the Hundred Years' War', *English Historical Review*, 54 (1939), 608–31, at 608–13; Ormrod, *Edward III*, p. 201.

[56] Thompson (ed.), *Chronicon Galfridi le Baker*, p. 97; Martin (ed. and trans.), *Knighton's Chronicle*, pp. 90–3.

France in 1359–60. The intention, as the chroniclers expressed it, was to put an end once and for all to Edward's dispute with the Valois by a massive show of strength that would rapidly force the regime of John II into submission.[57] If *W&W* reverberates with prophecy, then it may represent the reflections of a man who knew what Edward III planned in 1360: not only to take Rheims, the traditional coronation place of French kings, but also to lay siege to the city of Paris, the political capital of the Valois' kingdom.[58]

Finally, if we push the date of composition of *W&W* firmly into the 1360s, then the judgment meted out upon the two protagonists by the king at lines 456–503, and the final references to Edward III's destinies in France and the Empire at lines 496–503, could be seen as an important part of a public debate that developed over the wisdom and success of the diplomatic settlement made with the French in and after 1360.[59] Edward's failure to draw his enemies into open battle forced him to cut short the 1359–60 campaign and to sue for peace, first under terms set out in the Treaty of Brétigny and subsequently in the Treaty of Calais, both of 1360. In return for the promise of a huge ransom of £500,000 for the release of John II and full sovereign control over Calais and a great swathe of territories in south-west France, Edward III would agree to renounce his claim to the French throne.[60] The English polity seems initially to have been enthusiastic about

---

[57] Viard and Déprez (eds), *Chronique de Jean le Bel*, vol. 2, pp. 298–9; Jean Froissart, *Chroniques*, ed. S. Luce *et al.* (15 vols, Paris, 1859–1975), vol. 5, pp. 198–9; Tait (ed.), *Chronica Johannis de Reading et Anonymi Cantuariensis*, p. 133.

[58] For accounts of this campaign, see Clifford Rogers, *War Cruel and Sharp: English Strategy under Edward III, 1327–1360* (Woodbridge, 2000), pp. 407–8; Sumption, *Hundred Years War*, vol. 2, pp. 405–48; Ormrod, *Edward III*, pp. 400–4.

[59] Gollancz claimed that the reference to an impending military campaign in France means that *W&W* must have been written in a period when there was no truce in operation, and argued that the poem referred to a campaign fought by Edward III during a lapse between truces from September 1352 to March 1353: see the convoluted arguments analysed by Trigg, p. xxiv and n. 3. Trigg appears to believe this argument, to the extent that she assumes the king was abroad during the relevant months. In fact, while the various truces contracted during this period did indeed lapse between September 1352 and March 1353, the whole argument for the renewal of taxation put before the parliament of January–February 1352 was that the French had broken the truce and that impending war was inevitable: Thomas Rymer (ed.), *Foedera, conventiones, literae et cujuscunque generi acta publica* (3 vols in 6 parts, London, 1816–30), vol. 3(i), pp. 232, 254; *PROME*, vol. 5, p. 40. In spite of the renewal of hostilities in various theatres of war during 1352, however, no campaign was fought in France under royal leadership in 1352–3. Edward's continued presence in England throughout this year and the next can be firmly established by reference to his itinerary: Ormrod, *Edward III*, p. 623.

[60] For full details of the 1360 treaties and their interpretation by historians, see the

the prospect of lasting peace offered by this settlement, and the parliament of 1361 approved the Treaty of Calais without any obvious demur.[61] As time went on, however, and it became apparent just how difficult it was going to be to force the French into paying the ransom and ceding jurisdiction over the continental territories newly allocated to Edward, an element of disillusionment clearly developed in the domestic polity.

One of the main voices left for us from this debate is that of Sir Thomas Gray, who had participated in the earlier wars and began writing his Anglo-Norman prose chronicle, the *Scalacronica*, shortly after the Treaty of Calais. Gray spoke quite self-consciously for the many English knightly captains and men-at-arms who had invested themselves so deeply in the king's wars over the previous two decades. He claimed that Edward III's apparently cynical decision to renounce his ancestral rights in return for money amounted to a gross betrayal of everything for which he and his fellows thought they had been fighting since Edward had declared himself king of France in 1340.[62] In the first version (the A-text) of *Piers Plowman*, usually dated to the 1360s (though with passages that may have been added in the 1370s), William Langland seemingly shared in that same collective shock, denouncing a king who had been prepared to sell his 'lordsshipe' ('lordship' or 'sovereignty') of the 'riccheste reaume' ('richest realm') (i.e., France) for the 'litel silver' ('small amount of silver') generated from the ransom of John II.[63] After John's death in 1364, the prospect of the Valois maintaining the commitment of 1360 and paying the remainder of the ransom became still more unlikely, and the expectation of a peace dividend in which Edward and his subjects might share shrank away.[64]

---

review in Ormrod, *Edward III*, pp. 404–10.

[61] *PROME*, vol. 5, p. 133.

[62] Gray, *Scalacronica*, pp. 187–8; Andy King, 'War and Peace: A Knight's Tale. The Ethics of War in Sir Thomas Gray's *Scalacronica*', in Chris Given-Wilson, Ann J. Kettle and Len Scales (eds), *War, Government and Aristocracy in the British Isles, c.1150–1500: Essays in Honour of Michael Prestwich* (Woodridge, 2008), pp. 148–62, at pp. 153–4, 155–8.

[63] A-text, Passus III, lines 194–5: see George Kane (ed.), *Piers Plowman: The A Version. Will's Vision of Piers Plowman and Do-Well* (London, 1960), p. 245. For commentary on the dating and significance of this passage, see B. F. Huppé, 'The A-Text of *Piers Plowman* and the Norman Wars', *PMLA*, 54 (1939), 37–55; J. A. W. Bennett, 'The Date of the A-Text of *Piers Plowman*', *PMLA*, 58 (1943), 566–72, at 569; Ben Lowe, *Imagining Peace: A History of Early English Pacifist Ideas, 1340–1560* (Philadelphia, 1997), pp. 91–2; Denise M. Baker, 'Meed and the Economics of Chivalry in *Piers Plowman*', in Denise M. Baker (ed.), *Inscribing the Hundred Years' War in French and English Cultures* (Albany, New York, 2000), pp. 55–72.

[64] Ormrod, *Edward III*, pp. 423–4, 435. For details on the payments of this ransom, see below, p. 91.

Diplomatic setbacks also compounded the growing sense of English vulnerability. Pope Urban V's blatant manoeuvres during 1364 to block Edward III's bold plan to make his fourth son, Edmund of Langley, heir to the county of Flanders provoked public frustration in England that vented itself in the re-issue of the Statutes of Provisors and Praemunire in the parliament of January 1365 and the symbolic abolition of Peter's Pence in the next assembly, of May 1366.[65] The general mood of these assemblies is nicely articulated on the parliament roll for 1366, which recounts how the lay Lords and Commons reported back to the king that the homage performed by King John to Innocent III in 1213, on which basis the annual tribute of Peter's Pence had since been levied, was null and void since it broke the coronation oath to maintain the rights and dignities of the crown of England:

> Et outre ce, les ducs, countes, barons, grantz et communes accordant et granterent qe en cas qe le pape so afforceroit ou rien attempteroit par process ou en autre manere de fait, de constreindre le roi o uses subgitz de perfaire ce q'est dit q'il voet clamer celle partie, q'ils resistront et contreesterront ove toute leur peussance.
>
> (And in addition to this, the dukes, earls, barons, great men and Commons agreed and granted that in the event that the pope would assert or attempt anything, by process or in other manner of deed, to constrain the king and his subjects to do what is said he will claim in this matter [that is, to enforce the collection of Peter's Pence], they will resist and oppose it with all their power.)[66]

All of this serves to reinforce a suggestion that the king's exhortation to Wynnere to 'wayte to me' ('look to me') (line 496) until the moment when he attacks the 'proude pales of Parys the riche' ('proud walls of great Paris') (line 498), rather than predicting the campaign of 1359–60, is actually an expression of hope written after the diplomatic settlement that followed, to the effect that Edward might yet recognise the defects of the peace settlement and re-launch a war intent on the full-scale conquest of France. Without the lines that comprised the remainder of the text of *W&W*, we cannot be absolutely sure of the valences of the king's remarks on such a prospect. But the general tone may suggest that the author had a rather

---

[65] *PROME*, vol. 5, pp. 172–3, 177–81, 190, 193–4. For full discussion of Edward's ambitions in Flanders and his resulting conflict with Urban V, see J. J. N. Palmer, 'England, France, the Papacy and the Flemish Succession, 1361–69', *Journal of Medieval History*, 2 (1976), 339–64; J. J. N. Palmer and A. P. Wells, 'Ecclesiastical Reform and the Politics of the Hundred Years War during the Pontificate of Urban V (1362–70)', in C. T. Allmand (ed.), *War, Literature and Politics in the Late Middle Ages* (Liverpool, 1976), pp. 169–89.

[66] *PROME*, vol. 5, p. 194.

different and more hopeful vantage point from those adopted by Gray and Langland. Lacking any particular sense of overt criticism of the terms of peace, *W&W* seems instead to retreat into the prophetic fantasies that saw Edward as the new Arthur, and thus sought to uphold the otherwise rather desperate belief that he was indeed still capable of world domination.[67] In this sense, the poem may also align more closely with the collective sense of denial that continued to prevail in the inner circles of the court and the military elite until the mid-1370s over the possibility that a return to war could be anything but beneficial for Edward III's cause.

This chapter has argued that *W&W* made a series of references to recognisable social and political events over the course of the later 1350s and first half of the 1360s. The inference that the tournament envisioned at the beginning of the poem was to take place in the king's Great Park of Windsor, together with the powerful representation of foreign knights present in anticipation of the affair, strongly suggests that the poem effectively re-creates the special tournament held at the Garter feast at Windsor in 1358 in celebration of the Black Prince's victory at Poitiers and the resulting confinement in England of John II of France. The general anti-mendicant sentiment of the poem, moreover, can be linked with two controversies sparked in the mid-1350s over the place and rights of the friars in England. In terms of the poem's wider anti-papal stance, however, and its specific references in the final extant lines to the king's ambitions on the continent, it seems to read more as a text of the early 1360s, looking back on events over the previous decade and a half, rather than one composed in the immediate context, for example, of the 1358 Windsor tournament. This is a reminder of the point made in the Introduction that the well-informed poet of *W&W* seems to have had a good memory, and had a tendency to conjure up images of people and events from the relatively recent past as though they were contemporary with his writing. This point is worth further consideration in relation to the poem's references to aspects of the law and law enforcement, to which we next turn.

---

[67] Compare the high-flown Latin dedication found in some manuscripts of Mandeville's *Travels*, which present Edward III as the model Christian prince and imply his right to rule throughout the western world: Jean de Mandeville, *Le livre des merveilles*, ed. Christine Deluz (Paris, 2000), p. 483. For studies that argue the credibility of a presentation of the *Travels* to Edward III in the later 1350s or early 1360s, see Michael J. Bennett, 'Mandeville's *Travels* and the Anglo-French Moment', *Medium Aevum*, 75 (2006), 273–92; W. Mark Ormrod, 'John Mandeville, Edward III, and the King of Inde', *Chaucer Review*, 46 (2012), 314–39.

= 2 =

Treason, Public Order and Dispute Settlement: The Statute of Treasons of 1352 and Royal Arbitration

The aim of this chapter is to demonstrate the fallibility of two previously central arguments in the dating and interpretation of *W&W*: first, that the poem explicitly references the Statute of Treasons of 1352; and secondly that it commemorates the Black Prince's eyre (judicial visitation) of Cheshire in 1353. More generally, the chapter calls into question the degree to which the poet was concerned with more general issues of public order, and instead emphasises the particular challenges created by the desire of landed society to take matters into its own hands and resolve disputes through armed force. Seeing the 'trial' of Wynnere and Wastoure not as a formal judicial process with a plaintiff and a defendant, but rather as a form of royal arbitration between two equally matched (and equally implicated) protagonists, allows a more general discussion of Edward III's record and achievement in providing informal dispute resolution between his high-status subjects. As in the previous chapter, so in this: a reading of *W&W* that assumes a composition in the later 1350s or the 1360s allows us to move away from the sometimes reductive nature of previous historicist scholarship on the poem and to offer a new range of possible allusions to contemporary events and controversies surrounding the rule of law.

Early in the poem, we are told that the great assembly gathered before the king includes the forces of two rivals who have already technically broken the king's peace by unfurling their banners in a state of private war:

> In aythere holte was ane here in hawberkes full brighte,
> Harde hates appon hedes and helmys with crestys;
> Brayden owte appon thaire baners bown for to mete;
> Schowen owte of the schawes in schiltrons they felle
> And bot the lengthe of a launde theis lordes bytwene.
>
> (lines 50–4)

(On either side were two armies in bright hauberks,
Hard hats on their heads, and helmets with crests;
Their banners were unfurled and lowered ready to meet;

Rushing out of the woods, they formed up in phalanxes;
There was only the length of a laund between these lords.)

It is only subsequently, when the second knight is despatched to warn the rivals that they should bring their cause before the king, that the specific offence is elaborated (the words are those of the second knight):

'... Loo! the kyng of this kyth, ther kepe hym oure Lorde!
Send his erande by me, als hym beste lyketh,
That no beryn be so bolde, one bothe his two eghne,
Ones to strike one stroke, no stirre none nerre
To lede rowte in his rewme, so ryall to thynke
Pertly with youre powers his pese to disturbe.
For this es the usage here and ever schall worthe:
If any beryn be so bolde with banere for to ryde
Withinn the kyngdome riche bot the kynge one,
That he schall losse the londe and his lyfe aftir.'

(lines 124–33)

('... Lo! The king of this land, may the Lord keep him,
Sends his errand by me, as it most pleased him,
That no man should be so bold, on pain of both his eyes,
To strike a single stroke, or to stir up others
To raise a rout in his realm, so royal it is,
Using your powers openly to disturb his peace.
For this is the custom here, and will ever stand:
If any man is so bold as to ride forth with a banner
Within this noble kingdom, except the king alone,
That he shall lose his land, and his life thereafter.')

Two elements of this passage have been used to pin the poem's concerns over law and order to the specific context of the parliament of 1352. First, there is the remarkably persistent claim, first made by Henry Bradley in 1903, that the phrase 'his pese to disturbe' ('to disturb his peace') at line 127, repeated verbatim in specific relation to Sir William Shareshull at line 318, consciously echoes Shareshull's opening speech to the 1352 assembly, recorded on the parliament roll.[1] Given the reliance of so many arguments on this point, it is appropriate here to provide the text of the relevant part of Shareshull's 1352 speech in full.

---

[1] Henry Bradley, '"Wynnere and Wastoure"', *The Athenaeum*, 120, no. 3948 (27 June 1903), 816–17; Gollancz, p. vi. For criticism of such a position, see Trigg, p. xxv.

[N]ostre seignur le roi ad entenduz qe la pees de son roialme n'est pas bien garde come ester deveroit, et qe les destourbours de la pees et meintenours des quereles et des roites faites en pais grevont trope a son poeple, sanz ceo qe due punissement est fait de eux.

(... [O]ur lord the king understands that the peace of his realm is not as well kept as it should be, and that the disturbers of the peace and maintainers of disputes and riots occurring in the land greatly grieve his people, without due punishment being made upon them.)[2]

In fact, then, this source gives a slightly different rendering of the basic word-set: the chief justice, in expressing concern at the fact that the king's peace was imperfectly observed, claimed that 'disturbers of the peace' (*destourbours de la pees*) were going free without punishment. This should already provide a clue to the fact that the idiomatic link between 'pese' and 'disturbe' is simply too generalised to bear out the argument of conscious repetition by the poet of *W&W*. 'To disturb the peace', 'disturbance of the peace' and 'disturber[s] of the peace' are completely stock phrases in fourteenth-century legal and quasi-legal language (both in Latin, where the verb form is *disturbare*, and in Anglo-Norman, where it is *destourber*), and find clear resonance both backwards and forwards in time from the 1350s. The relevant phrases occur repeatedly, for example, in the important speech on law and order made by one of Shareshull's predecessors as chief justice of the king's bench, Sir Geoffrey Scrope, in parliament in 1332, and in a multiplicity of special commissions to arrest suspected felons issued over the years immediately following.[3]

Similarly, the breaking of the king's peace and measures to restore law and order were explicitly cited as reasons for the summoning of parliament not just in 1352 but also during the 1340s and in the assemblies of 1351, 1362, 1365, 1366 and 1368.[4] (It should be noted in this respect that the parliament rolls for 1357–61 are missing; the relevant assemblies may also have borne upon this question.) Shareshull may well have been the royal justice most keenly associated with a campaign of law and order in the middle decades of the fourteenth century: his modern biographer, Bertha Putnam, saw him as the architect of a considerable body of legislation in the 1350s designed to eradicate corruption in the courts and to enforce a wide range of social and economic obligations.[5] But he was also working, as we shall see

---

[2] *PROME*, vol. 5, p. 40.
[3] *PROME*, vol. 4, pp. 166–8; Anthony Musson, *Public Order and Law Enforcement: The Local Administration of Criminal Justice, 1294–1350* (Woodbridge, 1996), p. 70.
[4] *PROME*, vol. 4, pp. 267, 280, 434; vol. 5, pp. 9, 140, 176, 192, 207.
[5] Bertha H. Putnam, *The Place in Legal History of Sir William Shareshull, Chief Justice of the King's Bench* (Cambridge, 1950), pp. 59–78.

below, in a tradition of law enforcement that stretched backwards and forwards in time.[6] The argument that *W&W* deliberately references, and was therefore written immediately after, Shareshull's speech in the parliament of 1352 is therefore extremely tenuous.

The critical literature has equally (and equally needlessly) fixated upon the politics of 1352 with regard to the specific offence of which Wastoure subsequently complains of being charged by Shareshull and others (lines 314–18): that he had 'prikkede with powere his pese to distourbe' ('pricked with armed power to disturb his [that is, the king's] peace'). This, together with the definition of the relevant crime as set out at lines 130–3, has been understood as a direct reference to the Statute of Treasons of 1352 and the status that it accorded to the criminal offence of private war:

> Si par cas ascun homme de cest roialme chivache arme descovert ou secrement od gentz armees contre ascun autre, pur lui tuer ou derober, ou pur lui prendre et retenir tanq'il face fyn ou ranceon pur sa deliverance avoir, n'est par l'entent du roi et de son conseil qe en tiel cas soit ajugge treson, einz soit ajugge felonie ou trespass solonc la lei de la terre auncienement usee et solonc ceo qe le cas demand.
>
> (If by chance any man of this realm shall ride armed, openly or secretly, with armed men, against any other in order to kill or rob him, or to take and keep him until fine or ransom is made for his deliverance, it is not the mind of the king, nor that of his council, that in such cases it be judged as treason, but it shall be adjudged felony or trespass according to the law of the land as customarily observed, and as the case requires.)[7]

The older critical literature tended to assume that this was the first time that the crown had taken cognisance of the act of raising an armed force for the purpose of prosecuting a private vendetta, and therefore sees 1352 as a necessary *terminus a quo* for the composition of *W&W*.[8] This, in fact, is quite wrong. The work of historians such as Maurice Keen, John Bellamy and Richard Kaeuper has demonstrated very clearly that the precocity and expansiveness of the English criminal law meant that private war, which was licensed extensively in other parts of Europe, came to be regarded as a serious offence against the crown in England at least by the end of the thirteenth century.[9] The second knight in *W&W* announces that England has a

---

[6] See below, pp. 46–8, 60.
[7] *PROME*, vol. 5, p. 45; *SR*, vol. 1, pp. 319–20, with quote at 320 (translation modified).
[8] Gollancz, n. to line 130.
[9] M. H. Keen, *The Laws of War in the Late Middle Ages* (London, 1965), *passim*; J. G. Bellamy, *Crime and Public Order in England in the Later Middle Ages* (London, 1973), *passim*; and Richard W. Kaeuper, *War, Justice, and Public Order: England*

usage – a custom or tradition – on these matters, not that a new law on the subject has recently been promulgated.[10] As Eleanor Johnson has argued, that usage need not be treason at all, but could simply be a reference to the crime of trespass *vi et armis*: a real or imagined attack 'by force and arms' by a hostile opponent, for which ready remedy (by financial penalty, rather than by death) was provided in the criminal courts.[11]

Still greater unnecessary confusion has arisen from Salter's argument that the author of *W&W* actually made an error in assuming that riding with hostile intent against a rival was treason, when the Statute of Treasons of 1352 emphatically declared it to be outside the normal definition of the term and fixed it at a lesser order of offence, either a felony or a trespass.[12] In fact, the poet was emphatically not in error. First, he describes as treasonous not the simple act of 'riding' but the specific crime of riding 'with banere' ('with a banner') (line 131) – that is, with the heraldic achievements of the relevant party formally displayed on a rectangular banner. 'Riding with banners unfurled/displayed' was one of the standard ways in which an act of civil war or private war was defined in the fourteenth century; developments in both common and statutory law over the first half of that century made it clear that uprisings of this type were to be regarded as acts of treason.[13] Secondly, and more dramatically, the hostile figures of Wynnere and Wastoure are gathered with their supporters and other onlookers on the laund within sight of the king; by unfurling their banners in pursuit of their quarrel (line 52), they are therefore directly threatening the person and office of the monarch, in a clear act of *lèse majesté*.[14] And thirdly, Wynnere and Wastoure and

---

and France in the Later Middle Ages (Oxford, 1988), pp. 195–9, 225–31, 260–8.

[10] See also the comments of Richard Firth Green, *A Crisis of Truth: Literature and Law in Ricardian England* (Philadelphia, 1999), p. 212.

[11] Eleanor Johnson, 'The Poetics of Waste: Medieval English Ecocriticism', *PMLA*, 127 (2012), 460–76, at 463. I cannot accept Johnson's wider view that the debate between Wynnere and Wastoure is itself a form of trespass trial.

[12] Elizabeth Salter, *English and International: Studies in the Literature, Art and Patronage of Medieval England*, ed. Derek Pearsall and Nicolette Zeeman (Cambridge, 1988), pp. 181–3.

[13] Maurice H. Keen, 'Treason Trials under the Law of Arms', *Transactions of the Royal Historical Society*, 5th ser., 12 (1962), 85–103, at 93–6; J. G. Bellamy, *The Law of Treason in England in the Later Middle Ages* (Cambridge, 1970), pp. 92–5; Andy King, 'False Traitors or Worthy Knights? Treason and Rebellion against Edward II in the *Scalacronica* and the Anglo-Norman Prose *Brut* Chronicles', *Historical Research*, 88 (2015), 34–47, at 46; and Andy King, '"War", "Rebellion" or "Perilous Times"? Political Taxonomy and the Conflict in England, 1321–2', in Rémy Ambühl, James Bothwell and Laura Tompkins (eds), *Ruling Fourteenth-Century England: Essays in Honour of Christopher Given-Wilson* (Woodbridge, 2019), pp. 113–32.

[14] For the seriousness with which English law approached breaches of the king's per-

many of the others present are subsequently noted by the second knight as being foreigners (lines 138–41); the remarks on English *usage* ('custom') at lines 130–3 are simply meant to point up for their benefit that the notion of the king's peace in England did not encompass the right of one subject to make war on another.[15]

The classic comparator in this respect is France, where, by stark contrast, aristocratic society clung resolutely to its right to prosecute private wars; in spite of a series of royal initiatives by Louis IX and his immediate successors, the principle continued to prevail into the later fourteenth and fifteenth centuries.[16] The second knight in *W&W* was not therefore announcing some deeply nuanced point of law, and certainly not referring to any technical changes that might recently have been made to that law; what was relevant was that those schooled in other customs knew that in England it was unacceptable to make war against one's neighbour. In short, there is no reason why the definition of private war provided by the Statute of Treasons should be taken as a *terminus a quo* for *W&W*, that the passage at lines 130–3 should be seen as consciously referencing the legislation of 1352, or indeed that *W&W* is in any substantive sense 'about' the crime of treason at all.[17]

In just the same way as the supposed referencing of the Statute of Treasons proves to be something of a red herring both for the dating and for the meaning of *W&W*, so too is it unnecessary to suppose that the wider framework of law and order represented in the poem should be restricted to a unique historical moment in 1352–3. The argument that Wastoure's outburst against Shareshull and the lawyers at lines 329–33 specifically references the Black Prince's eyre of Cheshire, presided over by Shareshull in 1353, is especially tenuous. Trigg has already successfully discredited Gollancz's efforts to read the figure of the second knight in *W&W* as Edward of Woodstock, revealing the editor's all too eager efforts to compliment the

---

sonal peace and offences against his person and household, see Warren C. Brown, *Violence in Medieval Europe* (London, 2011), p. 201.

[15] For more on this point see below, pp. 42–3.

[16] Kaeuper, *War, Justice, and Public Order*, pp. 231–60. See also the useful summary by Richard W. Kaeuper, 'Private War', in William W. Kibler, Grover A. Zinn, Lawrence Earp and John Bell Henneman, Jr. (eds), *Medieval France: An Encyclopedia* (New York, 1995), p. 760.

[17] This approach obviates the necessity felt by Jana Mathews, 'The Case for Misprision in *Wynnere and Wastoure*', *Notes & Queries*, 46 (1999), 317–21, to see the offence committed by the two parties as misprision, which originally had the generic meaning of a misdemeanour but later, under the name of misprision of treason, came to denote the action of concealing one's knowledge of an act of treason committed by another. Even if we feel the need to look for other forms of treason in *W&W*, Mathews' argument falters on her failure to find any mid-fourteenth-century material to support the specific association between misprision and treason.

Prince of Wales of his day, the future Edward VIII.[18] Even if we suppose that the allusion to 'the West' at line 32 and the possible traces of a North-Western dialect in the poem imply that the poet had an eye to events in this area, we should remember that the poet did not know in what part of the country his dream was set (line 47).

Furthermore, it is quite incorrect to argue, as Scattergood does, that the only notable outbreak of lawlessness occurring in 'the West' (whatever precise area that term may encompass) between 1349 and 1365 took place in Cheshire.[19] As P. H. W. Booth has shown, the idea that the Cheshire eyre of 1353 was prompted by an armed uprising in the county is actually a fallacy of nineteenth-century antiquarianism. Although the inquiries that ensued certainly revealed a high level of disorder in the area, the motivating force behind the eyre of 1353 was emphatically fiscal, in that it offered the Black Prince the chance to levy a very heavy communal fine on the political community of the county in lieu of individual and collective prosecutions.[20] Much more serious in terms of a directed campaign against disorder in the areas where the Black Prince had special interests, in fact, were the subsequent judicial inquiries that Shareshull organised in Devon and Cornwall in 1354, in Cheshire (again) in 1358, and in the lordship of Denbigh in 1362 (with Shareshull coming out of retirement in this latter case to head the sessions).[21]

---

[18] Stephanie Trigg, 'Israel Gollancz's "Wynnere and Wastoure": Political Satire or Editorial Politics?', in Gregory Krutzmann and James Simpson (eds), *Medieval English Religious and Ethical Literature: Essays in Honour of G. H. Russell* (Cambridge, 1986), pp. 115–27, *passim*.

[19] John Scattergood, '*Winner and Waster* and the Mid-Fourteenth-Century Economy', in Tom Dunne (ed.), *The Writer as Witness: Literature as Historical Evidence*, Historical Studies, 16 (Cork, 1987), pp. 39–57, at p. 51, followed by Ginsberg, p. 3, and Britton J. Harwood, 'The Displacement of Labor in *Winner and Waster*', in Kellie Robertson and Michael Uebel (eds), *The Middle Ages at Work: Practicing Labor in Late Medieval England* (New York, 2004), pp. 157–77, at p. 166.

[20] P. H. W. Booth, 'Taxation and Public Order: Cheshire in 1353', *Northern History*, 12 (1976), 16–31, at 21. The point is acknowledged by Britton J. Harwood, 'Anxious over Peasants: Textual Disorder in *Winner and Waster*', *Journal of Medieval and Early Modern Studies*, 36 (2006), 291–319, at 305. See also, in general, P. Hall and P. Booth (eds), *The Chester County Court Indictment Roll, 1354–1377: Dealing with Serious Crime in Late Medieval Cheshire*, Chetham Society 3rd series 53 (2009).

[21] Putnam, *Shareshull*, pp. 1, 39–40, 67, 72–74, 163; Booth, 'Taxation and Public Order', p. 23; W. Mark Ormrod, *Edward III* (London, 2011), p. 361 and n. 22. Carter Revard, 'The Papelard Priest and the Black Prince's Men: Audiences of an Alliterative Poem, ca. 1350–1370', *Studies in the Age of Chaucer*, 23 (2001), 359–406, argues (at p. 379 n. 44) that *W&W* may be associated with the 1358 visitation of Cheshire.

The idea that the author of *W&W* was impressed solely or principally by the eyre of Cheshire (or by these latter initiatives) falters, too, when we appreciate the subjective nature of the evidence linking him personally to the North-West. It suits the purposes of literary historians to locate *W&W* in this area since it also apparently produced the four great poems of the *Pearl* manuscript and was a recruiting ground for the retainers of the Black Prince who went on to form a distinct provincial court in Cheshire under the presidency of Richard II.[22] In fact, however, as we saw in the Introduction, it has been argued that, like a significant number of other texts in the Thornton manuscripts, the dialect of *W&W* matches most closely that of an area of the North-East Midlands at the intersection of the counties of Nottinghamshire, Lincolnshire and Yorkshire.[23] In light of the assumptions that have been made about the original poet's close links to the royal court, it might be added that it was precisely the same area – Nottinghamshire, north Lincolnshire and a specific portion of Yorkshire bounded by York, Selby and Howden – that produced the single largest number of clerks operating in the royal chancery and other departments of government between the reigns of Edward I and Edward III.[24] A poet from this area might well have been less interested in events in 'the West' than he was with other law-enforcement initiatives that had taken place in his own region, such as the important sessions of the king's bench held at Lincoln and York under the presidency of Shareshull's predecessor, William Thorpe, in 1348–9, or the long sojourn of the same court at York during the Trinity and Michaelmas terms of 1362 under the direction of his successor, Henry Green.[25]

The universalising instinct and national reach of the author of *W&W*, which become most evident in his discussion of economic matters, also make it highly unlikely that he sought to use the poem as a detailed commentary on

---

[22] Michael J. Bennett, '*Sir Gawain and the Green Knight* and the Literary Achievement of the North-West Midlands: The Historical Background', *Journal of Medieval History*, 5 (1979), 63–88; Michael J. Bennett, 'The Court of Richard II and the Promotion of Literature', in Barbara A. Hanawalt (ed.), *Chaucer's England: Literature in Historical Context* (Minneapolis, 1992), pp. 3–20.

[23] See above, p. 4.

[24] J. L. Grassi, 'Royal Clerks from the Archdiocese of York in the Fourteenth Century', *Northern History*, 5 (1970), 12–33.

[25] For the scale and importance of the 1348–9 sessions, see W. Mark Ormrod, 'Edward III's Government of England, c.1346–c.1356' (Unpublished D.Phil. thesis, University of Oxford, 1984), pp. 186–94; W. Mark Ormrod, 'Competing Capitals? York and London in the Fourteenth Century', in Sarah Rees Jones, Richard Marks and A. J. Minnis (eds), *Courts and Regions in Medieval Europe* (York, 2000), pp. 75–98, at pp. 88–9. For the 1362 sessions, see Anthony Musson and W. Mark Ormrod, *The Evolution of English Justice: Law, Politics and Society in the Fourteenth Century* (Basingstoke, 1999), p. 202.

a specific campaign of law and order in any one region of the realm.[26] Shareshull continued Thorpe's practice of a peripatetic king's bench acting with comprehensive powers in the shires, but he actually concentrated his efforts on the South and the East, and particularly the Home Counties and East Anglia, where he held such sessions in virtually every year from 1351 to 1358. Henry Green maintained this tradition of an itinerant court of special jurisdiction through the king's bench's sessions at York in 1362, in the South-West Midlands in 1363, and in East Anglia in 1364–5.[27] These judicial visitations, which were regarded by the landed gentry of the relevant counties as an intrusion into their rights of self-government, proved controversial, and parliament several times tried to persuade the king to put a stop to them.[28] In this respect, Wastoure's belief that Shareshull and the justices had unfairly hounded him and his like (lines 314–18) could be read as expressing the frustration of a whole range of local elites about the heavy-handedness of the officials of the central courts, as well as the argument, which came to prevail by the end of the 1360s, that public order should be upheld through a form of self-policing represented by the commissions of the peace, staffed by nobility, gentry and men of law, and all drawn from the relevant locality.[29]

These major initiatives within the more general campaign of law and order conducted throughout the middle years of Edward III's reign provide the final clue as to the statement in *W&W* of the involvement of William Shareshull in proceedings against Wastoure, articulated in the latter character's second speech:

'And thies beryns one the bynches with howes one lofte
That bene knowne and kydde for clerkes of the beste,

---

[26] For further comment on the national reach of the poem, see John Speirs, *Medieval English Poetry: The Non-Chaucerian Tradition*, 2nd edn (London, 1971), pp. 264–6; Salter, *English and International*, pp. 101–3; Thomas H. Bestul, *Satire and Allegory in* Wynnere and Wastoure (Lincoln, Nebraska, 1974), pp. 103–7; Elizabeth Salter, *Fourteenth-Century English Poetry: Contexts and Readings* (Oxford, 1983), pp. 76–7.

[27] Musson and Ormrod, *Evolution of English Justice*, pp. 200–2.

[28] *PROME*, vol. 5, pp. 42–3, 182–3; Putnam, *Shareshull*, pp. 110–11; Ormrod, 'Competing Capitals?', p. 88.

[29] See the various accounts of this process (with significant differences of detail) provided by Bertha H. Putnam, 'The Transformation of the Keepers of the Peace into the Justices of the Peace, 1327–1380', *Transactions of the Royal Historical Society*, 4th ser., 12 (1929), 19–48; A. J. Verduyn, 'The Attitude of the Parliamentary Commons to Law and Order under Edward III' (Unpublished D.Phil. thesis, University of Oxford, 1991), *passim*; Robert C. Palmer, *English Law in the Age of the Black Death, 1348–1381: A Transformation of Governance and Law* (London, 1993), pp. 1–56; and Musson and Ormrod, *Evolution of English Justice*, pp. 1–2, 42–74.

> Als gude als Arestotle or Austyn the wyse,
> That alle schent were those schalkes and Scharshull itwiste
> That saide I prikkede with powere his pese to disturbe!'
>
> (lines 314–18)

> ('And these men on the benches with their lawyers' caps,
> Known far and wide as the best of learned men,
> As good as Aristotle or Augustine the wise,
> So all of them should be ruined, and Shareshull too,
> Who said I pricked with armed power to disturb his peace!')

The crucial element here is the use of the past tense in relation to the 'beryns one the bynches' (that is, senior judges sitting in the court of king's bench and the common bench, or court of common pleas) (line 314). These men are not making the accusation of disorder against Wastoure in the present moment, but have done so at some point in the past: Shareshull '*saide* I prikkede with powere his pese to disturbe' (line 318: emphasis added). The choice of the past tense here is not forced on the poet by the demands of metre, since the present tense would have worked just as well. Rather, Wastoure's use of Shareshull's name is taken to exemplify the more generalised proceedings that he claims have been made against him (the inference is, for some time) by successive 'beryns one the bynches'. Shareshull was simply the chief justice associated with one such law-enforcement initiative, and is to be taken as a type rather than as the sole example of the phenomenon. It might be added that his surname, with its own internal assonance, was much more useful to the author of an alliterative poem (at line 317) than were the rather bland names of Thorpe and Green.

There is one further element to the second knight's speech at lines 124–35 of *W&W* that adds to our understanding of the legal context of the poem. The passage ends with the second knight's statement:

> 'Bot sen ye knowe noghte this kythe ne the kynge ryche
> He will forgiffe yow this gilt of his grace one.'
>
> (lines 134–5)

Here, *kythe* is usually read as meaning custom or practice, while the *kynge ryche* is taken variously as the 'king's right' (Gollancz), the 'powerful king' (Trigg) or the 'noble king' (Millett). Such readings are problematic. Given that these two lines lead straight into the description of the international gathering of knighthood at lines 136–42 as analysed in Chapter 1, a more reasonable reading of lines 134–5 might be that the king and his messenger believe all or most of those gathered on the laund to be foreigners from outside the realm. In such a reading, *kythe* takes on its more usual sense of 'people', and the *kynge riche* becomes (at Turville-Petre's suggestion) the *kyngriche* or 'kingdom'. The lines may therefore be rendered in modern English as:

> 'But since you do not know this people, or the kingdom [of England],
> He will forgive this offence, of his own prerogative.'[30]

The idea that the assembled forces 'do not know this people, or the kingdom' therefore suggests that they are predominantly of a different political allegiance.[31]

Nothing in particular is made of such foreignness once Wynnere and Wastoure emerge as the chief protagonists at lines 202–15. It might be argued that the poet set up the two figures in the debate as foreigners in order to distance them from the king and make it easier to criticize their various stances on the political economy.[32] In historical terms, though, there is certainly nothing inherently odd about seeing Wynnere and Wastoure as foreign-born servants of the king.[33] Edward III's links via his mother, his wife and other members of his court to the aristocratic and military elites of northern France, the Low Countries and the western areas of the Empire, coupled with the king and queen's prolonged period of residence in Flanders in 1338–40, meant that a significant number of people from these regions were recruited as knights, esquires, ladies and lesser functionaries of the king's and queen's households.[34] Some, indeed, went on to distinguished

---

[30] Millett suggests 'But since you do not know this country, or the noble king/ He will forgive this transgression, from his grace alone'.

[31] Cara Hersh, '"Wyse wordes withinn": Private Property and Public Knowledge in *Wynnere and Wastoure*', *Modern Philology*, 107 (2010), 507–27, at 522, argues that the king is in error in initially assuming that Wynnere and Wastoure are foreigners and that their statement of long service at lines 205–6 represents a correction to his knowledge.

[32] For the argument that Wynnere and Wastoure are used to personify elements in the character of Edward III, see pp. 92–3.

[33] *Pace* Stephanie Trigg, 'The Rhetoric of Excess in *Winner and Waster*', *Yearbook of Langland Studies*, 3 (1989), 91–108, repr. in Stephanie Trigg (ed.), *Medieval English Poetry* (London, 1993), pp. 186–202, at p. 190 (with subsequent page citations from the reprint of this work).

[34] The foundational study is Bryce D. Lyon, *From Fief to Indenture: The Transition to Non-Feudal Contracts in Western Europe* (Cambridge, Massachusetts, 1956), with detailed prosopographical analysis in Mary Lyon, Bryce Lyon, Henry S. Lucas and Jean de Sturler (eds), *The Wardrobe Book of William de Norwell: 12 July 1338 to 27 May 1340* (Brussels, 1983); and Elsbeth Andre, *Ein Königshof auf Reisen: Der Kontinentaufenthalt Eduards III von England, 1338–40* (Cologne, 1996). See also further analysis and context in Malcolm Vale, 'England, France and the Origins of the Hundred Years War', in Michael Jones and Malcolm Vale (eds), *England and her Neighbours, 1066–1453: Essays in Honour of Pierre Chaplais* (London, 1989), pp. 199–216; and W. Mark Ormrod, 'The Royal Nursery: A Household for the

careers: among the founding and early members of the Order of the Garter, for example, were three Hainaulters closely associated with Edward III and Queen Philippa: Eustace d'Aubrichecourt, Henry Eam and (most famously) Walter Mauny.[35] It might be mischievous to point this out, but foreigners recruited into royal service during Edward III's time in the Low Countries in 1338–40 would have been approaching the twenty-fifth anniversary of their royal employment in the early 1360s (cf. line 206).

The main significance that attaches to the specific identification of Wynnere and Wastoure as people from other lands retained in the king's service relates to the king's decision to avoid their inadvertent breach of his laws by absolving them of blame and allowing them to petition him to preside over the trial of their dispute. The king's offer to 'forgiffe' ('forgive') (line 135) represents one of those instances where the monarch specifically declared a direct interest in a private dispute in such a way as to remove it from normal common law jurisdiction and to require that it be determined entirely by his prerogative judgment.[36] Such interventions were deemed especially appropriate when made on behalf of members of the royal household.[37] The king's own open acknowledgement of Wynnere and Wastoure as his followers – 'welcome, heres, as hyne of oure house bothen' ('welcome, both, as members of our household') (line 212) – therefore opens the way to a personal resolution that sits entirely outside the normal bounds of common or statute law.

Two possibilities then arise as to how the quarrel between Wynnere and Wastoure is to be ended. On the one hand, the king quite clearly favours a form of peaceful arbitration. The second knight calls upon the parties to put themselves upon the king's mercy on the understanding that the monarch will remove the threat of retributive justice: 'Thare nowthir wye be wrothe to wirche als he demeth' ('Let neither man be angry to act according to his [that is, the king's] judgment') (lines 196–201, with quote at line 201). The dispute will thereafter be couched as a purely private affair; the king's decision to accept the role of arbitrator (lines 218–20) arises not from the fact that a direct offence (treason or otherwise) has been committed against him and his peace, but because of the monarch's acknowledged function, as

---

Younger Children of Edward III', *English Historical Review*, 120 (2005), 398–415.

[35] Richard Barber, *Edward III and the Triumph of England: The Battle of Crécy and the Company of the Garter* (London, 2013), pp. 301–6, 511–19.

[36] W. Mark Ormrod, *The Reign of Edward III: Crown and Political Society in England, 1327–1377* (London, 1990), pp. 54–6.

[37] See, for example, G. O. Sayles (ed.), *Select Cases in the Court of King's Bench, Edward I–Richard III*, Selden Society, 55, 57, 58, 74, 76, 82, 88 (7 vols, London, 1936–71), vol. 6, no. 44.

a good lord, in resolving feuds between his followers.[38] This is entirely cognisant with Edward III's management of important ceremonial and political occasions at which he or his sons acted as president. Throughout the 1340s, for example, parliaments usually opened with a formal announcement that no-one except members of the peerage could bear arms in London or Westminster during the relevant session, in order to prevent the outbreak of 'debatz, riotz et conteks' ('debates, riots and quarrels') and the resulting disruption to the business of the king and country.[39] In such contexts, arbitration became the state's preferred means of reducing violence between its subjects and promoting harmonious relationships between actively or potentially hostile parties.

The second possible means of finding a solution to the dispute between Wynnere and Wastoure, and the one to which the two protagonists (by contrast) seem more drawn, is via the judicial combat or duel, governed by the law of arms.[40] By *c.*1380 cases of this nature, covering accusations of treason as well as private quarrels, went before a recognisable Court of Chivalry, presided over by the constable and marshal of England and occasionally by the king himself.[41] The frequent assumption in the critical literature that the second knight in *W&W* was a king's herald may have contributed to the belief that the poem represents a hearing before such a court. But there is very little to suggest that such an institution was at work either in the poem or in the England of the 1350s and 1360s, and in point of fact heralds (whose existence is still very ill documented in the mid-fourteenth century) never acted as agents of such a court, so the inferred connection

---

[38] There is a very large modern scholarship on late medieval arbitration. The seminal works are: M. T. Clanchy, 'Law and Love in the Middle Ages', in J. A. Bossy (ed.), *Disputes and Settlements: Law and Human Relations in the West* (Cambridge, 1983), pp. 47–67; Edward Powell, 'Arbitration and the Law in England in the Later Middle Ages', *Transactions of the Royal Historical Society*, 5th ser., 33 (1983), 49–67; Edward Powell, 'Settlement of Disputes by Arbitration in Fifteenth-Century England', *Law and History Review*, 2 (1984), 21–43. See also, most recently, Derek Roebuck and Arthur L. Marriott, *Mediation and Arbitration in the Middle Ages: England, 1154–1558* (Oxford, 2013).

[39] *PROME*, vol. 4, pp. 239, 266, 280–1, 306, 329, 359–60, 387, 411.

[40] 143 *Calendar of the Patent Rolls Preserved in the Public Record Office, 1350–54* (London, 1907), pp. 63, 540; Thomas Rymer (ed.), *Foedera, conventiones, literae et cujuscunque generi acta publica* (3 vols in 6 parts, London, 1816–30), vol. 3(i), p. 258.

[41] Maurice H. Keen, 'The Jurisdiction and Origins of the Constable's Court', in J. Gillingham and J. C. Holt (eds), *War and Government in the Middle Ages: Essays in Honour of J. O. Prestwich* (Woodbridge, 1984), pp. 159–69; and see most recently Anthony Musson and Nigel Ramsay, 'Introduction', in Anthony Musson and Nigel Ramsay (eds), *Courts of Chivalry and Admiralty in Late Medieval Europe* (Woodbridge, 2018), pp. 1–13.

is fallacious.[42] The kinds of courts put together under royal or delegated presidency to try cases under the law of arms in the mid-fourteenth century were, instead, *ad hoc* affairs deriving the essence of their authority from the judicial powers of the royal council.

In considering whether the 'trial' of Wynnere and Wastoure was in fact one such case of a dispute brought to judgment under the law of arms, it is particularly instructive to note that judicial duels of this kind were deemed especially suitable for cases in which one or both parties was an alien. In such cases, the president of the court, normally the king, acted less upon the basis of a formal jurisdiction and more in terms of his general reputation within the ranks of European knighthood. The invocation of the international law of arms then allowed for a more binding judgment than could be provided under the normal sovereign jurisdiction of the secular power.[43]

Two such 'international' duels were remarked with an unusual level of detail and interest by English chroniclers in the middle of the fourteenth century. The first, held before Edward III at Westminster Palace in October 1350, arose when Thomas de la Marche, the illegitimate son of King Philip VI of France, accused a Cypriot knight named John de Viscount (or Visconti) of slandering him during the time that both men had been in service in the eastern Mediterranean.[44] The second occasion came in the spring

---

[42] For the development of the office of herald and its associated responsibilities, see Anthony Richard Wagner, *Heralds of England: A History of the Office and College of Arms* (London, 1967); John A. Goodall, 'Some Aspects of Heraldry and the Role of Heralds in Relation to the Ceremonies of the Late Medieval and Early Tudor Court', *Antiquaries Journal*, 82 (2002), 69–91. I owe the point about the absence of heralds from the judicial work of the royal courts to Richard Barber.

[43] J. G. Bellamy, 'Sir John de Annesley and the Chandos Inheritance', *Nottingham Mediaeval Studies*, 10 (1966), 94–106, at 99–100; W. Mark Ormrod, Helen Killick and Phil Bradford (eds), *Early Common Petitions in the English Parliament, c.1290–c.1420*, Camden Society, 5th ser., 52 (Cambridge, 2017), p. 268.

[44] The official records of this event are *Foedera*, vol. 3(i), pp. 199, 205. A contemporary account was given in Edmund Maunde Thompson (ed.), *Chronicon Galfridi le Baker de Swynebroke* (Oxford, 1889), pp. 112–13, trans. in David Preest (trans.), *The Chronicle of Geoffrey le Baker of Swinbrook* (Woodbridge, 2012), pp. 97–8, though some of le Baker's details (including the supposition that la Marche was subsequently put to death in France for treason) are erroneous: see the editorial notes in Thompson (ed.), *Chronicon Galfridi le Baker*, pp. 281–3; and Ariella Elema, 'Trial by Battle in France and England' (Unpublished PhD dissertation, University of Toronto, 2012), p. 81 and n. 64. Briefer notices of the affair are found in James Tait (ed.), *Chronica Johannis de Reading et Anonymi Cantuariensis* (Manchester, 1914), p. 112; Thomas Walsingham, *Chronicon Angliae*, ed. Edward Maunde Thompson, Rolls Series, 64 (London, 1874), p. 29; and Thomas Walsingham, *Historia Anglicana*, ed. Henry T. Riley, Rolls Series, 28 (2 vols, London,

of 1352 when, on his way back from crusade with the Teutonic Knights, Edward III's cousin Henry of Grosmont, duke of Lancaster, challenged Otto III, duke of Brunswick-Lüneburg, for scheming to capture and hold him to ransom. The parties journeyed to Paris to seek permission for a duel before King John II, which was eventually granted; Grosmont's encomiast, Henry Knighton, celebrated his hero's prowess before the lacklustre Otto and praised him for insisting on a full vindication of his honour.[45]

Which of these processes – arbitration or a trial of arms – seems more apposite for *W&W*? The debate section seems to be framed largely in terms of the king's own preference for peaceful arbitration. Yet it is also punctuated by requests from the two rivals that they be allowed to resolve their disagreement once and for all by force and arms, either in hand-to-hand combat or, indeed, in a general mêlée akin to the team tournament. At the end of his first speech, Wynnere specifically requests that the king allow both parties '[t]o fighte further with oure folke to owthire fey worthe' ('[t]o fight on with our people till one of us falls') (line 245). Later, when Wastoure realises towards the end of his second speech that he seems to be losing the argument, he too calls upon the king to allow a resort to armed force:

'Forthi, comely kynge, that oure case heris,
Late us swythe with oure swerdes swyngen togedirs
For nowe I se it es full sothe that sayde es full yore -
"The richere of ranke wele, the rathere will drede:
The more hauande that he hathe, the more of hert feble."'
(lines 319–23)

('Therefore, comely king, having heard our case,
Let us swiftly with swords strike now together,
For what was said long ago, I now see is true,
"The richer a man is, the more will he fear;
The more he has of his own, the feebler his heart becomes."')

Wynnere is so derisory of Wastoure's meagre support, amounting (he claims) to no more than 'foure felawes or fyve' ('four or five fellows') (line 329), that the king does not even need to declare against Wastoure's proposal. The

---

1863–4), vol. 1, p. 275. For a silver-gilt ewer 'enamelled with diverse images' given to Thomas de la Marche by the king, presumably on this occasion, see TNA, SC 8/246/12280. M. J. Russell, 'Trial by Battle in the Court of Chivalry', *Journal of Legal History*, 29 (2008), 335–57, at 351, is not reliable on the details of the case.

[45] Tait (ed.), *Chronica Johannis de Reading et Anonymi Cantuariensis*, pp. 121–2; Geoffrey Martin (ed. and trans.), *Knighton's Chronicle, 1337–1396* (Oxford, 1995), pp. 114–19; and Kenneth Fowler, *The King's Lieutenant: Henry of Grosmont, First Duke of Lancaster, 1310–1361* (New York, 1969), pp. 105–10.

debate therefore continues until Wastoure, once more impatient and anxious, calls upon the king to declare an end by delivering his judgment, since the enmity between the two sides is simply too great to be reconciled:

> 'Now kan I carpe no more, bot Sir Kyng, by thi trouthe,
> Deme vs where we duell schall, me thynke the day hyes.
> Yit harde sore es myn [hert] and harmes me more
> Euer to see in my syghte that I in soule hate.'
>
> (lines 452–5)

> ('Now I can go on no longer; but Sir King, by your troth,
> Tell us where we should be; I think the day is flying.
> My heart is still sore, and it does me harm
> Ever having in my sight the one that I hate.')

Throughout the debate, moreover, the level of verbal aggression deployed by the two parties in their efforts to discredit each other is sufficient to suggest that rational argument might at any moment descend into physical attacks and open violence. (It might be added in this respect that the drawing of swords on the point of open violence would offer dramatic interludes in a staged performance of the poem, where otherwise the debate section offers few opportunities for on-stage action.)[46] Many arbitrations of the period involved a similar sense of simmering violence: part of the art of the arbitrator was to hold the peace sufficiently long that he could bring forward a judgment on which both parties were content to settle peacefully. *W&W* therefore bears striking witness to the constant pressure that the public authorities, represented in this instance by the king, felt about managing the expectations of a chivalric society that continued to seek vindication of its code of values through acts of real or ritualised violence.[47]

In light of this active tension between arbitration and arms, or between rational argument and brute force, we may give some further consideration to the way in which the poet of *W&W* uses the debate to reflect on Edward III's own record in maintaining peaceful accord between members of his household and retinue. Early in the reign there had been a particular *cause célèbre* between Sir John Grey of Rotherfield and Sir William de la Zouche of Ashby that left a lasting legacy in terms of the young king's abilities as peace-giver. The two lords became embroiled in a bitter legal contest over the right to marry one of the great heiresses of her generation, Eleanor Despenser (née Clare). In 1332 the two men, brought before the

---

[46] For the argument that *W&W* was performed *viva voce*, see p. 16, n. 6.
[47] See especially in this regard Kaeuper, *War, Justice, and Public Order*, pp. 134–268; and Richard W. Kaeuper, *Chivalry and Violence in Medieval Europe* (Woodbridge, 2001), pp. 89–120.

king and his council to negotiate a resolution, exchanged 'chaudes paroles' ('hot words'); Grey also committed a serious offence against the king's person by seeming to be about to draw his dagger in violent rage. The matter was eventually resolved in Zouche's favour. Importantly, though, the king also decided to pardon Grey for his crime of *lèse majesté*.[48] Grey clearly learned his lesson, and the rest of his career was the very model of honourable service to the monarchy. Sir John subsequently emerged as one of the innermost group of the 'knights of the chamber', personally attendant upon the king, and was a founder member of the Order of the Garter. He also held the office of steward of the king's household from 1350 to his death in 1359, and was thus the master of operations for the court during or shortly before the time that *W&W* was composed.[49]

The evident tension, found both in *W&W* and in the dispute between Lords Grey and Zouche, between the king's strong preference for peacemaking and the protagonists' frustrated outbursts of verbal and/or physical violence also allows us to re-evaluate the final judgment given by the figure of the king at the end of the extant text of the poem. Some critics have read the apparent lack of clarity and decisiveness in the penalties imposed on Wynnere and Wastoure as reflecting contemporary concerns over Edward III's mismanagement of his household and/or of the nation's prosperity: we shall return in Chapter 3 to whether this is an appropriate reading of the economic arguments in the debate section of the poem.[50] Other literary scholars, by contrast, have seen the poem's apparent prevarication simply as a matter of genre: equivocation is evident in many debate poems of the period, and serves in this instance to emphasise that both of the parties' arguments have some merit.[51] The Aristotelian model

---

[48] *PROME*, vol. 4, p. 169. For further details on the case, see J. Enoch Powell and K. Wallis, *The House of Lords in the Middle Ages: A History of the English House of Lords to 1540* (London, 1967), pp. 319–21; Ormrod, *Edward III*, pp. 139–40.

[49] Henry Summerson, 'Grey, John, First Lord Grey of Rotherfield (1300–1359)' 'Oxford Dictionary of National Biography' (online): https://doi.org/10.1093/ref:odnb/11544 (accessed 23 January 2019). For the significance of the rank of 'knight of the chamber', a term in occasional use from the beginning of Edward III's reign, see Chris Given-Wilson, *The Royal Household and the King's Affinity: Service, Politics and Finance in England, 1360–1413* (London, 1986), pp. 280–1; Ormrod, *Edward III*, pp. 134, 319.

[50] See below, pp. 61–82.

[51] See, *inter alia*, Nicolas Jacobs, 'The Typology of Debate and the Interpretation of *Wynnere and Wastoure*', *Review of English Studies*, NS, 36 (1985), 481–500; David V. Harrington, 'Indeterminacy in *Winner and Waster* and *The Parliament of the Three Ages*', *Chaucer Review*, 20 (1986), 246–57; and Thomas L. Reed, Jr, *Middle English Debate Poetry and the Aesthetics of Irresolution* (Columbia, Missouri, 1990), esp. pp. 284, 269. Scattergood, '*Winner and Waster*', p. 45, argues

that has been widely recognised as providing the intellectual framework of the debate assumes the search for a mean between the virtue of generosity and the vice of prodigality.[52] Following up on this scholastic context, Lois Roney has explicitly proposed that the *refrayte* between Wynnere and Wastoure reflects more the disputations of the university schools than the pleadings of the courtroom, with accompanying justification for its complex and conditional conclusions.[53]

While the cutting off of the text before a final resolution makes it almost impossible to tell whether the poem originally moved towards a more decisive ending, the general thrust of the critical literature is that the matter at odds between Wynnere and Wastoure is simply too complicated to be settled by declaring one or other party unilaterally victorious. Indeed, Wastoure at least seems to acknowledge this fact: at the end of his third speech, he comments (in what may be an aphorism known to the audience):[54]

> 'Whoso wele schal wyn a wastour moste he fynde
> For if it greves one gome it gladdes another.'
>
> (lines 390–1)

> 'He who wants to win wealth must find a waster,
> For what saddens one man, gladdens another.'

And the king himself refers to this symbiotic relationship between winning and wasting in his final speech, when addressing Wastoure: 'The more thou wastis thi wele the better the Wynner likes' ('The more you waste your money, the better Winner likes it') (line 495). These statements point the way persuasively to a resolution of compromise in the lost ending of the poem.

We may now add to these points by emphasising two further features of the poem's final fitt relating specifically to the king's personal interventions in private conflicts. The first is that the king's judgment upon the debate between Wynnere and Wastoure is quite different from that provided in a normal suit under the common law or other forms of prerogative justice, wherein one party 'won' and the other 'lost'. In certain types of judicial combat (the form of contest that Wynnere and Wastoure ultimately favour), the outcome could be brutally clear, with the victory accorded to the party who either killed his opponent on the battleground or brought him to the point of abject submission. In 1350, Edward III allowed the hand-to-hand

---

that the poet's intention 'is to raise issues, not to provide answers'.
[52] See, for example, Trigg, 'Israel Gollancz's "Wynnere and Wastoure"', p. 125.
[53] Lois Roney, '*Winner and Waster*'s "Wyse Wordes": Teaching Economics and Nationalism in Fourteenth-Century England', *Speculum*, 69 (1994), 1070–1100, at 1097–8.
[54] Note how Wynnere's preceding speech ends with an explicit reference to an aphorism at line 365.

combat on a point of honour between Thomas de la Marche and Jean de Viscount to run its course until the very point where de la Marche was about to take his rival's life; only then did the king declare that Viscount was to be spared and handed over to de la Marche, who might keep him permanently as his prisoner or levy a ransom for his release.[55] In arbitration (the form of dispute resolution that the figure of the king seeks to impose and enforce in W&W), however, final settlements tended to concentrate less on the apportioning of blame and much more on the setting up of an elaborate range of obligations upon both parties that would ensure the restoration of harmony between them.[56] All of this suggests that the audience for W&W was more conditioned than is sometimes assumed to a judgment that deliberately creates a kind of stalemate between the protagonists and puts off any final resolution of their dispute *sine die*.

Secondly, the king's judgment tells us much about contemporary understandings of the control that Edward III exercised over the real-life members of his household. Wynnere and Wastoure identify themselves, and are recognised by the king, as his own household servants (lines 205–6, 212). Given their status as '[k]nyghtis full comly one coursers attired' ('[k]nights full comely, on caparisoned steeds') (line 203) whom the king 'clothes' and whom he has 'fosterde and fedde' ('fostered and fed') for a quarter century (lines 205–6), they are seemingly part of the contingent of men-at-arms who received robes, fees and *bouche de court* from the royal household and who divided their time between attendance at court and running their private affairs in the localities where they had their own landed interests.[57] The

[55] Elema, 'Trial by Battle', p. 81.
[56] Powell, 'Settlement of Disputes', p. 28.
[57] Given-Wilson, *Royal Household and the King's Affinity*, pp. 204–12; Caroline Shenton, 'The English Court and the Restoration of Royal Prestige, 1327–1345' (Unpublished D.Phil. thesis, University of Oxford, 1995), *passim*; Alistair Tebbit, 'Royal Patronage and Political Allegiance: The Household Knights of Edward II', in Michael Prestwich, Richard Britnell and Robin Frame (eds), *Thirteenth Century England X* (Woodbridge, 2005), pp. 197–208; J. S. Hamilton, 'A Reassessment of the Loyalty of the Household Knights of Edward II', in W. Mark Ormrod (ed.), *Fourteenth Century England VII* (Woodbridge, 2012), pp. 47–72; Christopher A. Candy, 'A Growing Trust: Edward III and his Household Knights, 1330–1340', in L. J. Andrew Villalon and Donald J. Kagay (eds), *The Hundred Years War, III: Further Considerations* (Leiden, 2013), pp. 49–62; Matthew Hefferan, 'Edward III's Household Knights in War and Peace, 1327–1377' (Unpublished Ph.D. thesis, University of Nottingham, 2018); and Matthew Hefferan, 'Family, Loyalty and the Royal Household in the Fourteenth Century', in David Green and Chris Given-Wilson (eds), *Fourteenth Century England XI* (Woodbridge, 2019), pp. 129–54. The more general importance of the theme of the well-regulated household for all members of landed society in W&W is emphasised by Smith, *Arts of Possession*, pp. 2–4, 64–6, 72–107.

second knight represents just such a figure: rather than reading him as a herald, we need to give him the proper status of 'beryn' (or 'baroun', meaning a man of reputation and means) as accorded him in the poem (line 101) and to note that the king had himself dubbed him to knighthood (line 103).[58] Vitally, this same group of knights and esquires of the household made up the core of the royal army when the king led a military expedition in person; such was the case, for example, in Edward III's campaigns of 1338–40, 1346–7 and 1359–60.[59]

Early in the reign, at least some of Edward's household knights had a reputation for lawlessness. Sir Thomas Bradestone was accused of behaving like a 'seinturel' ('little saint') at court but as a 'lyon rampaunt' ('rampant lion') on his own home turf in Gloucestershire, where it was said that more than a thousand people had grievances against him.[60] And in 1341 another household knight, Sir John Molyns, was exposed for running a regime of terror and corruption in his native Buckinghamshire.[61] In the 1350s and 1360s there were fewer such scandals. But the author of *W&W* may well have had the same long memory as his protagonists, and could still remember the cases of notoriety in the previous generation. In his charge to the rivals to make account of their dispute, the figure of the king alludes to the general dangers of a resort to violence: paralleling Zouche and Grey's 'hot words' in 1332, he demands that the protagonists explain 'whi the hates aren so hote youre hertis betwene' ('why the hostility is so hot between your two hearts') before he will formally agree to 'deme yow this day' ('judge you today') (lines 219–20). Furthermore, the king's decision at the end of the poem to dismiss both Wynnere and Wastoure from his service in order to establish a safe distance between them may reflect some of the concern

---

[58] For the prevailing sense of *beryn* as a person of armigerous and courtly status, possibly also with an inferred personal connection to the king, see also lines 126, 131, 214, 278, 328, 457, 476. At line 314, by contrast, the term is linked to the 'barons' or senior justices of the common law courts.

[59] Andrew Ayton, 'English Armies in the Fourteenth Century', in Anne Curry and Michael Hughes (eds), *Arms, Armies and Fortifications in the Hundred Years War* (Woodbridge, 1994), pp. 21–38; Alistair Tebbit, 'Household Knights and Military Service under the Direction of Edward II', in Gwilym Dodd and Anthony Musson (eds), *The Reign of Edward II: New Perspectives* (York, 2006), pp. 76–96; and Matthew Hefferan, 'Edward III's Household Knights and the Crécy Campaign of 1346', *Historical Research*, 92 (2019), 24–49. See also David Green, 'The Military Personnel of Edward the Black Prince', *Medieval Prosopography*, 21 (2000), 133–52.

[60] TNA, SC 8/97/4826, transcribed by Nigel Saul, *Knights and Esquires: The Gloucestershire Gentry in the Fourteenth Century* (Oxford, 1981), pp. 266–7.

[61] Natalie M. Fryde, 'A Medieval Robber Baron: Sir John Molyns of Stoke Poges, Buckinghamshire', in R. F. Hunnisett and J. B. Post (eds), *Medieval Legal Records Edited in Memory of C. A. F. Meekings* (London, 1978), pp. 197–221, at pp. 201–2.

felt in England after the peace of 1360 about the consequences for public order of the demobilisation of significant numbers of both men-at-arms and infantrymen.[62] By the middle of the 1360s, furthermore, the steward of the household, Sir John atte Lee, was running an increasingly controversial campaign for the recovery of the king and queen's feudal rights, in which he became associated with other notorious figures with links to the household, including the still active Sir John Molyns and the deeply unsavoury John Bampton of Essex.[63] If W&W was indeed written in the 1360s, then the author may well have reflected on the true wisdom of a policy which, by releasing men from the normal forms of supervision they would receive in the household, would allow all their baser instincts to come to the fore. That, indeed, seems to be the ultimate message of the dismissals of Wynnere and Wastoure, sent to wallow in corruption and excess with their own kind, variously in the wanton court of Rome and the fleshpots of London.

As a consequence, the elements of W&W that may reflect on the household of Edward III seem to descend, by the end of the poem, into something akin to a state of critical resignation. Gone, by this stage, is the exuberant picture of a king at the height of his powers, presiding in magnificent estate over an international gathering of chivalry, as in the echoes of the Garter feast of 1358 that we earlier identified in the poem. Instead, the picture is somewhat darker, and the verdict on the figure of the king altogether more foreboding. It is not so much that the monarch lacks the sense of judgment to decide once and for all on whether his future lies with Wynnere or with Wastoure. Rather, his equivocation speaks to the habitual and simmering unruliness of the knightly members of his own household, whether aliens or denizens. In 1368, Sir John atte Lee, who had been steward of the king's household since 1361, was finally brought to book in parliament for his misdemeanours: abusing the common law by having various people brought to answer before the prerogative courts of the crown and his own court of the Marshalsea; allowing approvers (criminals who turned king's evidence) to go free on the basis of highly dubious claims alleged against other parties; and exploiting the feudal rights of the crown for his own personal gain.[64] This represented the biggest public scandal over the machinations of royal officers since Edward III's arbitrary dismissal and attempted trial of a group of ministers and judges in 1340–1; for the first time in the reign, moreover, the public forum of parliament was now held as the appropriate place in which

---

[62] See further discussion in Musson and Ormrod, *Evolution of English Justice*, p. 84.

[63] W. Mark Ormrod, 'Parliamentary Scrutiny of Royal Ministers and Courtiers in Fourteenth-Century England: The Disgrace of Sir John Atte Lee (1368)', in Richard W. Kaeuper (ed.), *Law, Governance and Justice: New Views on Medieval Constitutionalism* (Leiden, 2013), pp. 161–88.

[64] 167 *PROME*, vol. 5, pp. 214–15.

to conduct such trials.⁶⁵ As in most similar cases, the end result was a compromise: Lee was dismissed permanently from office, but was allowed to pay a fine in lieu of further investigation and thus to go free of the accusations made against him.⁶⁶ If we wish to push chronological boundaries further and suggest that the author of *W&W* was writing as late as 1368, then both Lee's trial and the messiness of its conclusion might well have prompted consideration that the knights of the king's household were indeed a class apart, capable of multiple wrongs and apparently impervious to the full force of the law.

This chapter has argued strongly that the common assumption that *W&W* references the Statute of Treasons of 1352 cannot be true, and that using this legislation as a means to date the poem is therefore erroneous. It has also rejected the notion that the issues of public order raised in the poem have anything precisely to do with the eyre of Cheshire of 1353, and has proposed that the poem provides commentary on the much broader programme of law enforcement associated not just with Sir William Shareshull but also with his predecessors in the 1330s and 1340s and his immediate successor in the 1360s. Most importantly, the chapter has considered the type of 'court' and process represented by the hearing of Wynnere and Wastoure before the figure of the king, and has seen in this a deliberate mismatch between the monarch's desire for peaceful arbitration and the protagonists' efforts to turn their quarrel into a duel under the law of arms. In this respect, the concerns of the poem about law enforcement are much less to do with generalised debates on the state of public order and much more with the abiding suspicion of royal servants, especially household knights, who abused their intimacy with the king to overturn the rights of others and pursue their own vendettas in such a way that publicly challenged the principles of social responsibility and good order. The thrust of the poem, however, is less concerned with lawlessness *per se* than it is with the debate on the political economy in which Wynnere and Wastoure engage before the king. It is to that debate and its implications that we next turn.

---

[65] For the arrests of 1340, see Natalie M. Fryde, 'Edward III's Removal of his Ministers and Judges, 1340–1', *Bulletin of the Institute of Historical Research*, 48 (1975), 149–61; Ormrod, *Edward III*, pp. 227–46.

[66] *PROME*, vol. 5, pp. 215–16.

═ 3 ═

Landed Society, Conspicuous Consumption and the Political Economy: The Sumptuary Laws of 1363

W&W has always tended to be viewed as expressing a tension between two different sub-orders of medieval society: on the one hand (exemplified in the figure of Wynnere) those who amassed wealth, assumed to represent the mercantile or wider 'commercial' classes; and on the other (in the person of Wastoure) those who spent all their resources in conspicuous consumption, usually regarded as members of the landed elite of nobles and gentry. Gollancz argued that 'the rise of the new merchant class – the new rich, with all the power of wealth, is an outstanding feature of the poem, and perhaps the main point at issue'.[1] His view has prevailed upon virtually every subsequent critic of the poem.[2] As S. H. Rigby has recently shown, however, the strong emphasis in modern literary scholarship on 'the rise of a "bourgeoisie" inhabiting a "new world" of money, trade, profit and economic individualism', and the implicit assumption of a tension between it and an 'old world' based on land and lordship, rest on a nineteenth-century, liberal-progressive view of the late Middle Ages and the idea that it was at this moment that the market became the primary agent of economic growth and social change.[3] In recent generations, historical scholarship has tended

---

[1] Gollancz, p. ix.
[2] See, most recently, Michael Johnston, 'Thornton Manuscripts', in Siân Echard and Robert Rouse (eds), *The Encyclopaedia of Medieval Literature in Britain* (4 vols, Chichester, 2017), vol. 4, pp. 1785–9, at p. 1786.
[3] S. H. Rigby, 'Introduction', in Rosemary Horrox and W. Mark Ormrod (eds), *A Social History of England, 1200–1500* (Cambridge, 2006), pp. 1–30, at p. 12. See also the conceptualisation of urban society in S. H. Rigby, *English Society in the Later Middle Ages: Class, Status and Gender* (Basingstoke, 1995), pp. 150–60, and the specific comments on literary interpretations of *W&W* by Christopher Dyer, *Standards of Living in the Later Middle Ages: Social Change in England, c. 1200–1520* (Cambridge, 1989), pp. 87–8. For the topos of the rise of the middle class, see M. M. Postan, *Essays on Medieval Agriculture and General Problems of the Medieval Economy* (Cambridge, 1973), p. 29; and J. H. Hexter, *Reappraisals in History*, 2nd edn (London, 1979), pp. 117–62. Much of the modern characterisation

to emphasise that the processes of urbanisation and commercialisation were well under way before the supposed 'rise of the middle class' in the fourteenth century.[4] And the same scholarship has been much more disposed to view the restructuring of society in the later Middle Ages not as the widening of a gulf between the urban and the rural but in terms of a fundamental shift in the socio-legal relationship between lords and peasants.[5] The collapse of serfdom and the rise in the prosperity of tenant farmers and wage labourers after the Black Death created a social hierarchy that was more finely nuanced and more flexible than ever before, and generated unparalleled opportunities for social advancement – not simply through the redistribution of land but also through service in the Church, in government and in

---

of Wynnere appears to draw on the figure of the Merchant in Chaucer's *Canterbury Tales*, whom the critical tradition has cast as 'an avaricious, shady, usurious, dishonest, and secretive social climber, one who is attempting, unsuccessfully, to ape his aristocratic and ecclesiastical social superiors': Richard Goddard, 'The Merchant', in Stephen H. Rigby, with the assistance of Alastair J. Minnis (eds), *Historians on Chaucer: The 'General Prologue' to the* Canterbury Tales (Oxford, 2014), pp. 170–86 (quotation at p. 170). For a further recent analysis that emphasises the supposed concerns provoked by the rise of a money economy and its threat to the social hierarchy, see David Sweeten, '"Whoso wele schal wyn, a wastour moste he fynde": Intereliant Economies and Social Capital', in Craig E. Bertolet and Robert Epstein (eds), *Money, Commerce, and Economics in Late Medieval English Literature* (Basingstoke, 2018), pp. 31–46.

[4] R. H. Britnell, *The Commercialisation of English Society, 1000–1500*, 2nd edn (Manchester, 1997), *passim*; Mark Bailey, 'Historiographical Essay: The Commercialisation of the English Economy, 1086–1500', *Journal of Medieval History*, 24 (1998), 297–311.

[5] See the summaries of modern debates on the explanation of socio-economic change in Rigby, *English Society*, pp. 1–14; John Hatcher and Mark Bailey, *Modelling the Middle Ages: The History and Theory of England's Economic Development* (Oxford, 2001); Mark Bailey, *The Decline of Serfdom in Late Medieval England: From Bondage to Freedom* (Woodbridge, 2014); John H. A. Munro, 'The Late Medieval Decline of English Demesne Agriculture: Demographic, Monetary, and Political-Fiscal Factors', in Mark Bailey (ed.), *Town and Countryside in the Age of the Black Death: Essays in Honour of John Hatcher* (Turnhout, 2012), pp. 299–348. For fuller reviews of the multiple factors influencing economic performance in the fourteenth century, see Barbara F. Harvey, 'Introduction: The Crisis of the Early Fourteenth Century', in Bruce M. S. Campbell (ed.), *Before the Black Death: Studies in the 'Crisis' of the Early Fourteenth Century* (Manchester, 1991), pp. 1–24; J. L. Bolton, '"The World Upside Down": Plague as an Agent of Economic and Social Change', in W. Mark Ormrod and Phillip G. Lindley (eds), *The Black Death in England, 1348–1500* (Stamford, 1996), pp. 17–78; Rigby, 'Introduction', pp. 1–30; Mark Bailey, 'Introduction: England in the Age of the Black Death', in Bailey (ed.), *Town and Countryside in the Age of the Black Death*, pp. xix–xxxvii.

the law and through involvement in manufacturing, retailing and wholesale trade.[6] Pinning down the figure of Wynnere such that he exclusively represents an assertive merchant class is therefore to close the other avenues that were acknowledged routes to social mobility in the fourteenth century and which are, of course, directly represented among Wynnere's followers on the laund, whether as clergy, lawyers, soldiers or merchants.

It comes as no surprise, then, that a poem written just after the middle of the fourteenth century, when these new forces and changes were still in their infancy, should have consciously seen land, its possession and its management as the *primum mobile* of economic and social development. Repeatedly and overwhelmingly in the debate section, *W&W* returns to key aspects of the rural economy. Wynnere and Wastoure hold agricultural estates that they either farm directly or lease out and, *in extremis*, mortgage or sell (lines 234–5, 401, 407). They grow and sell grain (lines 233, 274), produce wool (line 250), and maintain livestock and game to provide both food and sport (lines 251, 402–6). They have responsibility for their farms' infrastructures (barns, fences, dovecotes, etc) (lines 235, 288–9, 438). The poet is particularly exercised about the habit of selling off the timber cut down from trees on the estate, which was a common device among the landed classes in lean years; he points out the dangers of this kind of asset-stripping for the agrarian ecosystem and, in the longer term, for the sustainability of the estate (lines 396–400, 449–51).[7] In addition to exercising economic and seigniorial power over agricultural labourers who provide the essential manpower on their estates (lines 288, 370, 388, 438), the protagonists of the poem also maintain lower-ranking followers as personal servants and retainers, in the proper manner of gentility (lines 270, 327–31, 433).[8]

---

[6] F. R. H. Du Boulay, *An Age of Ambition: English Society in the Late Middle Ages* (New York, 1970); Michael J. Bennett, 'Careerism in Late Medieval England', in Joel Rosenthal and Colin Richmond (eds), *People, Politics and Community in the Later Middle Ages* (Gloucester, 1987), pp. 19–39; Philippa C. Maddern, 'Social Mobility', in Horrox and Ormrod (eds), *Social History*, pp. 113–33; and S. H. Rigby, 'English Society in the Later Middle Ages: Deference, Ambition and Conflict', in Peter Brown (ed.), *A Companion to Medieval English Literature and Culture, c. 1350–c. 1500* (Oxford, 2007), pp. 25–39.

[7] For the selling of timber as a cash crop, see Mavis Mate, 'The Agrarian Economy of South-East England before the Black Death: Depressed or Buoyant?', in Campbell (ed.), *Before the Black Death*, pp. 79–109, at pp. 102–3. Following the great storm of January 1362, known as St Maurus' Wind, the crown estates actively sought to profit by selling off fallen wood: W. Mark Ormrod, *Edward III* (London, 2011), p. 473. See also Eleanor Johnson, 'The Poetics of Waste: Medieval English Ecocriticism', *PMLA*, 127 (2012), 460–76, at 464–5; and Sweeten, '"Whoso wele schal wyn"', pp. 31–46.

[8] D. Vance Smith, *Arts of Possession: The Middle English Household Imaginary* (Min-

For all these reasons, it seems much more reasonable to argue that the figures of Wynnere and Wastoure, rather than being from contrasting ranks of society and epitomising some inherent conflict between the commercial and landed classes, are actually of the same sort. Indeed, the very force of the argument that ensues between them depends, in some measure, on the fact that they both have the same kind of resources and the same range of choices about how they manage their wealth. J. A. Burrow has recently challenged the prevailing view of Wynnere as a merchant by arguing that 'both disputants speak ... as members of the landed gentry, addressing, in accordance with their different natures, issues common to that class: the management of their estates and the conduct of their households'.[9] To follow this line slavishly would, of course, be to revert to the same kind of reductivism about old and new money that we have just criticised. As Trigg has emphasised, 'the poem marks out the conflict between [liberality and parsimony] by constantly altering the representations of its two personifications ... At different times, [Wastoure] is the leader of a mercenary army, a knight of the king's household, a disaffected aristocrat who squanders his inheritance, a labourer who refuses to work, a wealthy man with due concern for the poor, a glutton, and a courtly lover.'[10] It is true that Wynnere, whom Trigg simply defines as 'a bourgeois merchant concerned only with personal profit', has fewer valences to his character than does his rival.[11] But both figures have capacious meanings within any reading of the poem – so much so, indeed, that some critics have been disposed to see the form of *W&W* as too complex to be hidebound even by allegory.[12] The important point to be made here, however, is that, in storing up his goods, possessions and wealth against a rainy day, Wynnere is a representation not primarily of

---

neapolis, 2003), pp. 11, 80–1, argues that line 356 of *W&W* signifies the practice of estimating the average cost of a serving in the accounting systems of aristocratic households.

[9] J. A. Burrow, 'Winning and Wasting in *Wynnere and Wastoure* and *Piers Plowman*', in Carol M. Meale and Derek Pearsall (eds), *Makers and Users of Medieval Books: Essays in Honour of A. S. G. Edwards* (Cambridge, 2014), pp. 1–12, at pp. 5–10, with quotation at p. 5.

[10] Stephanie Trigg, 'The Rhetoric of Excess in *Winner and Waster*', *Yearbook of Langland Studies*, 3 (1989), 91–108, repr. in Stephanie Trigg (ed.), *Medieval English Poetry* (London, 1993), pp. 186–202, at p. 188. See also John Scattergood, '*Winner and Waster* and the Mid-Fourteenth-Century Economy', in Tom Dunne (ed.), *The Writer as Witness: Literature as Historical Evidence*, Historical Studies, 16 (Cork, 1987), pp. 39–57, at p. 50; and Helen Barr, *Socioliterary Practice in Late Medieval England* (Oxford, 2001), pp. 20–1.

[11] Trigg, 'Rhetoric of Excess', p. 188.

[12] Katharine Breen, 'The Need for Allegory: *Wynnere and Wastoure* as an *Ars poetica*', *Yearbook of Langland Studies*, 26 (2012), 187–229, at 211–19.

a social category (whether merchant or landholder) but of a moral attribute (in its purest form, prudent stewardship, but in its worst manifestation, aggressive avarice). While the predominantly agrarian imagery deployed to represent the getting and spending of Wynnere and Wastoure therefore reflects contemporary understandings about the social hierarchy, the poem certainly never descends into a mere discourse upon husbandry, since the allegorical tone of the debate serves to universalise both the instincts and the experiences of the protagonists.

That the author of W&W understood the management of the land to be the primary determinant of economic success or failure means that he may be assumed to have had a special interest in the challenging economic environment that prevailed after the Black Death.[13] The decade following the first arrival of the plague in 1348–9 was one of extreme volatility in the agrarian economy. The problem of securing sufficient labour on manorial estates meant that the amount of land set to the plough was significantly reduced. This, coupled with a sequence of hard winters and wet summers in the 1350s and 1360s, meant that, in spite of the reduction of the population by as much as forty per cent, there still continued to be occasional crises of resources both for peasants and for their lords. The Ordinance of Labourers of 1349, reinforced by the Statute of Labourers of 1351, aimed to address some of these issues by requiring that both wages and prices be set at the levels that had been the norm in 1346.[14] While this legislation failed in the long term, there is evidence that wage rates in the 1350s were significantly lower than they might have been without such artificial constraints.[15] This changed with the onset of further outbreaks of plague in 1361–2, 1368 and 1375, events that forced the proprietary elite to become more flexible over the wages that they allowed; and by the mid-1370s the post-plague economy was set on a clear long-term course of high wages and low prices.[16]

---

[13] For the demographic effects of the plague, see P. J. P. Goldberg, *Medieval England: A Social History, 1250–1550* (London, 2004), pp. 71–87, 163–7; Stephen Broadberry, Bruce M. S. Campbell, Alexander Klein, Mark Overton and Bas van Leeuwen, *British Economic Growth, 1270–1870* (Cambridge, 2015), pp. 8–27.

[14] *SR*, vol. 1, pp. 307–8, 311–13; Rosemary Horrox (ed. and trans.), *The Black Death* (Manchester, 1994), pp. 287–9, 312–16; Anthony Musson and W. Mark Ormrod, *The Evolution of English Justice: Law, Politics and Society in the Fourteenth Century* (Basingstoke, 1999), p. 93.

[15] Bruce M. S. Campbell, *The Great Transition: Climate, Disease and Society in the Late-Medieval World* (Cambridge, 2016), p. 317, fig. 4.14.

[16] Wages: S. A. C. Penn and Christopher Dyer, 'Wages and Earnings in Late Medieval England: Evidence from the Enforcement of the Labour Laws', *Economic History Review*, 2nd ser., 43 (1990), 356–76; John Hatcher, 'England in the Aftermath of the Black Death', *Past & Present*, 144 (1994), 3–35; Anthony Musson, 'Reconstructing English Labor Laws: A Medieval Perspective', in Kellie Robertson and

W&W was therefore written at a time when the landed elite was somewhat Janus-like in its approach to the agrarian economy. On the one hand, it was aware that the profit margins of landholders were coming under significant threat, and observed with concern that the labouring classes, growing confident in their newly found scarcity, could already afford to work less and still have more.[17] On the other hand, the erratic behaviour of the markets led it to believe that there was still some hope of preserving the clear socio-economic advantage that lords had enjoyed before 1348, and of re-establishing the authority and access to wealth enjoyed by the seigniorial elite in the accustomed social hierarchy.

It is fruitful, then, to reconsider the precise mood of those parts of the *refrayte* between Wynnere and Wastoure in which the parties address the contemporary experience of socio-economic change. Where it engages with the economics of labour and the accompanying social ethics, *W&W* does so within the traditional trope of a 'world upside down'. This is already signalled in the Prologue, where the dreamer comments on a land that is out of joint: one where a 'western wy' ('western man') dares not send his son south (lines 8–9), where mere 'boyes of blode' ('boys of low birth') marry women of high estate (lines 15–16), and where skilled minstrels are replaced by those who jangle like jays and do nothing more than tell poor jokes (lines 20–8).[18] It is

---

Michael Uebel (eds), *The Middle Ages and Work: Practicing Labor in Late Medieval England* (New York, 2004), pp. 113–32; and Broadberry, Campbell, Klein, Overton and Leeuwen, *British Economic Growth*, pp. 253–4. Prices: David L. Farmer, 'Prices and Wages, 1350–1500', in Edward Miller (ed.), *The Agrarian History of England and Wales III: 1348–1500* (Cambridge, 1991), pp. 431–525, at pp. 434, 502; R. H. Britnell, 'English Agricultural Output and Prices, 1350–1450: National Trends and Regional Divergences', in Ben Dodds and Richard H. Britnell (eds), *Agriculture and Rural Society after the Black Death: Common Themes and Regional Variations* (Hatfield, 2008), pp. 20–39; and Broadberry, Campbell, Klein, Overton and Leeuwen, *British Economic Growth*, p. 256. For the debate on the relative agility of the seigniorial and peasant economies to adapt in the light of changes in prices during the era of the Black Death, see Eric B. Schneider, 'Prices and Production: Agricultural Supply Response in Fourteenth-Century England', *Economic History Review*, 2nd ser., 67 (2014), 66–91.

[17] Bruce M. S. Campbell, 'The Land', in Horrox and Ormrod (eds), *Social History*, pp. 179–237, at pp. 215–18; Bruce M. S. Campbell and Cormac Ó Gráda, 'Harvest Shortfalls, Grain Prices, and Famines in Preindustrial England', *Journal of Economic History*, 71 (2011), 859–86.

[18] For the literary significance and analogues of the Prologue, see Thorlac Turville-Petre, 'The Prologue of *Wynnere and Wastoure*', *Leeds Studies in English*, NS, 18 (1987), 19–29; and for upward mobility through marriage and land, see Simon J. Payling, 'Social Mobility, Demographic Change, and Landed Society in Late Medieval England', *Economic History Review*, 2nd ser., 45 (1992), 51–73.

not, however, until Wastoure's speech at lines 368 that the poet addresses the specifics of the new post-plague economy. Wastoure comments that Wynnere is miserable at the prospect of low prices for his grain and actively hopes for a bad harvest in order to keep his profits high: in an image later deployed by Shakespeare, the proverbial miserly farmer finds a plentiful harvest such a damaging prospect that he contemplates hanging himself:[19]

> 'Thurgh the pure plente of corne that the peple sowes,
> That God will graunte of his grace to grow on the erthe,
> Ay to appaire the pris, and it passe notte to hye,
> Schal make the to waxe wod for wanhope in erthe,
> To hope aftir an harde yere to honge thiselven.'
> (lines 370–4).

> ('Through the plenty of corn that the people sow,
> Which God will grant of His grace to grow on the Earth
> To prevent the price from rising too high,
> You will go mad and in wild despair,
> Hoping for a hard year, and thus hang yourself.')

The consequence of a regime of low prices and high wages is seen in quite standard terms as a type of social inversion: lords will end up on a diet of bacon, beef, gruel and rye bread, while 'laddes' – meaning servants and other employees – will indulge in bitterns, swans, rich sauces and the best wheat bread:[20]

> 'Late lordes lyfe als tham liste, laddes as tham falles;
> Thay the bacon and beef, thay botours and swannes,
> Thay the roughe of the rye, thay the rede whete,
> Thay the grewell gray, and thay the gude sewes;
> And then may the people hafe parte in povert that standes,
> Sum gud morsel of mete to mend with their chere.'
> (lines 378–83).

[19] *Macbeth*, Act II, Scene 3: 'Here's a farmer, that hanged himself on the expectation of plenty.' See also James Davis, *Medieval Market Morality: Life, Law and Ethics in the English Marketplace, 1200–1500* (Cambridge, 2012), pp. 117–18.

[20] For peasant consumption of foodstuffs after the Black Death, see Christopher Dyer, 'Changes in Diet in the Late Middle Ages: The Case of the Harvest Workers', *Agricultural History Review*, 36 (1988), 22–37; and, more generally, Christopher M. Woolgar, *The Culture of Food in England, 1200–1500* (London, 2016). For food as a marker of social (in)stability, see Miriam Müller, 'Food, Hierarchy and Class Conflict', in Richard Goddard, John Langdon and Miriam Müller (eds), *Survival and Discord in Medieval Society: Essays in Honour of Christopher Dyer* (Turnhout, 2010), pp. 231–48.

('Let lords live as they please, servants as befits them,
The one [servants] on bacon and beef, the other [lords] on bitterns and swans,
They [servants] on husks of rye, those [lords] on fine wheat,
They [servants] on thin gruel, they [lords] on the good stews;
And let the people have a share, who stand in poverty,
With a good morsel of meat to cheer them.')

The implications of this scenario remain largely implicit, though they are glimpsed at the end of the passage: when a hen can be bought for a halfpenny (that is, very cheaply), '[s]chold not a ladde be in the londe a lorde for to serve' ('there wouldn't be a servant in the land to serve a lord') (lines 384–8, with quotation at line 388).[21]

These kinds of comments on the destabilising social effects of economic change are part of the stock in trade of English moralisers and polemicists of the later Middle Ages, before as well as after the plague.[22] *W&W*, however, is notably silent on the common topos of blaming the lower orders for the new dispensation. From the 1370s onwards, the official and unofficial discourses that had developed in the 1350s reached a new level of vehemence, very explicitly criticising the greed and laziness of the peasants who, exploiting their own scarcity value, were supposedly pushing their lords and other employers into financial ruin and social humiliation.[23] Harwood has suggested that the author of *W&W* (whom be believes to have been writing in 1353) began his project as a critique of the resistance of the lower orders to their lords' efforts to enforce traditional seigniorial rights, but withdrew from this exercise when he realised that the literary genres within which he had chosen to write (as Harwood defines them, the *chanson de geste* and satire) did not permit the representation of open conflict between the ranks of society.[24] The present study takes a different approach, seeing the general absence of any sustained hostility towards the labouring classes as a reflec-

---

[21] The meaning of this passage is difficult to disentangle; the reading here follows the spirit of Turville-Petre, p. 411 n. 16, and Ginsberg, p. 25 n. 2. Millett, lines 384–8, is unhelpful since she supposes that the 'henne at ane halpeny' (line 387) represents a high, rather than a low, price. See also the evidence of poultry prices from 1363 discussed below, p. 73.

[22] Thomas H. Bestul, *Satire and Allegory in* Wynnere and Wastoure (Lincoln, Nebraska, 1974), pp. 55–9.

[23] W. Mark Ormrod, *Political Life in Medieval England, 1300–1450* (Basingstoke, 1995), pp. 115–17.

[24] Britton J. Harwood, 'The Displacement of Labor in *Winner and Waster*', in Kellie Robertson and Michael Uebel (eds), *The Middle Ages at Work: Practicing Labor in Late Medieval England* (New York, 2004), pp. 157–77; and Britton J. Harwood, 'Anxious over Peasants: Textual Disorder in *Winner and Waster*', *Journal of Medieval and Early Modern Studies*, 36 (2006), 291–319.

tion of the poet's understanding that lords, too, had a necessary part to play in the process of post-plague reconstruction, and that the privileged audience for which he wrote was more confident than Harwood supposes of its own ability to resolve the matter.

In 1368, the parliamentary Commons called for the reinforcement of the labour laws:

> A nostre seignur le roi; prient la commune qe vivent par geynerie de lours terres our marchandie et qe n'ont seignuries ne villeins pur eux servir: que lui plese par son sage conseil ordiner remedie encontre la maicle et grevouse cherte touchantz servantz, laborers et artificers, queux chescun an de plus et plus par lour exces et outrageouses prises et salaries destruent et enpoverissent a demesure le poeple, issint qe ceux qe vivont de lour terres achetent la vesture de lour terre apoy a la value.

> (To our lord the king; the commons who live by husbandry of their lands or trade, and who do not have lordships and villeins to serve them, pray: that it may please him by his wise counsel to ordain remedy against the malice and burdensome costs relating the servants, labourers and artisans, who each year, more and more, by their excessive and outrageous prices and salaries, destroy and impoverish a great number of people, so that those who live off their lands sell the produce of their land at scarcely its value.)

The remedy, the petitioners proposed, was a re-issue of the Statute of Labourers and newly reinforced commissions for its enforcement in the shires. The crown agreed to the general proposal, but refused to apply a specific recommendation that those who demanded excessive wages should re-pay twice what they had asked of the original employers.[25]

A number of aspects of this petition call for our attention. The Commons claimed that they were acting not principally for their own kind, the gentry, but for those 'who live by husbandry of their lands': that is, substantial peasant farmers who were heavily reliant on waged labour to work on their holdings. The Commons supposed that those who had 'lordships or villeins to serve them' – that is, those who exercised traditional seigniorial rights over unfree tenants – could still potentially compensate for the greater expense involved in hiring workers by reinvigorating the unpaid labour services required of unfree tenants on the manor.[26] The petition is therefore expressed in relatively optimistic terms, reflecting a belief, sustained through three outbreaks of plague, that the habitual structures and functions of rural society were bound to survive and that those who were dependent both on villein services and on waged labour would in the end prevail.

[25] *PROME*, vol. 5, p. 211. For the new peace commissions of 1368, see Ormrod, *Edward III*, p. 478.
[26] M. M. Postan, *The Medieval Economy and Society* (Harmondsworth, 1970), p. 170.

Wishful thinking this may have been, but it chimes quite well with the social thinking of the author of *W&W*. It is particularly noticeable that whereas William Langland and other commentators of the later fourteenth century personified the vices of sloth and gluttony in terms of an uppity peasantry grown lazy and fat since the plague, the *W&W* poet (speaking through Wynnere) reserved his criticism of such behaviours for those men of his own kind who make off to the tavern to get drunk on wine (rather than the peasants' drink of ale) and cavort with women of low degree.[27]

> 'And thou wolle to the taverne, byfore the tonne-hede,
> Iche beryne redy with a bolle to blerren thyn eghne,
> Hete the whatte thou have schalte ad whatt thyn hert likes,
> Wyfe, wedowe, or wenche that wonnes there aboute.
> Then es there bott "fille in" and "feche for the", florence to schewe,
> "Wee hee", and "worthe up", words ynewe.'
> (lines 277–82).

('And you will go to the tavern, with the wine-casks,
And everyone serves you with a bowl to blur your eyes.
You order your drinks, and what your heart desires,
Wife, widow or wench, whatever may be had.
Then there is nothing but "Fill it up!" and "Fetch forth" to get your money,
"Wee-hee!" And "Climb up!" and not a word more.')

Here and elsewhere, *W&W* suggests that the poverty into which Wastoure is in danger of driving his kind is not simply or principally the consequence of adverse market forces, but instead the result of his own wilful profligacy. If he would only give up on his heavy spending on wine at the tavern (line 283), on ostentatious feasting in his hall (lines 332–65), and on fine trappings and clothing for his womenfolk and servants (lines 270–2, 392–4, 408–14), then all may yet be well.

Pace Harwood, then, the inability of the author of *W&W* to represent the peasantry as poised upon some collective act of resistance may be said to arise not from the limits of genre but from a conservatism which readily assumed that a hierarchical social order could still prevail against the economic stresses of the 1350s and 1360s. The Prologue, like the passage at

---

[27] For the wider trope on the laziness of the peasantry after the plague, see Christopher Dyer, 'Work Ethics in the Fourteenth Century', in James S. Bothwell, P. J. P. Goldberg and W. Mark Ormrod (eds), *The Problem of Labour in Fourteenth-Century England* (York, 2000), pp. 21–41; Mavis E. Mate, 'Work and Leisure', in Horrox and Ormrod (eds), *Social History*, pp. 276–92, at pp. 281–3; and Emma Martin, 'The Performance of Idleness in Late Medieval English Society: Work, Leisure and the Sin of Sloth' (Unpublished Ph.D. thesis, University of York, 2017), pp. 114–19.

lines 368, may present a picture of a socially disrupted world, both now and yet to come, but it also sees it as one in which the worst excesses might still be avoided. In particular, there is no hint in the poem of looming revolution. Harwood, who favours the idea that *W&W* commemorates the eyre of Cheshire of 1353, supposes that the poet was influenced by the organised resistance mounted by the villein tenants of Vale Royal Abbey in Cheshire on the manor of Darnhall during the 1320s and 1330s.[28] What is striking about the generation immediately after the plague, however, is not the prevalence but the scarcity of such peasant uprisings.[29] Whether we see *W&W* as written in the 1350s or the 1360s, we are still a long way from the position that arose from the mid-1370s, when a sudden hike in wages and an equally dramatic drop in grain prices resulted in a much more vehement political rhetoric against the lower orders and the application of new and more severe punitive measures against both free and unfree peasants.[30] It was this shift that, in turn, raised the prospect of the kind of widespread, organised resistance that became terrifying realities in the so-called 'Great Rumour' of 1377 and the Peasants' Revolt of 1381.[31]

In representing Wastoure's habits of extravagance and ostentation, the author of *W&W* is inevitably preoccupied with the question of conspicuous consumption. In comparison with the intense interest that critics have shown in the supposed public order issues represented in the poem, it is striking that no-one has previously followed up fully on Gollancz's comment about 'questions of labour, wages, prices, dress, food, which call forth the Statute of Labourers, 1351, *and various sumptuary and economic enactments of about this time*'.[32] Part of the reason for this neglect is Gollancz's own insistence that the poem must have been written in 1352–3; assuming these 'enactments' were mainly put in place after the plague, the window of relevant legislation is thereby rendered extremely narrow, and many scholars have assumed that the only germane legislation is the Statute of Labour-

[28] Harwood, 'Anxious over Peasants', pp. 307–9.

[29] R. H. Hilton, 'Peasant Movements in England before 1381', *Economic History Review*, 2nd ser., 2 (1949), 117–36; and E. B. Fryde and Natalie Fryde, 'Peasant Rebellion and Peasant Discontents', in Miller (ed.), *Agrarian History of England and Wales, III*, 744–819.

[30] See in particular the notably strident common petitions directed against the interests of the lower orders in the parliaments of 1376–7: *PROME*, vol. 5, pp. 337–40; vol. 6, pp. 36–7, 47–8.

[31] R. J. Faith, 'The "Great Rumour" of 1377 and Peasant Ideology', in R. H. Hilton and T. H. Aston (eds), *The English Rising of 1381* (Cambridge, 1981), pp. 43–73; and Andrew Prescott, '"Great and horrible rumour": Shaping the English Revolt of 1381', in Justine Firnhaber-Baker and Dirk Schoenaers (eds), *The Routledge History Handbook of Medieval Revolt* (London, 2017), pp. 76–103.

[32] Gollancz, p. iv (emphasis added). See also Trigg, p. xxiv.

ers of 1351 (which, as we have noted, aimed to regulate prices, as well as wages). There are, in fact, a number of lesser elements in the poem that can be tied to previously unnoticed statutory instruments and judicial reforms of the 1350s and early 1360s. For example, Wastoure's criticisms of Wynnere's habit of storing up, rather than selling, his goods – whether wool (line 250), bacon (line 251), or grain (lines 368–74) – carry an insinuation of the offence of forestalling: that is, the interception and hoarding of goods in order to create artificial scarcity and to push up their price once they were released onto the open market.[33] In 1351 the crown issued an important new statute against forestalling, which was first applied with notable rigour as part of Shareshull's campaign of economic enforcement via the king's bench and later, in 1364, was absorbed into the powers of the local justices of the peace.[34] A similarly important initiative in economic regulation arose from the new legislation of 1352 on the standardisation of weights and measures, which was again prosecuted actively in the king's bench in the 1350s and then delegated to the justices of the peace from 1361.[35] These instances provide another reminder that the economic issues represented in *W&W* cannot adequately be addressed simply by reference to the Ordinance and Statute of Labourers.[36] Indeed, by giving cognisance to some of the principal economic issues at odds in the courts during the 1350s and 1360s, *W&W* provides unwitting testimony of the more general process whereby, over the second half of the fourteenth century, both common law and statute law were coming to take on more and more responsibility for an ever wider range of basic economic functions and associated social obligations.[37]

[33] Gwen Seabourne, *Royal Regulation of Loans and Sales in Medieval England: 'Monkish Superstition and Civil Tyranny'* (Woodbridge, 2003), pp. 73–159; Davis, *Medieval Market Morality*, pp. 222–31; and Robert Braid, 'Behind the Ordinance of Labourers: Economic Regulation and Market Control in London before the Black Death', *Journal of Legal History*, 34 (2013), 3–30, at 7–8.

[34] Horrox (ed. and trans.), *Black Death*, p. 289; *SR*, vol. 1, pp. 321–2; *PROME*, vol. 5, pp. 36–7; Bertha H. Putnam, 'Chief Justice Shareshull and the Economic and Legal Codes of 1351–1352', *University of Toronto Law Journal*, 5 (1943–4), 251–81; and Musson and Ormrod, *Evolution of English Justice*, pp. 84–5. The true foci for the setting and enforcement of reasonable prices, however, remained the urban courts: R. H. Britnell, 'Price-Setting in English Borough Markets, 1349–1500', *Canadian Journal of History*, 31 (1996), 1–15.

[35] *PROME*, vol. 5, pp. 37, 46–7; *SR*, vol. 1, pp. 321–2; W. Mark Ormrod, 'Edward III's Government of England, *c*.1346–*c*.1356' (Unpublished D.Phil. thesis, University of Oxford, 1984), pp. 172–3, 204–5; and Musson and Ormrod, *Evolution of English Justice*, pp. 84–5.

[36] As emphasised by Trigg, 'Israel Gollancz's "Wynnere and Wastoure"', p. 123.

[37] Robert C. Palmer, *English Law in the Age of the Black Death, 1348–1381: A Transformation of Governance and Law* (London, 1993), *passim*; Anthony Musson,

If, however, we are prepared to countenance the notion that *W&W* could have been written in the 1360s, then the range of referents in the poem to economic activity as a whole, and particularly to patterns of consumption, becomes both significantly greater and arguably still more relevant. In that decade, public concern as expressed in parliament became much more strident about the problem of prices and the expectation that the state might do something about them. In October 1363, the parliamentary Commons asked that the crown expand upon the general idea of holding prices to their pre-plague levels by requiring that a *covenable pris* ('suitable price') be set on victuals which they perceived as overly expensive. They suggested their own scale of maximum prices, taking poultry as their exemplar: 4d for a goose or a mature capon, 3d for a young capon, 2d for a hen and 1d for a chicken. The government put the petition into statutory form and seems to have expected that it would be enforced by the justices of the peace, as part of their generally increasing responsibility for economic legislation.[38]

More novel and momentous was the Commons' other complaint in 1363, to the effect that the makers and sellers of a wide range of quality goods were attempting to manipulate the market in order to keep prices artificially high:

> Item, pur ce qe grandes meschiefs sont avenuz de novel, sibien a nostre seignur le roi, les grauntz et communes come autres de la terre, de ce qe les marchantz nomez grossers engrossent toutes maneres de marchandies vendables; et ceux as qeux le marchandie est le pris levent sodeinement dedeniz la terre, mettantz a vente, par covyn et ordinance entre eux faite appelle fraternite et gilde de marchant, et par lour conseil et assent mettont les autres marchandises en repose tanqe au temps qe chierte ou defaute soit d'ycelles en la dite terre, et adonqes par lour dit accorde les mettent a vente en la fourme avantdit ... Et par les enchesons susdites les vitailles sont ensi encherrez de jour en autre qe trope damages sont avenuz a nostre seignur le roi, grantz, nobles et communes ...

Medieval Law in Context: The Growth of Legal Consciousness from Magna Carta to the Peasants' Revolt (Manchester, 2001), *passim*; John Watts, *The Making of Polities: Europe, 1300–1500* (Cambridge, 2009), pp. 233–8; and W. Mark Ormrod, 'Parliament, Political Economy and State Formation in Later Medieval England', in Peter Hoppenbrouwers, Antheun Jansen and Robert Stein (eds), *Power and Persuasion: Essays on the Art of State Building in Honour of W. P. Blockmans* (Turnhout, 2010), pp. 123–39.

[38] *PROME*, vol. 5, p. 164; *SR*, vol. 1, pp. 378–9; Musson and Ormrod, *Evolution of English Justice*, pp. 52–3. For the medieval notion of the 'just price', see the useful summary of a large literature by Davis, *Medieval Market Morality*, pp. 55–65. Other aspects of the 1363 legislation are discussed by Cara Hersh, '"Wyse wordes withinn": Private Property and Public Knowledge in *Wynnere and Wastoure*', *Modern Philology*, 107 (2010), 507–27, at 522–4.

(Also, because great misfortunes have recently arisen, both to our lord the king, the great men and the commonalty as well as to others of the land, because the merchants called forestallers engross all manner of saleable merchandise; and those to whom the merchandise belong raise the price suddenly within the land, putting it to sale by agreement and ordinance made between those called the fraternity or guild of merchants; and by their counsel and consent they put the other merchandise in store until there is a scarcity or lack of the same in the said land, and then by their said accord they put it up for sale in the aforesaid form ... And for the aforesaid reasons the victuals thus rise in prices from day to day, so that great damages have come to our said lord the king, the great men, nobles and commonalty ...)[39]

This common petition provides testimony of the consumer revolution that had been brought on by the plague, and which was already resulting in a significant increase in imports of luxury goods as well as in the development of native industries, especially the manufacture of cloth.[40] The implication was that such production could not keep up with demand and that providers of the goods favoured by Wastoure and his sort – fine food and wine, fancy clothing, shoes and jewellery, carpets and tapestries to adorn their homes, and so on – were exploiting scarcity to push up prices. The crown accepted the Commons' startling proposal that both artisans and merchants should be restricted to dealing in only one commodity each: 'vineters as vins, marchantz des leines as leines, drapers a draperie, chaucours au chacerie, [etc]' ('vintners to wine, wool merchants to wool, drapers to cloth, shoemakers to shoes, [etc]'); only female craftspeople and 'toutes autres qe usent et oeverent overeignes manueles' ('all others who work and labour at manual tasks') would be permitted to work across a range of occupations.[41] The logic was that manufacturers and merchants reliant on single commodities would need ready turnover and be less inclined to try to make excessive profits from other sidelines.

Finally, and still more remarkably, the Commons of 1363 demanded that something be done about the wearing of clothing appropriate to social status:

Item, monstrent les communes: qe come diverses vitailles dedeinz le roialme sont grandement encherrez, par cause qe diverses gentz de diverses condicions usent diverse apparaill nient appertenant a lour estat; c'estassaver, garceons usent apparaill des gentz de mestire, et gentz de mestire apparaile des valletz, et valletz apparaile des esquires, et esquires apparaill de chivalers, l'un et l'autre pellure qe seulment de reson appertienent as seignurs et chivalers, femmes povres et autres apparaile des

---

[39] *PROME*, vol. 5, p. 164.
[40] Maryanne Kowaleski, 'A Consumer Economy', in Horrox and Ormrod (eds), *Social History*, pp. 238–59.
[41] *PROME*, vol. 5, p. 165; *SR*, vol. 1, pp. 379–80.

dames, povres clercs pellure come le roi et autres seignurs. Issint sont les marchandises susdites a plus grant pris qe ne soleient ester, et le tresor de la terre destruit, a grant damage des seignurs et communes. Dont ils priont remede …

(Also, the Commons declare: that whereas the prices of various victuals within the realm are greatly increased because various people of various conditions wear various apparel not appropriate to their estate; that is to say, grooms wear the apparel of craftsmen, and craftsmen wear the apparel of gentlemen, and gentlemen wear the apparel of esquires, and esquires wear the apparel of knights, the one and the other wear fur which only properly belongs to lords and knights, poor and other women wear the dress of ladies, and poor clerks wear clothes like those of the king and other lords. Thus the aforesaid merchandises are at a much greater price than they should be, and the treasure of the land is destroyed, to the great damage of the lords and the commonalty. Wherefore they pray remedy …)[42]

The notion of a society in which rank is no longer clearly demarcated and repeatedly challenged by those from below is also remarked in near-contemporary historical writing: the reference to men of lowly birth marrying wealthy women in the Prologue to *W&W* (lines 14–15), for example, finds a close analogue in the Middle English *Brut* chronicle's remark on the rush of marriages of widows with men of 'lowe degree et litele reputacion' ('low status and small reputation') following the plague of 1361–2.[43] One clear way to avoid such social ambiguities was to have all men and women present themselves in dress that accorded clearly with their relative status in life.

The Commons' aspiration to this end in 1363 did not include any specific proposals for the new dress code. But the government decided to act on the prompt, issuing a new law to deal with 'l'outrageouse et excessive apparaille des plusours gentz, contre lour estat et degree, a tresgraunt destruccion et empoverissement de tote la terre' ('the outrageous and excessive apparel of diverse people, against their estate and degree, to the great destruction and impoverishment of all the land').[44] The legislation demarcated some seven categories of society below the rank of peer (which itself remained unrestricted), and provided equivalences between landed and rural society on the

---

[42] *PROME*, vol. 5, pp. 165–6. For the background, see Frédérique Lachaud, 'Dress and Social Status in England before the Sumptuary Laws', in Peter R. Coss and Maurice Keen (eds), *Heraldry, Pageantry and Social Display in Medieval England* (Woodbridge, 2002), pp. 105–23.

[43] F. W. D. Brie (ed.), *The Brut, or, The Chronicles of England*, EETS OS, 131, 136 (2 vols, London, 1906–8), vol. 2, p. 314. See also Turville-Petre, 'Prologue', p. 24.

[44] *SR*, vol. 1, pp. 380–2, with quote at p. 380. The statute was also written up on the parliament roll: *PROME*, vol. 5, pp. 166–8.

one hand, and urban society and the clergy on the other. This is especially important in showing the way that contemporary authorities viewed the relationship between landed and urban society:

> Item, qe marchantz, citeseyns et burgeys, artificers, gentz de meistere, sibien deinz la cite de Loundres come aillours, q'ont clerement biens et chateux a la value de cynk centz livres, et lour femmes et enfantz, puissant prendre et user en manere come les esquires et gentils gentz q'ont terre ou rente a la valu de cent livres par an; et qe les marchantz, citeseyns et burgeys q'ont clerement biens et chateux outre la value de mille livres, et lour femmes et enfantz, puissant prendre et user en manere come les esquires et gentils gentz qi ont terre ou rent a la value de deux centz livres par an; et qe nul garson, yoman ne servant des marchaunz, artificer ou gentz de meistere ne use altrement en apparaille qe n'est ordeigne des garsons et yomen des seigneurs paramont.

> (Item, that merchants, citizens and burgesses, artificers, people of handicraft and as within the city of London as elsewhere, who clearly have goods and chattels to the value of £500, and their wives and children, may take and wear in the same manner as esquires and gentlemen who have lands or rents to the value of £100 a year; and that the same merchants, citizens and burgesses, who clearly have goods and chattels to the value of £1,000 a year, and their wives and children, may take and wear in the same manner as esquires and gentlemen who have lands and rents to the value of £200 a year; and no groom, yeoman or servant of a merchant, artificer, or craftsperson shall wear other in apparel than is ordained above for yeomen of lords.)

In each category, rules were then laid down as to the types of cloth, fur and jewellery that the group was permitted to wear, as well as placing some restriction on the consumption of food. The manner in which the legislation equates the hierarchies of urban and landed society allows us to question whether the supposed tension between traditional, 'feudal' society and the new 'commercial' interest, which scholars have so often seen as an attribute of *W&W*, really existed. Whether the king's council consulted with the Commons on the social gradations that emerged in the legislation remains unrecorded, and we have to assume that the principal influence upon the details of this new law came from those royal councillors who, as bishops, aristocrats and senior lawyers, would themselves be free of its specifications. On the other hand, there is nothing to suggest that the king's council skewed the equivalences in such a way as to prejudice for or against 'new wealth'. While even the super-rich merchants and craftspeople who held over £1,000 in goods and chattels could only aspire to the same rank as wealthier esquires and gentlemen, the superior rank of knight (the highest to be put to regulation under this legislation) was also, by exception, open to the mercantile class: in 1339, Edward III had made his principal financier, the merchant-banker William de la Pole (d.1366), a knight banneret (a more exclusive title than that of simple knight), and just before William's death in 1366 his son Michael received a personal summons to parliament that made him *de facto* a member of the peerage.[45]

The ways in which the 1363 sumptuary legislation differentiated the levels of society have made it a particularly well-known document of social history, analysed alongside a similar list of grades in the poll tax of 1379 to provide detailed evidence of how the fourteenth-century governing elite regarded, and aimed to preserve, the social hierarchy.[46] Quite how the elaborate edifice of the laws of 1363 was to be policed and enforced remained, however, unstated – and perhaps deliberately so. The fact that this 'solution' to the Commons' complaint went almost entirely unremarked by chroniclers strongly suggests that very few people were actively involved in its application in the public arena and that few men of estate had the inclination to apply it as a self-denying ordinance in their families and households.[47]

The act on apparel of 1363 was part of a wider phenomenon, known by historians as sumptuary legislation, found across much of Europe in the later Middle Ages.[48] Other measures had already been put in place before this date to limit the wearing of specific imported commodities and thus promote domestic manufactures in England: in 1337, for example, parliament had banned the wearing of foreign-made cloth by anyone other than members of the royal family, as part of Edward III's strategy of fostering the native woollen cloth industry.[49] Nor was the debate on the supposed dangers of excess in clothing altogether new in 1363. A marked shift away from loose-fitting garments to figure-hugging fashions for men and women

---

[45] E. B. Fryde, *William de la Pole, Merchant and King's Banker* (London, 1988), pp. 133, 229.

[46] For a full analysis of these social equivalences, see Dyer, *Standards of Living*, pp. 88–9; Maurice H. Keen, *English Society in the Later Middle Ages, 1348–1500* (London, 1990), pp. 9–16.

[47] For a rare reference to the legislation in a contemporary chronicle, see John Taylor, *English Historical Literature in the Fourteenth Century* (Oxford, 1987), p. 292.

[48] Frances Elizabeth Baldwin, *Sumptuary Legislation and Personal Regulation in England* (Baltimore, 1926); Alan Hunt, *Governance of the Consuming Passions: A History of Sumptuary Law* (Basingstoke, 1996); Andrea Denny-Brown, *Fashioning Change: The Trope of Clothing in High- and Late-Medieval England* (Columbus, Ohio, 2012).

[49] *SR*, vol. 1, pp. 280–1; Ormrod, *Edward III*, p. 117. For the mechanisms deployed by the government of Edward II to control prices in the late 1300s and 1310s, see Wendy R. Childs, 'Government and Market in the Early Fourteenth Century', in Rémy Ambühl, James Bothwell and Laura Tompkins (eds), *Ruling Fourteenth-Century England: Essays in Honour of Christopher Given-Wilson* (Woodbridge, 2019), pp. 37–57, at pp. 40–7.

from the 1340s onwards had already caused moralisers to comment on the indecency and decadence of elite clothing before the plague. The passage in W&W where Wastoure's kind are berated for allowing their wives to spend to excess on the new fashions, and specifically on long, slashed sleeves trimmed with ermine (lines 408–14), links quite closely, for example, with the anonymous continuation of the Westminster chronicle, written in the mid-1340s, which derides the new obsession with decoration in male clothing in the form of slashes, laces, straps and buttons and fixates on garments with elaborate buttoning and 'cum manicis ac tipetis supertunicarum et caputiorum nimis pendulis tortoribus' ('with the sleeves of the gowns and the tippets of the hoods hanging down to absurd lengths').[50] In terms of the specifics of fashion and the moralising on its excesses, then, W&W does not have to be linked directly to the sumptuary law of 1363, and could quite reasonably be said to reflect the more general practices and debates of the 1350s.

There are other signs, however, to suggest that the particular ways in which W&W reflects on clothing as a form of social display chime more precisely with a new social and political rhetoric developing after the second plague in the 1360s. The two most detailed attacks on the decadence of elite clothing in the generation of the Black Death, made by the anonymous Malmesbury continuator of the *Eulogium historiarum* and the Westminster chronicler John of Reading, consciously locate themselves within the 1360s.[51] Both claimed that there was now a new craze for excess and ornament, which the former dated quite specifically as beginning in 1361–2 and the latter in 1365. The author of the passage in the continuation of the *Eulogium historiarum* betrays a general concern about the social hierarchy that nicely echoes the criticisms expressed both by the parliamentary Commons in 1363 and by W&W. He claims that esquires (lesser gentry) and freeholders (yeomen) indulge themselves so much in the fashion for ornate belts that they will spend anything up to £5 on such showy items, even though they could really only afford less than two shillings. Twice in W&W, Wynnere directs criticism against Wastoure for over-generous provision of

---

[50] James Tait (ed.), *Chronica Johannis de Reading et Anonymi Cantuariensis* (Manchester, 1914), pp. 88–9, translated in Horrox (ed. and trans.), *Black Death*, pp. 88–9 (a passage written in the mid-1340s). For the new fashions of the 1340s, see Stella Mary Newton, *Fashion in the Age of the Black Prince: A Study of the Years 1340–1365* (Woodbridge, 1980).

[51] For what follows, see Frank S. Haydon (ed.), *Eulogium historiarum*, Rolls Series, 9 (3 vols, London, 1858–63), vol. 3, pp. 230–1, translated in Horrox (ed. and trans.), *Black Death*, pp. 131–3; Tait (ed.), *Chronica Johannis de Reading et Anonymi Cantuariensis*, pp. 166–8, translated in Horrox (ed. and trans.), *Black Death*, pp. 133–4. For further discussion of the dating and content of these passages, see Antonia Gransden, *Historical Writing in England, II: c. 1307 to the Early Sixteenth Century* (London, 1996), pp. 101–8.

attire and accoutrements ('girdills of golde', 'sadills of sendale' and 'sercles full riche') ('girdles of gold', 'silken saddles' and 'rich circlets') to dependants, with the implication that people of lesser estate are adorned in a way more appropriate to their superiors (lines 270–2, 392–4). And in the passage mentioned above on the way that husbands indulge their fashion-conscious wives, there is a strong sense of outrage over people who go beyond their rightful station: far from being genuine 'fine ladies', the wives of Wastoure's associates are but 'nysottes of the new gett' (line 410) (engagingly rendered by Millett as 'fashion victims') who can no more carry off their fantastic attire than can a 'cely symple wenche' ('poor, simple girl') (line 414):

> 'That are had lordes in londe and ladyes riche
> Now are thay nysottes of the new gett, so nyseley attired,
> With side slabbande sleves, sleght to the grounde,
> Ourlede all umbtourne with ermyn aboute,
> That es as harde, as I hope, to handle in the derne,
> Also a cely symplye wenche that never silke wroghte.'
> (lines 409–14).[52]

> ('Those who would be lords in land and fine ladies
> Are now foolish girls of the new fashion, so excessively dressed
> With broad trailing sleeves that sweep to the ground,
> The lining and borders edged around with ermine,
> That is as hard, I think, to handle in the dark
> As a poor, simple girl who never worked silk.')

Most striking of all in this respect is the passage in *W&W* where Wastoure turns on Wynnere and challenges his right of self-determination in the styles of dress of his dependants:

> '... Thou Wynnere, thou wriche, me woundirs in hert
> What hafe oure clothes coste the, caytef, to by
> That though schal birdes vpbrayd of thaire bright wedis,
> Sythen that we vouchesafe that the siluer payen.
> It lyes wele for a lede his lemman to fynde,
> Aftir hir faire chere to forthir his herte.

[52] There is much scribal corruption, modern editorial variation, and consequent confusion of meaning in lines 409–15: for details, see Trigg, p. 42. I broadly follow the suggestions on the meaning of the passage provided by Ginsberg, p. 26, marginal n. to line 409 and n. 2, and Millett, n. to lines 413–14. Compare the more complicated rendering of the passage by Turville-Petre, p. 412 n. 22. For the gender implications of the 1363 statute, see Kim Phillips, 'Masculinities and the Medieval English Sumptuary Laws', *Gender & History*, 19 (2007), 22–42.

...
'And if my peple ben prode, me payes alle the better
To [s]ee tham faire and free tofore with myn eghne.'

(lines 424–9, 433–4)[53]

(... 'Winner, you wretch, I wonder in my heart
What our garments have cost you, wretch, to buy,
That you should upbraid ladies for their bright clothes,
Since we guarantee to pay in silver.
It is proper for a man to provide for his loved one,
To follow her wishes and thus win her favour.
...
'And if my people are finely arrayed, it pleases me all the better
To see them with my own eyes looking fair and free.')

Wastoure's assertive claim that he has the right to clothe himself, his womenfolk and his followers in whatever way his resources allow resonates remarkably closely with the public debate that followed the issue of the 1363 sumptuary law. The crown had already expressed concern about its ability to enforce this legislation at the time when it was issued: the chancellor, noting that such a level of intrusion into the personal lives of the king's subjects represented things 'novels et nounpas veues avant ces heures' ('new and never before witnessed'), had persuaded the Commons that the law should be considered to have the status of an ordinance in order that it could be readily amended in future without the formalities attaching to fully-fledged parliamentary statutes.[54] In the event, the parliament that met in January 1365 declared that the attempts to dampen demand for high-quality clothing and other accoutrements had completely failed, and requested that 'celle ordinance sot reherce et examine en cest present parlement, and par bon avis du parlement, touz les pointz par qeux touz les povres communes sont mis en daunger et en subjeccion soient repellez et adnullez' ('this ordinance [of 1363] shall be recited and examined in this present parliament, and that, by the good advice of the parliament, all the points by which all the poor commons are put in danger and subjection shall be repealed and annulled'). The Commons claimed that prices had risen, rather than fallen, as a result of the initiatives of 1363, and now decided to support the complete withdrawal both of the legislation requiring trade in only one commodity and of the ordinance on clothing. In doing so, they declared that 'toutez gentz, de quele estat ou condicioun q'ils soient, puissant franchement ordeiner lour sustenance en vivre et en apparail pur eux, lour femmes, enfantz et servantz

---

[53] For the problem of the word 'see' at line 434 and the possibility that it could be read as 'fee', see Turville-Petre, line 434; Trigg, pp. 43–4.

[54] *PROME*, vol. 5, p. 170.

en manere come meltz lour semble pur lour profit demesne' ('all people, of whatever estate or condition they may be, may freely determine their consumption of victuals and apparel for themselves, their wives, children and servants in the manner that seems best to them for their own profit').[55] The kinds of qualifying statements that one might expect on such an occasion – in particular, that heads of household should observe self-control and due propriety in order to ensure that they and their families live according to their estate – are strikingly lacking. It was the libertarian position adopted by Wastoure that therefore ultimately prevailed in parliament: it is worth pointing out that further sumptuary legislation designed to limit and differentiate the clothing and food of the various ranks of society was not, in fact, issued for another century, until the time of Edward IV.[56]

It is the contention of this study, then, that the discussions of clothing in *W&W* directly capture something of the debate that occurred in the parliaments of 1363 and 1365 over whether the state had either the practical ability or, indeed, the moral authority to intervene in people's lives at the level of personal adornment and domestic display. In 1363, parliament, and following it the crown, took the side of Wynnere, promoting a policy of abstention and moderation in order to establish a balance between production and demand, especially in luxury goods. In 1365, however, the Commons persuaded the king to return to the previous policy of *laissez faire*, and made quite an emphatic statement in support of what, in effect, is Wastoure's basic precept: people should have the right, regardless of degree, to dress and feed themselves, their families and followers as they wished. It may even be seen as credible to argue that *W&W* was written in direct response to this debate by someone with a close eye to parliamentary business and the public mood. Certainly, that would provide *W&W* with a ready audience both in officialdom and in fashionable society.

The close parallels between the parliament rolls and the chronicles on the one hand and the text of *W&W* on the other therefore reinforce the suggestion made in earlier chapters that the poem should be considered a composition of the 1360s. Indeed, the linkages with the legislation on clothing seem in several respects more precise than do some of the supposed allusions within the poem that have previously been read as evidence of a dating in 1352–3. The world that the poet presents to us in the opening scenes immediately after the Prologue may well be an invitation to cast the mind back to the time, in 1358, when not just France but the whole of Europe had seemed to be in obeisance to the glorious Edward III. The poet may also have reflected on some of the major cultural achievements and legal and economic reforms that this king had instituted in the immediate

---

[55] *Ibid.*, vol. 5, p. 182.
[56] Kowaleski, 'Consumer Economy', p. 248.

aftermath of the first plague. Through the debate section, however, both the chronological frame of reference and the mood change, as we move to address the principal universalising theme of the poem: the ability of the landed elite to uphold its traditional primacy in society by reinforcing its rights and living within its means. The final element of that more sombre analysis is provided by the allusions to Edward III's imperfect fulfilment of public expectations in relation to his management of the crown's finances. It is to that theme that we next turn our attention.

=4=

The Private and the Public Spheres: The Royal Household and State Finance under Edward III

The aspect of the political economy that has attracted the most enduring attention of scholars working on the social meanings of *W&W* relates to Edward III's household management and war finances. The idea that the poem provides a commentary on the financing of the Hundred Years War goes back to a short article by Gardiner Stillwell published in 1941.[1] Stillwell argued that Wynnere's opening speech represented Wastoure as the personification of the state, unjustly extracting hard-earned resources from its subjects to finance its own proud ambitions:

> 'Bot this felle false thefe that byfore yowe standes
> Thynkes to strike or he styntt and stroye me for euer.
> All that I wynn thurgh witt he wastes thurgh pryde,
> I gedir, I glene and he lattys goo sone,
> I pryke and I pryne and he the purse opynes.
> Why hase this cayteffe no care how men corne sellen?'
> (lines 228–33)

> ('But this wicked, false thief who stands before you
> Thinks to strike me down and destroy me for ever.
> All that I win by my wits, he wastes through pride,
> I gather, I glean, and he lets it all go,
> I pinch and I save, and he opens the purse.
> Why does this scoundrel have no care how corn is sold?')

Convinced by Gollancz's dating of the poem to 1352–3, Stillwell compared this passage to the formal record on the parliament roll of 1352 of the grant made by the Commons to the king of a three-year fifteenth and tenth (the standard form of taxation that had been in place in England since 1334). This schedule included a statement that 'le commune people de la terre fut molt empovery, sibien par la pestilence mortiele qe nadgairs avient en

---

[1] Gardiner Stillwell, '*Wynnere and Wastoure* and the Hundred Years' War', *ELH*, 8 (1941), 241–7.

la terre come par autres soviers taxes, taillages et plusours autres chevances qe les ont survenuz' ('the common people of the land [are] greatly impoverished, as much by the deadly pestilence which they recently suffered in the land as by the frequent taxes, tallages and many other levies which have befallen them').[2] This was apparently enough to convince Stillwell that the passage in *W&W* just cited was a veiled allusion to public discontent with the unreasonable economic burden that the king's wars placed on the country at precisely the moment that the Commons made their tax grant in 1352. Stillwell's article, though lightly researched and lacking in any real understanding of the fiscal context, has nonetheless become a standard resort for literary scholars and has bred a general assumption, prevalent in the current generation, that the poem acts in some way as a critique of war taxation.[3]

Since Stillwell also took up Gollancz's idea that Wynnere represents the bourgeois elite, it was but a short leap from this position to the argument that the poem criticises the forms of credit finance that had been deployed in England since the opening of the French war in 1337. Wynnere certainly has wool and wine merchants among his supporters (lines 189–90); it was the former group that provided most of the credit on which Edward was able to launch his continental campaigns of the late 1330s and 1340s.[4] At the end of the poem, after the banishment of the protagonists, the king orders Wynnere to 'wayte to me' ('look to me') (line 496) and imagines a moment when he will reinstate the latter's services by giving him 'gyftes full grete of golde and of sil[uer]' ('great gifts, of gold and of silver') (line 500). Stillwell argued that this was a reference to the crown repaying its debts to merchant capitalists, and that the relationship between Wynnere and the king was therefore 'a financial one', rather like that of Edward III with Sir William de la Pole, the underwriter *extraordinaire* of so many of England's military enterprises in the first decade of the Hundred Years War. Consequently, Stillwell argued, Wynnere represents 'the increasingly wealthy and increasingly powerful middle classes' who drew their prosperity not from land and the exploitation of yeoman farmers and agricultural labourers, but from the worlds of commerce and finance.[5]

---

[2] *PROME*, vol. 5, p. 41.

[3] Eleanor Johnson, 'The Poetics of Waste: Medieval English Ecocriticism', *PMLA*, 127 (2012), 460–76, at 461–2, points to the importance of taxes raised for the Hundred Years War as part of the background to *W&W* and *Piers Plowman*, but does not otherwise pursue the point.

[4] E. B. Fryde, *Studies in Medieval Trade and Finance* (London, 1983).

[5] Stillwell, '*Wynnere and Wastoure*', pp. 241–7, with quotations at pp. 242, 247. For de la Pole and his associated merchant capitalists, see Rosemary Horrox, *The de la Poles of Hull*, East Yorkshire Local History Series, 38 (Beverley, 1983); E. B. Fryde, *William de la Pole, Merchant and King's Banker* (London, 1988).

From this slender base developed an article of faith, revived by D. V. Moran and Thomas Bestul in the 1970s and by John Scattergood in the 1980s, to the effect that W&W represents a particular phase, in the early 1350s, of a longer struggle for power between the landed and the commercial classes over the way in which Edward III's wars should be financed. There were two possible vehicles by which this might be achieved. On the one hand, there was the more traditional method of direct taxation based on the value of moveable property (grain and livestock in the countryside, and domestic furnishings and goods in trade in the towns); this was the type of financing preferred by parliament, because it had secured direct control over grants of such taxes since the time of Edward I. On the other hand, there was the still novel device of imposing heavy additional taxes on the export of wool and setting up merchant syndicates to generate royal profit from the wider system of charges levied since Edward I's time on overseas trade (the so-called customs and subsidies); these taxes were opposed by parliament because the king continued, until the 1350s, to insist that he had the power to impose them himself, without necessary parliamentary consent.[6]

The major difficulty with approaching the poem as a debate on public finance is that, as Stillwell himself had to recognise, there is nothing in W&W either by way of conscious description of the forms and logistics of royal taxation, or indeed of any obvious criticism of the deleterious social effects of direct and/or indirect levies.[7] In this respect, the poet's aims are very different from those of the generation before him: the authors of the

[6] D. V. Moran, 'Wynnere and Wastoure: An Extended Footnote', *Neuphilologische Mitteilungen*, 73 (1972), 683–5, at 683; Thomas H. Bestul, *Satire and Allegory in Wynnere and Wastoure* (Lincoln, Nebraska, 1974), pp. 48–50; John Scattergood, '*Winner and Waster* and the Mid-Fourteenth-Century Economy', in Tom Dunne (ed.), *The Writer as Witness: Literature as Historical Evidence*, Historical Studies, 16 (Cork, 1987), pp. 39–57, at pp. 41, 50, 52. Unlike the earlier authors in this debate, Scattergood consulted a seminal article on the topic: George Unwin, 'The Estate of Merchants, 1336–1365', in George Unwin (ed.), *Finance and Trade under Edward III* (Manchester, 1918), pp. 179–255. However, this had already been superseded by other important work on the political relationship between parliament and the semi-autonomous 'estate of merchants', usefully summarised by G. L. Harriss, *King, Parliament and Public Finance in Medieval England to 1369* (Oxford, 1975), pp. 420–49.

[7] Stillwell, '*Wynnere and Wastoure*', p. 246. For the systems of direct and indirect taxation, see W. Mark Ormrod, 'England in the Middle Ages', in Richard Bonney (ed.), *The Rise of the Fiscal State in Europe, c.1200–1815* (Oxford, 1999), pp. 19–52; and David Grummitt and Jean-Françoise Lassalmonie, 'Royal Public Finance (c.1290–1523)', in Christopher Fletcher, Jean-Philippe Genet and John Watts (eds), *Government and Political Life in England and France, c.1300–c.1500* (Cambridge, 2015), pp. 116–49.

Middle English *Song of the Husbandman* and the Anglo-Norman/Latin *Song against the King's Taxes*, both probably writing in the late 1330s, exhibit an altogether keener social conscience than ever does the poet of *W&W* over the inequities of the fiscal system and its punitive impact on the peasantry.[8] Indeed, it is almost as though the latter deliberately distances himself from such debates: with its emphasis on the good stewardship of the landed estate, *W&W*'s position is essentially a very conservative one, presuming that the peasantry exists primarily to generate seigniorial incomes and seemingly taking the view that matters of public finance are largely irrelevant to its *raison d'être*.

Similar difficulties attach to Stillwell's notion, taken up more recently by Christine Chism, that the promised gifts of gold and silver from the king to Wynnere at the very end of the poem represent a commercial relationship between crown and merchants:[9]

> 'And wayte to me, thou Wynnere, if thou wilt wele chefe,
> When I wende appon were my wyes to lede
> For at the proude pales of Parys the riche
> I think to do it in ded and dub the to knyghte
> And giff giftes full grete of sil[uver]
> To ledis of my legyance that lufen me in hert.'
>
> (lines 496–501)

> ('And look to me, Winner, if you want to gain wealth,
> When I go to the wars to lead my men;
> For in the proud walls of the great city of Paris
> I plan to have it done, and dub you to knight,
> And to give great gifts, of gold and of silver,
> To those of my allegiance who love me in their hearts.')

The vocabulary of exchange here is, in fact, entirely that of lordship. Although the king had previously recognised Wynnere and Wastoure as knights of his household (line 203), Wynnere (and, by implication, Wastoure) is here represented as not yet having assumed that rank. The anomaly is easily addressed, however, when we consider that an increasing number of men within the gentry preferred to maintain the status of esquire, which was gaining significantly in social prestige as the fourteenth century progressed; like knights, such men held land, maintained households, and provided a

---

[8] See below, p. 106.

[9] Christine Chism, *Alliterative Revivals* (Philadelphia, 2002), p. 205, argues that, in this passage, 'the poem completely divorces the aristocracy from military practice, while at the same time recruiting the rich, non-aristocratic, merchants, fraternal orders, and lawyers to the king's war efforts'.

range of services to the nobility and the crown.¹⁰ The king also promises gifts not simply to a group of unidentified creditors but to 'ledis of my legyance' ('those of my allegiance') (line 501): that is, to all those who exercise lordship and, in return for such rights, owe due allegiance to the king. This is the language of feudalism, or at least of the characteristic form of social organisation between great lords and gentry based in financial exchange that historians have dubbed 'bastard feudalism'; what it is not, very clearly, is some representation of the late medieval triumph of trade.¹¹

On a very different and much higher plane, however, there is much to be said for the engagement of *W&W* in debates about finance as part of a wider scrutiny of what, in the present study, is called the political economy. Lois Roney and Brantley Bryant have both observed that the poem situates its protagonists (and imagines its audience) in terms of a collective responsibility to what Roney calls the 'national economy' and Bryant (using reifying capitals) the 'Public Wealth'.¹² Speaking from the point of view not of peasant taxpayers but of those who actually helped make fiscal policy (particularly the minor landholders and merchants who dominated the Commons in parliament), the poet approaches questions about the acquisition and redistribution of wealth with a set of assumptions about the ways in which people of substance should manage their estates and businesses: spending only to a level they can properly afford; avoiding the disastrous effects of living on credit; and reinvesting their profits into productive activities that benefit both themselves and the economy at large. The context in which the *refrayte* between Wynnere and Wastoure is set may appear to be private and domestic, but this simply reflects the fact that both landed estates and commercial businesses were organised essentially as extensions of the master's household. This chapter picks up again

---

[10] Nigel Saul, *Knights and Esquires: The Gloucestershire Gentry in the Fourteenth Century* (Oxford, 1981), pp. 6–35; C. E. Morton, 'A Social Gulf? The Upper and Lower Gentry of Later Medieval England', *Journal of Medieval History*, 17 (1991), 255–62; Peter R. Coss, *The Origins of the English Gentry* (Cambridge, 2003), pp. 216–38.

[11] For bastard feudalism in the fourteenth century, see (among much else) Simon Walker, *The Lancastrian Affinity, 1361–1399* (Oxford, 1990); Michael A. Hicks, *Bastard Feudalism* (London, 1995); Christine Carpenter, 'Bastard Feudalism in England in the Fourteenth Century', in Steve Boardman and Julian Goodare (eds), *Kings, Lords and Men in Scotland and Britain, 1300–1625: Essays in Honour of Jenny Wormald* (Edinburgh, 2014), pp. 59–92; Gordon McKelvie, *Bastard Feudalism, English Society and the Law: The Statutes of Livery, 1390–1520* (Woodbridge, 2020).

[12] Lois Roney, '*Winner and Waster*'s "Wyse Wordes": Teaching Economics and Nationalism in Fourteenth-Century England', *Speculum*, 69 (1994), 1070–1100; Brantley L. Bryant, 'Talking with the Taxman about Poetry: England's Economy in "Against the King's Taxes" and *Wynnere and Wastoure*', *Studies in Medieval and Renaissance History*, 3rd ser., 5 (2008), 219–48. I am grateful to Brantley Bryant for providing me with a copy of his article.

on the possibility that *W&W* is a poem not of the early 1350s but of the 1360s and develops Roney and Bryant's lines of thinking in a more precisely historicised manner. In particular, the analysis below explores the ways in which the imagery of the household reflects the nature of royal government and the substance of national politics during the peacetime conditions that prevailed between 1360 and 1369.

The peace treaties established with the Scots (in 1357) and the French (in 1360) allowed for a period of continuous truce that prevailed until 1369 and created the longest period of effective peace for England since the late thirteenth century.[13] Whereas in times of war the realm was obliged, through the Romano-canonical doctrine of *necessitas* (necessity), to respond to the king's demands for financial assistance against his enemies, no such obligation existed in periods of peace.[14] In 1360, the political classes therefore had every expectation that the country would revert (to use the classic taxonomy in modern scholarship) from a 'tax state' to a 'domain state': that is, from a system of public taxation for the defence of the realm to a position in which the king might 'live of his own' from his private and seigniorial rights, and run the residual functions of government as an extension of his household.[15] Edward III and his ministers, however, had a very different view both of their commitments to the debts accumulated during the long years of war and of the responsibility of parliament to support a peacetime royal lifestyle suitable to the dignity of the monarchy. It is in the tension between these two approaches that we may productively assess the extent to which *W&W* reflects consciously on the income and expenditure of Edward III's court.

[13] On the conditional nature of the treaties, see Pierre Chaplais (ed.), 'Some Documents Regarding the Fulfilment of the Treaty of Brétigny, 1361–1369', in *Camden Miscellany XIX*, Camden Society, 3rd ser., 80 (London, 1952); A. A. M. Duncan (ed.), 'A Question about the Succession, 1364', in *Miscellany of the Scottish History Society XII*, Scottish History Society, 5th ser., 7 (Edinburgh, 1994), pp. 1–57; W. Mark Ormrod, *Edward III* (London, 2011), pp. 389–90, 405–13, 427–8.

[14] Harriss, *King, Parliament*, pp. 27–48, 313–55.

[15] J. A. Schumpeter, 'The Crisis of the Tax State', *International Economic Papers*, 4 (1954), 5–38 (a work originally published in 1918), provides the classic model. For subsequent criticism, see Richard Bonney and W. Mark Ormrod, 'Introduction. Crises, Revolutions and Self-Sustained Growth: Towards a Conceptual Model of Change in Fiscal History', in W. Mark Ormrod, Margaret Bonney and Richard Bonney (eds), *Crises, Revolutions and Self-Sustained Growth: Essays in European Fiscal History, 1130–1830* (Stamford, 1999), pp. 1–21; Karl-Heinz Schmidt, 'Schumpeter and the Crisis of the Tax State', in Jürgen G. Backhaus (ed.), *Joseph Alois Schumpeter: Entrepreneurship, Style and Vision* (Boston, Massachusetts, 2003), pp. 337–51. For the precept of the king living 'of his own', see William Stubbs, *The Constitutional History of England*, 4th edn (3 vols, Oxford, 1906), vol. 2, p. 543; G. L. Harriss, *Shaping the Nation: England, 1360–1461* (Oxford, 2005), p. 66.

In 1981, David Starkey suggested that the eponymous protagonists of W&W represent the embodiments of the two departments of the royal household as set out in the later fifteenth-century *Black Book of the Household*, a text which purported to replicate lost ordinances from the time of Edward III. On the one hand, there was the 'getting' or lower division, headed by the steward, and named in the *Black Book* as the *domus providencie* ('household of providence', or, less obliquely, 'household of provision'); and on the other hand, there was the 'spending' or upper division, headed by the chamberlain, and labelled the *domus magnificencie* ('household of magnificence'). Starkey was chiefly interested in the ways in which the poet universalises the theme of the household, and did not seek to argue that W&W is self-consciously critical of the domestic regime of Edward III.[16] But his study opens up the possibility that the debate between Wynnere and Wastoure represents a discussion going on in the 1360s about the king's peacetime, household-based government and whether its enterprises should be supported from the public purse.[17]

Following the Treaty of Calais of 1360, the political performance of the crown was such as to suggest that Edward III bore at least some of the attributes of both Wynnere and Wastoure. In the public finances, the king achieved a very remarkable sleight of hand. Observing the convention that no direct taxes should be collected outside periods of active war, he avoided making any requests for such charges. However, his attitude towards indirect taxation was very different.[18] Indirect taxes consisted of a complicated series of levies made mainly on the export of a range of goods, and especially of England's chief commercial commodity, wool. These consisted both of 'customs', which the king collected as of right on a permanent basis, without the need for parliamentary approval, and 'subsidies', which were extraordinary supplementary taxes granted only during wartime and levied only for fixed periods (normally of a few years).

---

[16] David Starkey, 'The Age of the Household: Politics, Society and the Arts, *c.*1350–*c.*1550', in Stephen Medcalf (ed.), *The Context of English Literature: The Later Middle Ages* (London, 1981), pp. 225–90. For the *Black Book* and its scheme of household organisation, see A. R. Myers (ed.), *The Household of Edward IV: The Black Book and the Ordinance of 1478* (Manchester, 1959); Kate Mertes, 'The *Liber niger* of Edward IV: A New Version', *Bulletin of the Institute of Historical Research*, 54 (1981), 29–39.

[17] For a parallel discussion of the theme of the household in W&W, with an emphasis on the idea of the non-disclosure of 'private' information, see Cara Hersh, '"Wyse wordes withinn": Private Property and Public Knowledge in *Wynnere and Wastoure*', *Modern Philology*, 107 (2010), 507–27.

[18] For what follows, see Harriss, *King, Parliament*, pp. 466–508; *PROME*, vol. 5, pp. 135–9, 155–7, 172–5, 189–91, 203–6.

By far the most valuable of these charges was the subsidy on wool.[19] The wool subsidy, only very intermittently imposed between the 1290s and the 1330s, had come to be a semi-permanent feature of wartime taxation after 1338, and was authorised in fixed-term grants that dovetailed with each other from the early 1340s onwards; it was levied at a much higher rate than the wool customs, representing anything between a third and a half of the market value of the commodity taxed.[20] When the last of this sequence of grants (made in 1355) expired in 1362, the crown asked parliament for a further, peacetime, extension of the subsidy; and it did so again on two further occasions during the years of truce, in 1365 and 1368.[21] This was therefore the first time that a hitherto extraordinary tax justified solely by a state of active war was sought, granted and collected during peacetime.[22]

This situation was all the more remarkable given the large amounts of money collected under the form of the wool subsidy. In the 1360s, when wool exports were high, the value of the wool subsidy to the crown was especially considerable. Depending on the scale of the trade and the rate at which the tax was levied, it brought in an annual income of between £20,000 and £80,000 during this decade. This was at a time when the other ordinary revenues of the crown (from land and feudal rights, the profits of justice, and the customs) scarcely amounted to £30,000 a year.[23]

---

[19] N. S. B. Gras, *The Early English Customs System*, Harvard Economic Studies, 18 (Cambridge, Massachusetts, 1918); Mabel H. Mills, 'The Collectors of the Customs', in J. F. Willard, W. A. Morris, J. R. Strayer and W. H. Dunham (eds), *The English Government at Work, 1327–1336* (3 vols, Cambridge, Massachusetts, 1940–50), vol. 2, pp. 168–200; R. L. Baker, *The English Customs Service, 1307–43: A Study of Medieval Administration* (Philadelphia, 1961); and W. Mark Ormrod, 'The Crown and the English Economy, 1290–1348', in Bruce M. S. Campbell (ed.), *Before the Black Death: Studies in the 'Crisis' of the Early Fourteenth Century* (Manchester, 1991), pp. 149–83, at pp. 167–75. Historians sometimes refer to the wool subsidy as the *maltolt/maltote*, or 'bad tax', which was the nickname that it acquired when first imposed, in 1294; in fact, the term was rarely used in the middle of the fourteenth century, by which time it had largely lost the original sense of a grievous or unreasonable levy. See Harriss, *King, Parliament*, p. 424; and Richard W. Kaeuper, *War, Justice, and Public Order: England and France in the Later Middle Ages* (Oxford, 1988), pp. 37–8.

[20] W. Mark Ormrod, *The Reign of Edward III: Crown and Political Society in England, 1327–1377* (London, 1990), p. 206.

[21] *PROME*, vol. 5, pp. 136–54, 172–5, 203–6.

[22] J. G. Edwards, *The Second Century of the English Parliament* (Oxford, 1979), pp. 17–31.

[23] Ordinary revenue: Kaeuper, *War, Justice, and Public Order*, pp. 62–3. Figures for the wool subsidy given here are estimates based on multiplying the numbers of wool sacks exported each year by the rate at which parliament set the tax in the

By turning an extraordinary wartime levy into a permanent part of the crown revenues, Edward III's government had indeed revolutionised the peacetime finances of the state.

That Edward was able to do this was all the more remarkable given that he was simultaneously building up a very large private treasure from the profits of the various ransoms and war indemnities that he had negotiated with the Scots and the French in 1357–60. Medieval convention allowed that such accidental profits of war could be treated as part of the king's private income, beyond the control both of the exchequer and of parliament.[24] Although Edward was prepared to hand over significant amounts from this fund during the 1360s to help support the regimes of his sons and other lieutenants in the remaining parts of the Plantagenet Empire in France and Ireland, he was emphatic that the money was his alone to spend.[25] Contemporaries aware of this private resource probably exaggerated its value, partly because the actual amounts of money that came in from ransoms were usually much smaller than the official sum demanded, and partly because such revenue (unlike the wool subsidy) was not, of course, a renewable resource. Nevertheless, all the evidence suggests that the king reserved a substantial proportion of this prerogative income in a cash hoard, kept under special surveillance at the Tower of London, and whose existence became something of a bone of contention both among his ministers and in parliament.

The largest of all the ransoms received by Edward in this way was that offered by the French in 1360 for the release of John II. In the end, the English received rather less than half of the £500,000 actually promised under the terms of the Treaty of Calais. Nevertheless, a one-off windfall of somewhere between £200,000 and £250,000 was clearly a major addition to the king's personal wealth, representing up to eight times the value of the crown's annual ordinary revenues.[26] Even after Edward had spent much of this private fund during the middle years of the decade, the total residue in his private coffers at the time of the reopening of the French war in 1369 was still at least £135,000, and probably considerably more. Taken as a whole, then, the private funds that he enjoyed during the 1360s marked

---

relevant year: Eleanor Carus-Wilson and Olive Coleman, *England's Export Trade, 1275–1547* (Oxford, 1963), p. 48; and Ormrod, *Reign of Edward III*, p. 206.

[24] Kenneth Bruce McFarlane, *The Nobility of Late Medieval England* (Oxford, 1973), p. 129.

[25] Harriss, *King, Parliament*, pp. 490–5.

[26] For the conflict between the English and the French claims (at the time and since) as to the total value of the sums received, see R. Delachenal, *Histoire de Charles V* (5 vols, Paris, 1909–31), vol. 2, pp. 325–31; Dorothy M. Broome (ed.), 'The Ransom of John II, King of France, 1360–1370', in *Camden Miscellany XIV*, Camden Society, 3rd ser., 37 (London, 1926), pp. ix–xiv; and Ormrod, *Edward III*, p. 435.

Edward III out as the richest peacetime ruler of England in the whole of the Middle Ages.[27] For members of the privileged circles in which the poet of *W&W* seemingly operated, Edward could well have been seen in the 1360s as the very epitome of Wynnere, who hoards his 'sterlynges' ('silver pennies') in strong, steel-bound chests (line 252).

At the same time, the king also showed attributes that could very clearly be associated with the figure of Wastoure. The later 1350s and early 1360s represented the most exuberant and lavish phase in Edward III's expenditure on buildings, décor, feasting, costume and other forms of display that commemorated and advertised the outstanding achievements of his monarchy.[28] Even while the French and Scottish wars were still being actively prosecuted in the 1350s, large sums of money from the profits of the customs and subsidies had already been siphoned off to help pay for this calculated campaign of magnificence, and especially for the ambitious programme of building and decoration at the palaces of Westminster and Windsor and a series of lesser royal residences, including Sheppey and Kings Langley.[29] With the administrative merger of the king's and queen's households in 1360, Edward III assumed responsibility both for Queen Philippa's debts and for most of her subsequent expenditure; at the same time, the king was paying out regular sums of money to support an increasing number of members of the next generation of the royal family.[30] As a result, the royal household swelled to a scale unprecedented in its recorded history, with a regular staffing of over 450 people and direct costs of at least £35,000 a year.[31] Here, as with the support of the overseas dominions, Edward was quite prepared to dip

---

[27] Harriss, *King, Parliament*, pp. 499–502, with the estimated figure revised upwards by Ormrod, *Edward III*, p. 485. For the belief that this royal treasure still existed in the 1370s and even the 1380s, see Ormrod, *Edward III*, p. 581 and n. 20.

[28] Harriss, *King, Parliament*, pp. 479–81; and Ormrod, *Edward III*, pp. 446–71. In particular, see the major building work at Windsor in these years: Christopher Wilson, 'The Royal Lodgings of Edward III at Windsor Castle: Form, Function, Representation', in Laurence Keen and Eileen Scarff (eds), *Windsor: Medieval Archaeology, Art and Architecture of the Thames Valley*, British Archaeological Association Conference Transactions, 25 (Leeds, 2002), pp. 15–94.

[29] W. Mark Ormrod, 'The English Crown and the Customs, 1349–63', *Economic History Review*, 2nd ser., 40 (1987), 27–40, at 35–6.

[30] Chris Given-Wilson, 'The Merger of Edward III and Queen Philippa's Households, 1360–9', *Bulletin of the Institute of Historical Research*, 51 (1978), 183–7.

[31] Ormrod, *Edward III*, pp. 447–8. The figure of £35,000 is a rounded total of the known expenditures of the wardrobe and the great wardrobe in the fiscal year 1363–4: Thomas Frederick Tout, *Chapters in the Administrative History of Mediaeval England* (6 vols, Manchester, 1920–33), vol. 6, pp. 92, 107. This total excludes the expenditure of the privy wardrobe and the chamber, neither of which were accountable to the exchequer in this period and for which expenditures are therefore unknown.

into his private treasure to help cover costs. Nevertheless, in insisting on the peacetime levying of the wool subsidy while at the same time holding on to substantial private resources, Edward could clearly be held up as the manifestation of Wastoure, exploiting the hard work of his subjects (lines 228–32) for no more end than to support his gluttonous feasting (lines 330–65) and his dalliance with vainglorious fashion (lines 408–14).

To follow this line of thinking is also to be drawn back to some specific details in *W&W* that may have carried particular associations for a courtly and politically aware audience in the 1360s. In his second speech during the *refrayte*, Wynnere responds to Wastoure's criticism of his instinct for hoarding by pointing out not merely that excessive spending quickly results in general impoverishment, but also that the consequence is a tendency to live on credit and accumulate debt:

'There is no wele in this werlde to wasschen thyn handes
That ne es gyffen and grounden are thou it getyn haue.'
                                                    (lines 268–9)

Millett nicely renders these lines as

'There is no source of wealth flowing through your hands
That is not given and granted before you have got it.'

A further example of the same phenomenon occurs at the end of Wynnere's condemnation of wine consumption at the tavern. Once all the jollification is over, 'the wyne moste be payde fore' ('the wine must be paid for') (line 283). In accordance with his preoccupation with the affairs of the elite rather than of the peasantry, the poet does not dwell particularly on the wider social consequences arising from the practice of living on credit. In fact, Wastoure is quick to respond with the counter-argument that prodigality has a beneficial trickle-down effect: 'With oure festes and oure fare we feden the pore' ('With our feasts and our fare we feed the poor') (line 295).

This latter argument only worked, however, if money actually changed hands: peasant suppliers of goods to great households could not live on IOUs, but needed the cash that represented the fulfilment of their transactions. This was a vital issue throughout the first half of the fourteenth century, when purveyors charged with collecting foodstuffs to support both royal and noble households were frequently accused of abusing their powers of requisition, offering prices significantly below the market rate and using credit instruments, in the form of wooden tally sticks, as a substitute for ready money.[32] The Statute of Purveyance of 1362, however, conceded

---

[32] J. R. Maddicott, *The English Peasantry and the Demands of the Crown, 1294–1341*, Past & Present Supplement, 1 (Cambridge, 1975), p. 26. For purveyance by mem-

by Edward III in return for the first peacetime grant of the wool subsidy, required that the king's purveyors, now to be known as buyers, would in future offer the going rate for the foodstuffs and other goods that they commandeered, and would pay for them in coin:

> Que sur tieux purveances desore affaire pur les hosteulx le roi at la reigne soit paiement fait en poigne, cestassavoir le pris pur quell autiels vitailles sont venduz communement, en marchees environ; et que le heignous noun de purveour soit chaunge et nome achatour; ... et qe les prises et achatz soient faitz es lieux et places ou greindre plentee yad, et ce en temps covenable; et qe plus ne soit pris qe ne busoigne en sa sesone, pur les ditz deaux hosteulx ...

> (That upon such purveyances from henceforth to be made for the households of the king and the queen, ready payment shall be made in hand, that is to say, the price for which such victuals be sold commonly in the markets about; and that the heinous name of purveyor be changed, and named buyer; ... and that the prises and purchases be made in such places where greatest plenty is, and that at a suitable time; and that no more be taken than shall be needful in the season for the said two households ...)[33]

While it might push credulity too far to suggest that *W&W* provides a specific lesson in the virtues of the 1362 statute, its more general preoccupation with the elite not over-extending its purchasing power could have provided a timely reminder that the king's new commitment to paying his way was also going to lead to higher costs both for the royal household and for those who funded it.

In similar fashion, the financing of the great feast that Wynnere imagines as the centrepiece of Wastoure's luxurious lifestyle may have some significance in relation to the fiscal politics of the 1360s (lines 332–63). This lavish affair, with its multiple courses of freshly slaughtered meat, game, fowl, custards, pastries and pies, costs (we are told, at line 356) the outrageous sum of a mark (13s 4d) for every two people. Wastoure should be ashamed and disgraced, says his rival, for paying a 'rawnsom of siluer' ('ransom of silver') (line 363) for a single meal: he should take note of the simple herdsman and understand the

---

bers of the nobility, see Ormrod, *Reign of Edward III*, pp. 98, 99, 112; and Wendy Scase, 'Satire on the Retinues of the Great (MS Harley 2253): Unpaid Bills and the Politics of Purveyance', in Anne Marie D'Arcy and Alan John Fletcher (eds), *Studies in Late Medieval and Early Renaissance Texts in Honour of John Scattergood* (Dublin, 2005), pp. 305–20.

[33] *PROME*, vol. 5, pp. 142–5; *SR*, vol. 1, pp. 371–3, with quote at p. 371 (translation slightly amended). For the significance of the statute of 1362, see Harriss, *King, Parliament*, pp. 376–83, 506; Chris Given-Wilson, 'Purveyance for the Royal Household, 1362–1413', *Bulletin of the Institute of Historical Research*, 56 (1983), 145–63.

virtues of the adage, 'Better were meles many than a mery nyghte' ('Better to have many meals than one merry night') (line 365). The phrase 'rawnsom of siluer' is conventional enough as a metaphor: in the fourteenth century, *raunsoun* in Middle English and *rançun* in Anglo-Norman French carried both the general meaning of an exaction or redemption and the modern meaning of a payment for the release of a prisoner.[34] In light of the arguments in Chapter 1 about the early passages of *W&W* possibly reflecting the Garter feast at Windsor in April 1358, however, we may also venture to suggest that the 'rawnsom of siluer' is a direct allusion to the large sums of money that Edward III had at his disposal in the 1360s from the ransom of John II. Certainly, the lavishness, and therefore the cost, of the 1358 Garter feast quickly became proverbial. John of Reading, writing in the 1360s, claimed that the French king had commented on Edward III's own tendency to live off credit by pointing out the irony of a banquet purchased with wood (that is, tally sticks) but served on silver and gold platters.[35] If *W&W* was indeed written during the political debate over public finance that spanned the parliaments of 1362–5, then the imputation would be that Edward III's 'house of magnificence' felt it perfectly appropriate to squander a king's ransom on the maintenance of an appropriately splendid royal lifestyle, even at a moment when the crown was pleading that it had insufficient resources to cover its war debts and ongoing public commitments and was accordingly demanding the continuation of the wool subsidy in times of peace.

Finally, a reading of *W&W* as a debate between two related and competing attributes of monarchy during the 1360s gives further possible meaning to the manner in which the figure of the king resolves the dispute between the protagonists at the end of the extant text of the poem. The passage has been addressed and cited a number of times above, but repays quotation *in extenso* here:

> 'Wende, Wynnere, thi waye ouer the wale stremys
> Pass forthe by Paris to the Pope of Rome,
> The cardynalls ken the wele, will kepe the ful faire
> And make thi sides in silken scheytys to lygge

[34] 'Middle English Dictionary', quod.lib.umich.edu, *s.v.* 'raunsoun'; 'The Anglo-Norman Online Hub: Anglo-Norman Dictionary', http://www.anglo-norman.net, *s.v.* 'rançun'.
[35] James Tait (ed.), *Chronica Johannis de Reading et Anonymi Cantuariensis* (Manchester, 1914), p. 130. See also the speech attributed to John II on the same occasion in a mid-fifteenth-century chronicle: Edward Tyrrell and Nicholas Harris Nicolas (eds), *A Chronicle of London from 1089 to 1483* (London, 1827), pp. 63–4. For further literary analogues, see Anthony Steel, *The Receipt of the Exchequer, 1377–1485* (Cambridge, 1954), pp. xxxiv–v; Given-Wilson, 'Purveyance for the Royal Household', p. 149; Hugh E. L. Collins, *The Order of the Garter, 1348–1461: Chivalry and Politics in Late Medieval England* (Oxford, 2000), pp. 238–9; and Ormrod, *Edward III*, p. 389 n. 23.

And fede the and foster the and forthir thyn hert
As leefe to worthen wode as the to wrethe ones.
Bot loke, lede, be thi lyfe, when I letters sende
That thou hy to me home on horse or one fote,
And when I knowe thou will co[me] he schall cayre vttire
And lenge with another lede til thou thi lefe [take].
For thofe thou bide in this burgh to thi ber[yinge-daye]
With hym happyns the neuer a fote for [to holde].
And thou, Wastoure, I will that thou wonn[e sholde]
Ther moste waste es of wele and wyng [ther vntill].
Chese the forthe into the Chepe, a chamber though rere,
Loke thi wundowe be wyde and wayte the aboute
Where any p[etit] beryn thurgh the burgh passe.
Teche hym to the tauerne till he tayte worthe,
Doo hym drynke al nyghte that he dry be at morow,
Sythen ken hym to the crete to comforth his vaynes,
Brynge hym to Bred Strete, bikken thi fynger,
Schew hym of fatt chepe scholdirs ynewe,
Hotte for the hungry, a hen other twayne
...
'Then passe to the Pultrie, the peple the knows
And ken wele the katour to knawen thi fode
...
'And wayte to me, thou Wynnere, if thou wilt wele chefe,
When I wende appon were my wyes to lede
For at the proude pales of Parys the riche
I think to do it in ded and dub the to knyghte
And giff giftes full grete of sil[uver]
To ledis of my legyance that lufen me in hert.'
      (lines 460–82, 490–1, 496–501)[36]

('Winner, wend your way far overseas,
Pass forth by Paris to the pope of Rome;
The cardinals know you well, and will keep you in fair estate,
Making your sides to lie in silken sheets;
They will feed you and foster you and further your desire,
Willing to go mad rather than to anger you at all.
But look, Sir, by your life, when I send you letters
That you should hurry home to me by horse or on foot,

[36] This final extant section of the poem has some lacunae, and the modern readings therefore vary: see for example, Turville-Petre, pp. 414–15 and nn. I continue here to use Trigg as the base text, but have accepted some elisions, spellings and punctuation from Turville-Petre and Ginsberg.

And when I know you intend to come, he [Wastoure] shall go away
And stay with another until you take your leave;
For though you stay in this town until the day of your death,
You will never have to walk a single foot with him.
And you, Wastoure, I order that you stay
Where wealth is wasted most, so wing your way there;
Go forth to Cheapside, and set up a room there,
Take care that your window is open wide, and wait there
Until anyone with a purse passes through the town.
Take him to the tavern, until he gets drunk,
Make him drink all night, so that he is dry the next day,
Then offer him some Cretan wine to comfort him.
Bring him to Bread Street, beckon with your finger,
Show his fat shoulders of mutton,
"Hot for the hungry", a hen or two.
...

'Then pass on to Poultry, where the people know you,
And direct your buyer to recognise the food you like.
...

'And look to me, Winner, if you want to gain wealth,
When I go to the wars to lead my men;
For at the proud walls of the great city of Paris
I plan to have it done, and dub you to knight,
And give great gifts, of gold and of silver,
To those of my allegiance who love me in their hearts.')

The tradition of criticism on *W&W* offers two main readings of the king's decision not to declare decisively in favour of one or other party. The less critical of these (favoured, for example, by Trigg) is the one that sees the king's equivocation as a tacit acknowledgement of his need to retain the services of both men and thus to have his court and household epitomise both the prudent frugality of Wynnere and the showy magnificence of Wastoure. The statement at lines 466–71 is especially important to this argument, for it suggests that the king understands the irreconcilability of the protagonists; if he calls Wynnere home (that is, on the outbreak of further war), then he will send Wastoure away (from London) to live under 'another lede' ('another lord') (line 469), presumably meaning his redeployment within England, but perhaps also suggesting exile to another land.[37] More judgmental is the reading favoured by Bestul and many of those who have followed him, which sees the king's prevarication either as an implied criticism of Edward III's failure to curb the unruliness of his retainers (which

---

[37] Millett translates the phrase 'another lede' at line 469 by the looser idea of 'someone else'.

leads us back into the debate about public order) or as exemplifying the economically damaging effects of the taxes and purveyances he continues to levy in order to cover his high expenditure on war.[38]

If, by contrast, the poem is set against the background of peace in the 1360s, then the final passage of the poem at lines 456–503 may be read as containing a rather different set of valences. First, the generally critical depiction of the activities to which Wastoure will apply himself when sent onto the streets of London may suggest something of the disquiet underpinning the parliamentary debates of the early 1360s over the notably high expenditure of the king's household, itself a major customer in the London markets for both luxury and staple goods.[39] Secondly, the later dating of the poem means that it becomes even less likely that the 'giftes full grete of golde and sil[uer]' ('great gifts, of gold and of silver') promised to Wynnere and his followers at line 500 represent the large debts that Edward III owed to the merchant financiers of the 1340s. The accompanying controversies had largely been resolved in the early 1350s when the crown agreed to dispense with the monopolies on wool exports that had caused so much controversy in the previous decade.[40] Although London-based capitalists were still lending to the crown in the later 1350s and through the years of peace in the 1360s, the scale of their operations was very much reduced – not least, it may be pointed out, because of the large stores of ready cash that Edward had at his disposal in his private treasure at the Tower.[41] Instead, the gifts

[38] Bestul, *Satire and Allegory*, pp. 3–4, 48–51, 78–80.

[39] For the importance of those London companies that dealt in luxury goods as suppliers to the royal household, see Pamela Nightingale, *A Medieval Mercantile Community: The Grocers' Company and the Politics of Trade in London, 1000–1485* (London, 1995); Anne F. Sutton, *The Mercery of London: Trade, Goods and People, 1130–1578* (Aldershot, 2005); and Jessica Lutkin, 'Goldsmiths and the English Court, 1360–1413' (Unpublished Ph.D. thesis, University of London, 2008).

[40] The means by which this was effected, under the terms of the Ordinance of the Staple of 1353, was radical: *all* denizen merchants were to be deprived of the right to export wool, which would now be handled solely by aliens. After 1357 the crown relaxed the ban on denizen exports, and its decision in 1363 to transfer the wool staple from England to Calais resulted in the creation of a company of twenty-six English merchants to govern the town; although they were given no formal monopoly, it was inevitable that the members of the company would come to dominate the wool trade. See Harriss, *King, Parliament*, pp. 446–7; R. L. Baker, 'The Government of Calais in 1363', in William Chester Jordan, Bruce McNab and Teofilo F. Ruiz (eds), *Order and Innovation in the Middle Ages: Essays in Honor of Joseph R. Strayer* (Princeton, 1976), pp. 207–14; T. H. Lloyd, *The English Wool Trade in the Middle Ages* (Cambridge, 1977), pp. 108–9; and Ormrod, *Reign of Edward III*, pp. 190–4.

[41] Ormrod, 'English Crown and the Customs', pp. 35–6.

of gold and silver that will be offered when the time comes to re-employ Wynnere and his cohorts seem to represent an understanding on the part of the poet that Edward III would indeed give up the remainder of this hoard as and when it was necessary to re-build the crown's military resources in preparation for the renewal of war. As in the discussion of the diplomatic and military context of the poem in Chapter 1, so here: the exiling of Wynnere seems to fit much more neatly with a period when formal hostilities by the English crown were actually suspended, during the 1360s.

In fine, then, the suggestions made by this study that *W&W* may have been composed after 1358, and most probably around debates taking place in parliament between 1362 and 1365, make it possible to see the figures of Wynnere and Wastoure as representing a commentary on the regime of Edward III not, as previously argued, because of the high costs of the Hundred Years War, but as a result of Edward III's own efforts to extend the fiscal conditions of war to the public finances of peace after the Treaty of Calais. In this reading, *W&W* reflects the unease of the polity at Edward's evident desire not to share the peace dividend of 1360 but to have all the benefits, private and public, for himself: if we may put it thus, to have his fiscal cake and eat it. And if this was the principal message intended by the poet of *W&W*, then the prevarication shown by the king at the end of the poem over the rights and wrongs of Wynnere and Wastoure's arguments could well be a fourteenth-century articulation of the idea of the false dilemma, epitomised in the principle later known as 'Morton's fork'. Named for Henry VII's chancellor, John Morton, and apparently having some currency in the sixteenth century, this idea held that a man who saved money and lived frugally had ample resources with which to pay his taxes, while he who spent lots of money on a lavish lifestyle thereby ironically also demonstrated his wealth and was equally able to pay tax.[42] The king, it seemed, might indeed have things both ways.

The strongest evidence in support of the existence of a public debate on this general position outside the confines of government and parliament in the 1360s is the *Commentary* that the Augustinian friar John Erghome wrote on the text known as the *Prophecy of John of Bridlington*, which had itself been composed *c*.1350. Bestul deployed the *Commentary* in support of his own extension of Stillwell's arguments about *W&W* as a critique of the financing of the Hundred Years War, but did so without consideration of the specific moment at which it was composed.[43] Erghome, who began

---

[42] For the possibility that the true originator of Morton's fork might have been Richard Foxe, lord privy seal to Henry VII, and that the principle was already known under Edward IV, see S. B. Chrimes, *Henry VII*, 2nd edn (London, 1999), p. 203 and n. 6.

[43] Thomas Wright (ed.), *Political Poems and Songs Relating to English History*, Rolls

his work shortly after the second plague of 1361–2 and had definitely completed it by 1373, aimed to demonstrate how Edward III's glorious successes in the middle years of his reign contained within them the seeds of his own downfall. Much of this was by way of generalised criticism of the decadence of the court, and more specifically of the emerging influence, by the later 1360s, of the king's controversial mistress, Alice Perrers.[44] But Erghome also referred specifically to the avarice that Edward demonstrated in his fiscal policies. He shared the sensibilities of other political commentators about the unjust nature of taxes that ground down the poorer members of society. Writing from the vantage point of the 1360s, however, he went further. The king's need for money had become a constant, whether the country was at war or not: '[Q]uando enim cessabit a guerris erit valde avarus pecuniae, et aliquando magis pencuniae quam honorum' ('[E]ven when he abandons his wars he will still be extremely greedy for money, and sometimes more greedy for money than for honour').[45] In the peculiarly exposed position that he had put himself in as a result of his decision to continue to seek public resourcing during peacetime, Edward III had therefore become the epitome of the avaricious ruler.

To consider the politics of the 1360s in light of Erghome's perspective is the better to understand the otherwise ill-documented fiscal debates during these years both in the confidential confines of the king's council and in the public arena of parliament. Edward III was almost certainly in conflict with some of his ministers over his insistence on retaining complete autonomy over the spending of the French ransom and other prerogative incomes, and both he and his government were evidently aware of the possible backlash in parliament over the unprecedented demands now made for peacetime taxation.[46] In particular, the accidental survival in the exchequer records of

---

Series, 14 (2 vols, London, 1859–61), vol. 1, pp. 123–215; Bestul, *Satire and Allegory*, pp. 62–4. I use Bestul's translations of the *Commentary*. Bestul wrote at a time when it was still assumed that both the *Prophecy* and the *Commentary* were written by Erghome; but it has since been demonstrated that the *Prophecy* was a separate (anonymous) Latin verse composition of *c.*1350, to which Erghome added his Latin prose glosses in *c.*1360–72. See A. G. Rigg, 'John of Bridlington's Prophecy: A New Look', *Speculum*, 63 (1988), 596–613.

[44] John Barnie, *War in Medieval English Society: Social Values and the Hundred Years War* (London, 1974), pp. 145–7. See also, more generally, Christopher D. Fletcher, 'Corruption at Court: Crisis and the Theme of *luxuria* in England and France, *c.*1340–1422', in Stephen Gunn and Antheun Janse (eds), *The Court as a Stage: England and the Low Countries in the Late Middle Ages* (Woodbridge, 2006), pp. 28–38.

[45] Wright (ed.), *Political Poems and Songs*, vol. 1, p. 139, translated by Bestul, *Satire and Allegory*, p. 63.

[46] Broome (ed.), 'Ransom of John II', pp. i–xxvi, argued that the exchequer protested

a series of carefully constructed 'balance sheets' purporting to represent the income and expenditure of the crown at various stages between 1362 and 1365 strongly suggests that Edward's treasurers felt the need to be armed with the fullest possible information when they put their requests to parliament for the renewal of the wool subsidy.[47] A large range of concessions was made on the first such occasion, in 1362, including the Statute of Purveyors; the famous legislation providing that the proceedings of the courts should be conducted in English; a guarantee that the king would continue to seek extensions of the wool subsidy by reference to parliament; and a general pardon for criminal offences committed in the past. This suggests that the (otherwise unrecorded) debates on this occasion were particularly hard-fought and that the Commons took full advantage of a release from the emergency of war to argue strongly, if ultimately unsuccessfully, their case for a self-financing royal regime.[48] The newly critical focus on the ways in which the royal court was using public money to support such displays of magnificence also yielded some victims. The trial of the steward of the royal household, Sir John atte Lee, in the parliament of 1368 was partly prompted by charges of corruption relating to his efforts to exploit the king's feudal rights and thus to increase the income of the main financial office of the royal household, the wardrobe.[49] In all of this, we see the glimpses of a more fundamental debate over who was meant to benefit from the making of peace: the king or his people.

And yet it would be a mistake to over-stress the wider political implications represented by a reading of *W&W* as an overt criticism of courtly luxury financed off the back of an impoverished and downtrodden realm. There is a significant difference in the political mood of the parliaments of the 1360s, which were prepared to negotiate and compromise, and those

---

at the king's claim to run the income from the ransoms and indemnities as part of his independent, private income. Harriss, *King, Parliament*, p. 500, preferred to see the technical changes effected in the administration of these revenues in 1364 as a direct shift in royal policy. Either way, there is evidence for changing positions arising from keen debate.

[47] Thomas Frederick Tout and Dorothy M. Broome, 'A National Balance Sheet for 1362–3', *English Historical Review*, 39 (1924), 404–19; and Harriss, *King, Parliament*, pp. 470–502, 527–30.

[48] Harriss, *King, Parliament*, pp. 504–7; W. Mark Ormrod, 'The Use of English: Language, Law and Political Culture in Fourteenth-Century England', *Speculum*, 88 (2003), 750–87; and Helen Lacey, *The Royal Pardon: Access to Mercy in Fourteenth-Century England* (York, 2009), pp. 114–15.

[49] W. Mark Ormrod, 'Parliamentary Scrutiny of Royal Ministers and Courtiers in Fourteenth-Century England: The Disgrace of Sir John Atte Lee (1368)', in Richard W. Kaeuper (ed.), *Law, Governance and Justice: New Views on Medieval Constitutionalism* (Leiden, 2013), pp. 161–88.

of the 1370s, which became more and more obdurate about the perceived deficiencies of government. After the renewal of the French war in 1369, dramatically escalating costs and a general shortage of credit available to the state allowed a small cabal of prominent courtiers, led by the chamberlain of the household, William Latimer, the steward, John Neville, and the now highly conspicuous royal mistress, Alice Perrers, to exploit the money markets for major personal gain.[50] It was during the 1370s, too, that the previously lone voice of Erghome began to find echoes and embellishments in the thinking of other moralising critics, as figures such as John Wyclif and John Gower began to question the whole legitimacy of Edward III's cause against the French.[51] In 1376 the implication became an ominous reality, when the so-called Good Parliament refused point-blank to grant any new direct taxes in support of the war.[52] The political rupture that ensued, in which the courtiers and other financiers were exposed and discredited, was of a directness and ferocity quite unknown in the 1360s.

Even if parts of *W&W* do indeed fixate on Edward III's explosion of expenditure in the aftermath of the Treaty of Calais, then, the element of criticism actually remains quite veiled, in line with the overall political mood of that decade. And it follows that, even though the author of *W&W* may have moved from a general adulatory image of Edward III in the opening sequences of his work to a more critical stance at the end, it was never his intention to turn the poem into a full-scale denunciation of Edward's monarchy. Ralph Hanna has suggested that the representation of the king at lines 456–503 is light-hearted and humorous: it 'comically ratifies one version of Edwardian policy … : [namely] to pillage folks on the continent in order to support domestic sumptuousness.'[53] Rather more generally and substantively, from the beginning of the debate to its end, the central issue of *W&W* remains firmly fixed on the way that all members of landed society – king, nobles and gentry alike – should work to promote the virtues of moderation and stability in an uncertain and fickle world.

---

[50] George Holmes, *The Good Parliament* (Oxford, 1975), pp. 69–79. For Alice Perrers' London connections, see most recently Laura Tompkins, 'Alice Perrers and the Goldsmiths' Mistery: New Evidence Concerning the Identity of Edward III's Mistress', *English Historical Review*, 130 (2015), 1361–91. Whereas Latimer, Neville and a number of London-based capitalists were impeached in this assembly, Perrers was simply expelled from the court. For the subsequent investigations of complaints against her in the early parliaments of Richard II, see W. Mark Ormrod, 'The Trials of Alice Perrers', *Speculum*, 83 (2008), 366–96, at 369–86.

[51] Michael Wilks, *Wyclif: Political Ideas and Practice* (Oxford, 2000), pp. 117–77.

[52] The justification for this refusal was apparently that a truce was running at the time: Ormrod, *Reign of Edward III*, p. 165.

[53] Ralph Hanna, *London Literature, 1300–1380* (Cambridge, 2005), p. 262.

This chapter has proposed that it is possible to unravel sections of *W&W* such as to reveal important political debates going on in the royal council and parliament during the 1360s. The question remains as to who might have had the knowledge and capacity to incorporate the substance of such debates into the highly coded forms in which, as the analysis has suggested, they are articulated within the poem. The relatively subdued nature of the arguments around the financing of the royal household during the years of peace in the 1360s means that the people most likely to understand the details and implications of the debate were those who discussed these matters in parliament and those whose job it was to apply the relating decisions in the offices of royal government. No evidence has ever been adduced to show that either laymen elected as Members of Parliament or clerks working in the royal chancery and exchequer wrote polemics, either political or poetical, on Edward III's record of government and fiscal policy in the 1360s. Among a wider group of writers, however, we should recall the point made in Chapter 1 about William Langland's sharp criticisms of the Treaty of Calais of 1360 and his specific reference to the ransom of John II in the first recension of *Piers Plowman*.[54] And by contrast, Clementine Oliver has shown that there was a significant market for 'political pamphleteering' in the 1370s and 1380s, when a number of men employed on the edges of the royal administration engaged in writing up the sensational events of the Good Parliament of 1376, the Wonderful Parliament of 1386 and the Merciless Parliament of 1388 for audiences fully engaged in the dramatic politics of the time.[55] As we have stressed, there was comparatively little in the 1360s of the sense of urgency and emergency that would overcome public debate in the 1370s. Nonetheless, it is possible to speculate that the author of *W&W* reveals his own keen interest in high politics, and fiscal policy in particular, by the very decision to engage in a debate about the getting and spending of wealth. Edward III's private treasure in the Tower of London stood, for those in the know, both as a marker of the king's great success in building up the wealth of the crown and as a reminder of his sometimes rather unscrupulous efforts to impose wartime taxes during a period of peace. Reading *W&W* as a composition of the 1360s thus reveals the ambivalence that at least some members of the polity felt about the peacetime fiscal policies of Edward III.

---

[54] See p. 35.
[55] Clementine Oliver, *Political Pamphleteering in Fourteenth-Century England* (York, 2010). See also Gwilym Dodd, 'Was Thomas Favent a Political Pamphleteer? Faction and Politics in Later Fourteenth-Century London', *Journal of Medieval History*, 37 (2011), 397–418.

5

Satire, Complaint and Authorship: *Winner and Waster* and the Alliterative Revival of the Fourteenth Century

It has long been appreciated that *W&W* presents a satire upon the behaviours of the ruling elite, exposing as it does both the greed of the upper orders of society and the recklessness of their lavish lifestyles.[1] The question therefore arises as to how *W&W* compares with other literary works of social commentary and political complaint of the period. The fourteenth century saw a flourishing of such works, many of which (like *W&W*) survive only in single manuscripts; had more of the ephemeral literature of the period come down to us, the modern understanding of the authorship, content and reception of complaint literature would not only be all the greater, but possibly rather different in its assumptions around such issues as authorship and audience.[2] There is a sufficient corpus of material, however, to give a strong indication of the nature of this genre over the reigns of the first three Edwards, and to provide the starting-point for a consideration of *W&W*'s own identity as a 'complaint' poem.

The previous chapters have emphasised that the immediate message of *W&W* relates not to the hardships of the lower orders but to the responsibilities of the higher levels of society, and to the lesser landed classes or gentry in particular. *Pace* Harwood's thesis about the anxiety of the poet over the presumptuousness of the peasantry in the aftermath of the Black Death, we have observed that direct criticism of the lower orders is generally omitted from the text.[3] Similarly, the representation of the merchant class is

---

[1] Thomas H. Bestul, *Satire and Allegory in* Wynnere and Wastoure (Lincoln, Nebraska, 1974), *passim*.

[2] For reviews of the genre of complaint literature, see Janet Coleman, *English Literature in History, 1350–1400: Medieval Readers and Writers* (London, 1981), *passim*; and Wendy Scase, *Literature and Complaint in England, 1272–1553* (Oxford, 2007), *passim*. See also the landmark essay of J. R. Maddicott, 'Poems of Social Protest in Early Fourteenth-Century England', in W. Mark Ormrod (ed.), *England in the Fourteenth Century: Proceedings of the 1985 Harlaxton Symposium* (Woodbridge, 1986), pp. 130–44.

[3] See above, pp. 68–9.

limited, and shies away from the stereotypes of contemporary literature that often present the commercial classes as unscrupulous profiteers and comical social climbers.[4] Instead, there sit within the poem a series of grounded assumptions about a well-ordered society in which peasants and lords (not to mention clerics and merchants) understand their own positions in the grand scheme of things and are properly mindful of their resulting social obligations towards others.

At first sight, this decidedly conservative viewpoint seems at odds with some recent interpretations of the complaint literature of the period. Modern criticism has served to radicalise some of the more outspoken social commentaries in fourteenth-century poetry, such as those found in the *Song of the Husbandman* and the *Song against the King's Taxes* in the first half of the fourteenth century and in William Langland's *Piers Plowman* and the literature sparked by the latter in the second half of the century. The fact that *Piers Plowman* acted as an inspiration to literate and illiterate rebels during the Peasants' Revolt of 1381 provides clear evidence of the way in which, during extraordinary circumstances, political poetry could help the lower orders both to understand their predicament and to articulate the radical reforms they required in the organisation of state and society.[5] Other less ambitious works of imagination, such as the mnemonic verses spread by the rebels of 1381 as ideological war cries, carry clear overtones of sedition and, perhaps, revolution:

> Iakke Mylner asket help to turne hys mylne aright. He hath gronden smal smal; the kyngus sone of heuen he schal pay for alle. Loke thi mylne go aright, with the foure sayles, and the post stande in stedfastnesse. With right and with myght, with skyl and with wylle. let myght help ryght, and skyl go before wille, and ryght before myght, than goth oure mylne aright, and if myght go before ryght, and wylle before skylle, than is oure mylne mys a dyght.

---

[4] For the social aspirations of merchants see, amongst much else, Rosemary Horrox, 'The Urban Gentry in the Fifteenth Century', in John A. F. Thomson (ed.), *Towns and Townspeople in the Fifteenth Century* (Gloucester, 1988), pp. 22–44; Philippa C. Maddern, 'Social Mobility', in Rosemary Horrox and W. Mark Ormrod (eds), *A Social History of England, 1200–1500* (Cambridge, 2006), pp. 113–33, at pp. 126–8; and Caroline Barron, 'Chivalry, Pageantry and Merchant Culture in Medieval London', in Peter R. Coss and Maurice Keen (eds), *Heraldry, Pageantry and Social Display in Medieval England* (Woodbridge, 2002), pp. 219–41.

[5] Steven Justice, *Writing and Rebellion: England in 1381* (Berkeley, California, 1994), pp. 102–39. For further discussion, see, *inter alia*, Maddicott, 'Poems of Social Protest', pp. 138–9; Richard Firth Green, 'John Ball's Letters: Literary History and Historical Literature', in Barbara A. Hanawalt (ed.), *Chaucer's England: Literature in Historical Context* (Minneapolis, 1992), pp. 176–200; and Ann W. Astell, *Political Allegory in Late Medieval England* (London, 1999), pp. 44–72.

(Jack Miller asks for help to turn his mill aright. He has ground things small, and small, the King's Son of Heaven shall pay for all. Take care that your mill turns well, with its four sails, and that the post stands steadfast. With might and with right, with skill and with will; let might help right, and skill go before will, and right before might, and then our mill will go aright. For if might go before right, and will before skill, then our mill will not go well.)[6]

Here, the mill takes the place of another metaphor used in contemporary literature, the ship of state, in what becomes a parable of good and bad society.[7] 'Right' (we might say, liberty and the rule of law) should prevail over 'might' (the exercise of force, implied perhaps as coming from seigniorial authority); and 'skill' (honest work) should take precedence over 'will' (the arbitrary use of prerogative power, again implied as coming from the higher orders of society). The general meaning, then, is that the lower orders have a greater sense of public morality and social responsibility than do their so-called betters, and that their own sense of 'right' and 'will' can give legitimacy to acts of defiance against acknowledged authority. This is not just the language of discontent: it is the lifeblood of insurgency.

The question nonetheless arises as to whether the wider body of complaint literature produced over the fourteenth century ever really supported some grander notion of social revolution. Much more common is a sense of resignation to the evils of the times, with trust in God being the only true and available refuge. Thus, for example, the Anglo-Norman/Latin macaronic text *The Song against the King's Taxes*, written some time between 1338 and 1341, shows strong support for the lower orders in the sense that it regards the crown's heavy impositions as deeply inequitable and regressive, burdening the poor rather than the rich:[8]

---

[6] Geoffrey Martin (ed. and trans.), *Knighton's Chronicle, 1337–1396* (Oxford, 1995), pp. 222–3. See also the rendering of this passage by Justice, *Writing and Rebellion*, p. 13.

[7] For the 'ship of state' topos, see W. Mark Ormrod, *Political Life in Medieval England, 1300–1450* (Basingstoke, 1995), p. 60.

[8] The most recent edition of this poem (with the translation given here) is found in Susanna Fein with David Raybin and Jan Ziolkowski (eds and trans.), *The Complete Harley 2253 Manuscript* (3 vols, Kalamazoo, 2015), vol. 3, pp. 290–9. For dating and context, see also Maddicott, 'Poems of Social Protest', pp. 130–44; John Scattergood, 'Authority and Resistance: The Political Verse', in Susanna Fein (ed.), *Studies in the Harley Manuscript: The Scribes, Contents, and Social Contexts of British Library MS Harley 2253* (Kalamazoo, 2000), pp. 163–201, at pp. 163–6; Scase, *Literature and Complaint*, pp. 30–41; and David Matthews, *Writing to the King: Nation, Kingship and Literature in England, 1250–1350* (Cambridge, 2010), pp. 125–34.

> Depus que le roy vodera
> > Tam multum cepisse,
> Entre les riches si purra
> > Satis invenisse.
> E plus, a ce que m'est avys,
> > Et melius fecisse
> Des grantz partie aver pris,
> > Et parvis pepercisse.
> > > Qui capit argentum,
> > > Sine causa, peccat egentum.
>
> (lines 61–70)

> (Since the king wants
> > To take so much,
> Among the rich he may thus
> > Find enough.
> And besides, in my opinion,
> > He would do better
> To have taken a portion from the great,
> > And have spared the lowly.
> > > He who, without cause, takes money
> > > From the needy commits sin.)

This, however, is no revolutionary voice. The poet is at pains to argue that the young king should not be blamed for a policy that he ascribes to the greybeards of the royal council (lines 71–80). And when it comes to organised resistance, he returns quickly to the assumptions and language of the social establishment:

> Tel tribut a nul feor
> > Diu nequit durare.
> De voyde qy puet doner,
> > Vel minibus tractare?
> Gentz sunt a tiel mischief
> > Quod nequeunt plus dare;
> Je me doute, s'ils ussent chief
> > Quod vellent levare.
> > > Sepe facit stultas
> > > Gentes vacuata facultas.
>
> (lines 121–30)

> (Such tribute can by no means
> > Last for long.
> Who can give from emptiness,

Or touch it with his hands?
People are in such bad straits
   That they cannot give more;
I fear that, had they a leader,
   They would rise in rebellion.
         Often people turn foolish
         For loss of possessions.)

A similar conscious effort to move back from the brink of open resistance is evident in the thinking of William Langland, whose great dream-poem, *Piers Plowman*, was one of the powerful influences upon the thought and action of rebel leaders during the revolt of 1381.[9] In the aftermath of the rising, Langland removed from the Prologue to *Piers* the notion that the king's legitimacy derived from the will of the people, thus distancing himself from the rebels' declared desire to abolish lordship and live in a kind of primitive communism with their own elected ruler.[10] Whether in direct criticism of royal policies or in more general assumptions about the right ordering of society, then, the author of *W&W* shared a widespread view that writing was quite different from direct activism, and was done, on the whole, within a mindset supportive of the monarch and critical only of the corruption that existed among the king's ministers and officials at Westminster and in the localities. To this extent, *W&W* conforms to what the literary scholar Anne Middleton calls the 'public poetry' of the Ricardian period: poetry that addressed the whole of secular society and called to mind the responsibilities of status, high and low, in the common pursuit of prosperity and stability.[11]

This view of complaint poetry as a kind of safety valve providing both an outlet for critical speech and a brake upon violent reaction is best exemplified in the attitudes of fourteenth-century authors towards the professional representatives of the Church and the law.[12] A number of political poems of the time dwell on the corruption of the ecclesiastical order in general and on the church courts and/or the king's common law courts in particular: for example, the *Satire on the Consistory Courts* (Latin, early fourteenth century); the *Song on the Venality of the Judges* (Latin, early fourteenth century); *The Simonie* (Middle English, c.1325); the *Outlaw's Song of Trailbaston* (Anglo-Norman French and Latin, c.1305, but copied in response to

[9] Justice, *Writing and Rebellion*, pp. 67–139.
[10] Anthony Musson and W. Mark Ormrod, *The Evolution of English Justice: Law, Politics and Society in the Fourteenth Century* (Basingstoke, 1999), p. 172.
[11] Anne Middleton, 'The Idea of Public Poetry in the Reign of Richard II', *Speculum*, 53 (1978), 94–114. For critiques of Middleton's thesis, see Astell, *Political Allegory*, pp. 2–7.
[12] See, in general, Jill Mann, *Chaucer and Medieval Estates Satire: The Literature of Social Classes and the* General Prologue *to the* Canterbury Tales (Cambridge, 1973).

a revival of trailbastons, or judicial inquiries, in 1341); and the *Song against the Friars* (Middle English, late fourteenth century) – not to mention *Piers Plowman* itself (Middle English, written in three recensions, *c.*1362–82) and that great set piece of medieval social satire, the 'General Prologue' to Chaucer's *Canterbury Tales* (Middle English, late fourteenth century).[13] A comparison of these and other texts with *W&W* can help reveal the mindset of the author of the latter poem and possibly something of the attitude of his intended audience.

There are two places where *W&W* explicitly considers the common law and its representatives. The first is in the identification of the group of men gathered under the second banner on the tournament field. Their emblem is the coif, the distinctive headgear worn by senior members of the legal profession and the judges in the common law courts (lines 149–51). The poet wonders (through the voice of the knight-messenger) why such men should be present if the purpose of the day is indeed to see a trial of arms between the forces of Wynnere and Wastoure:

'Thies are ledlis of this londe that schold oure lawes yeme,
That thynken to dele this daye with dynttis full many.
I holde hym bot a fole that fightis whils flyttynge may helpe,
When he hase founden his frende that fayled hym never.'
(lines 152–5)

('These are the men of this land who should protect our laws,
But are ready to fight today with many strokes.
I hold him but a fool who prefers to fight while he can dispute instead,
When he has found his friend that failed him never.')

The same tension between the lawyers' proper aim of peaceful resolution and the protagonists' preference for a trial under the law of arms becomes apparent in Wastoure's second speech during the debate, where he com-

[13] For editions of the first five texts listed here, see, respectively: Fein with Raybin and Ziolkowski (eds and trans.), *Complete Harley 2253 Manuscript*, vol. 2, pp. 188–92; Peter Coss (ed.), *Thomas Wright's Political Songs of England* (Cambridge, 1996), pp. 224–30; James M. Dean (ed.), *The Simonie* (Kalamazoo, 1996); Fein with Raybin and Ziolkowski (eds and trans.), *Complete Harley 2253 Manuscript*, vol. 3, pp. 144–9; and Thomas Wright (ed.), *Political Poems and Songs Relating to English History*, Rolls Series, 14 (2 vols, London, 1859–61), vol. 1, p. 268. For the argument that the *Outlaw's Song of Trailbaston* may have been copied into London, British Library Harley MS 2253 in response to Edward III's issuing of commissions of trailbaston in 1341, see Carter Revard, 'The Outlaw's Song of Trailbaston', in Thomas H. Ohlgren (ed.), *Medieval Outlaws: Ten Tales in Modern English* (Stroud, 1998), pp. 99–105, 302–4, 329–31; and Carter Revard, 'Scribe and Provenance', in Fein (ed.), *Studies in the Harley Manuscript*, pp. 21–109, at pp. 74–7.

ments both on the futility of the lawyers' attempts to bring his case to court and on his own strong desire to have the matter dealt with in a trial of force:

> 'And theis beryns one the bynches with howes one lofte,
> That bene knowen and kydde for clerkes of the beste,
> Als gude als Arestotle or Austyn the wyse,
> That alle schent were those schalkes and Scharschull itwiste,
> That saide I prikkede with powere his pese to distourbe!
> Forthi, comely kynge, that oure case heris,
> Late us swythe with our swerdes swyngen togedirs.'
> (lines 314–20)

('And these men on the benches with their lawyers' caps,
Known far and wide as the best of learned men,
As good as Aristotle or Augustine the wise,
So all of them should be ruined, and Shareshull too,
Who said that I pricked with armed power to disturb his peace!
Therefore, comely king, having heard our case,
Let us swiftly with swords strike now together.')

In respect of the representatives of the law, then, *W&W* is quite different from other political and satirical verse of the fourteenth century. It does not condemn judges and lawyers as corrupt, in the tradition of the *Song on the Venality of the Judges* or the *Outlaw's Song of Trailbaston*.[14] It twice contends that the proper way to dispute resolution is through a formal, peaceful process, and not – as Wastoure wants, and as is championed, for example, in the mid-fourteenth-century *Tale of Gamelyn* – by the parties taking matters into their own hands and descending into open hostility and bloodshed.[15] Rather, *W&W* chastises the lawyers for their countenancing of an assembly that was preparing for a general trial by combat, and seemingly reflects on the limits to which the common law could go in disciplining people of high status and royal connection. The fact that the poet does not produce accusations of venality with regard to the lawyers indicates either that he

---

[14] For a further text that dwells on corruption in the courts, see the early fourteenth-century Middle English 'Song on the Times' in Coss (ed.), *Thomas Wright's Political Songs*, pp. 195–205. For the venality topos more generally, see John A. Yunck, *The Lineage of Lady Meed: The Development of Mediaeval Venality Satire* (South Bend, 1963).

[15] For the *Tale of Gamelyn*, see Stephen Knight and Thomas Ohlgren (eds), *Robin Hood and Other Outlaw Tales* (Kalamazoo, 1997), pp. 184–226; and for its commentary on contemporary royal justice and administration, see Richard W. Kaeuper, 'An Historian's Reading of the *Tale of Gamelyn*', *Medium Aevum*, 52 (1983), 51–62; and John Scattergood, 'The *Tale of Gamelyn*: The Noble Robber as Provincial Hero', in Carole M. Meale (ed.), *Readings in Medieval English Romance* (Cambridge, 1994), pp. 159–94.

felt it unnecessary to introduce the corruption motif of the traditional complaint literature or that he was actually in sympathy with the king in the latter's efforts generally to enforce law and order and specifically to bring the dispute between Wynnere and Wastoure to peaceful arbitration. In this respect, then, *W&W* cuts against the grain of the near-contemporary complaint literature, exhibiting much more confidence in the formal structures of the law and implied sympathy for a peaceful way out of the *refrayte* between the two protagonists. This, too, suggests that the author of *W&W* took an 'establishment' view towards the ordering of society.

In its treatment of the clergy, by contrast, and more particularly of the mendicant orders, *W&W* shows much more in common with the general estates satire and complaint literature of the later Middle Ages. *The Simonie*, for example, sets up the topos of the corrupt regime over which the pope presides, and stresses that silver, not justice, is the driving force there.[16] This finds an analogue in the king's decision at the end of *W&W* to despatch Wynnere to Rome, where he would lead a life of luxury in the company of corrupt cardinals:

> 'Wende, Wynnere, thi waye ouer the wale stremys
> Pass forthe by Paris to the Pope of Rome,
> The cardynalls ken the wele, will kepe the ful faire
> And make thi sides in silken scheytys to lygge
> And fede the and foster the and forthir thyn hert
> As leefe to worthen wode as the to wrethe ones.'
>
> (lines 460–5)

> ('Winner, wend your way far overseas,
> Pass forth by Paris to the pope of Rome;
> The cardinals know you well, and will keep you in fair estate,
> Making your sides to lie in silken sheets;
> They will feed you and foster you and further your desire,
> Willing to go mad rather than to anger you at all.')

The Simonie's coverage of the various orders of the Church is quite comprehensive, but its reference to the friars shows some similarity with *W&W* in the way that both texts itemise the four principal mendicant orders and allege that their only motive (contrary to their official precepts, especially those of the Franciscans) is financial gain. Thus in *The Simonie*:

> And yit ther is another ordre, Menour and Jacobin,
> And freres of the Carme, and of Seint Austin,
> That wolde preche more for a bushel of whete

---

[16] Dean (ed.), *The Simonie*, lines 7–30.

Than for to bringe a soule fro helle out of the hete
    To rest.
And thus is coveytise loverd bothe est and west.
                                      (lines 162–7)

(And yet there is another order, Minorites and Dominicans,
And Carmelite friars, and those of St Augustine,
Who would preach more for a bushel of wheat
Than to bring a soul out of the heat of Hell
    To rest.
And thus is covetousness the lord of East and West.)

In *W&W*, this *coveytise* (covetousness) is broken down into caricatures of each of the four mendicant orders, represented in the devices upon the banners that they carry to the tournament field. The Franciscans are cast as wealthy, the Dominicans as ostentatious and self-important, the Carmelites as gluttons (and, by extension, lechers) and the Augustinians as revellers in luxury.[17]

The poet of *W&W* is especially occupied with the hypocrisy of the Franciscans, whose own internal divisions on the meaning of apostolic poverty made them easy prey for satirists. In the words of the king's knight-messenger:

'Thies are Sayn Franceys folke, that sayen alle schall fey worthe;
They aren so ferse and so fresche, thay feghtyn bot seldom.
I wote wele for wynnynge thay wentten fro home;
His purse weghethe full wele that wanne thaym all hedire.'
                                      (lines 159–62)

('These are St Francis's men, who say that all flesh shall soon pass.
They are so fierce and eager, though they fight only seldom.
I know it was for profit they went from their homes;
He who lured them here must have a full purse.')

Unlike the late fourteenth-century *Song against the Friars* and Chaucer's depiction of the Friar in the 'Prologue' to the *Canterbury Tales*, however, this writer's preoccupation is not with the way that the mendicants insinuate themselves into the homes and lives of the vulnerable or have illicit relationships with their female victims. Instead, his focus is firmly on the status that the mendicants, and particularly the Dominicans, had achieved for themselves in the hierarchy of the Church: his comment on this order at line 169 – 'And sythen the pope es so priste thies prechours to helpe' ('And

---

[17] Dinah Hazell, *Poverty in Late Medieval English Literature: The Meene and the Riche* (Dublin, 2009), p. 146; and Helen Barr, *Socioliterary Practice in Late Medieval England* (Oxford, 2001), pp. 21–2.

since the pope is so prompt to give these preachers help') – speaks to the links established in Chapter 1 between the mendicants and the papacy and insinuates that this order is present upon the tournament arena specifically to support the 'hede ... of holy kirke' ('head of Holy Church') (line 147).[18] The fact that the Dominican order provided the majority of Edward III's personal confessors may well be a point of detail of which our poet was aware. His establishment viewpoint might accommodate some critical comment; but it offers nothing of the more radical notions, articulated in *Piers Plowman* (B-text, Passus VIII) and its spawn, *Pierce the Ploughman's Crede*, that the mendicants are false Christians incapable of imparting the truths of their faith.[19] Again, then, we see the author of *W&W* drawing back from the more radical positions taken up in some complaint literature of the second half of the fourteenth century; his attacks on the Church are indeed by way of satirical jibe rather than a form of incitement to radical reform.

It is in the area of personal display that *W&W* can perhaps be contextualised most clearly in the near-contemporary literature. Chapter 3 argued that *W&W* may have been written in response to the public debate precipitated by the sumptuary laws of 1363 and their withdrawal in 1365, and analysed various narrative accounts of what seemed to their monastic authors as outrageous new fashions prevailing after 1361.[20] The fourteenth-century Middle English poem known as *On the Follies of Fashion* provides a vituperative critique of a new mode of hairdressing involving plaits and buns of hair being drawn up over the ears of trend-setting women.[21] The general effect, according to the poet, was to make females look like nothing more than baited pigs (lines 37–8). In a recent edition of this poem, Susanna Fein

---

[18] See above, pp. 29–30.

[19] For Edward III's confessors, see Alfred B. Emden, *A Survey of Dominicans in England* (Rome, 1967), pp. 448, 486. For the temporary confiscation of mendicant property by the crown in 1349–50, see A. G. Little, 'A Royal Inquiry into Property Held by the Mendicant Friars in England in 1349 and 1350', in J. G. Edwards, V. H. Galbraith and E. F. Jacobs (eds), *Historical Essays in Honour of James Tait* (Manchester, 1933), pp. 179–88; W. Mark Ormrod, 'The Personal Religion of Edward III', *Speculum*, 64 (1989), 849–77, at 874 n. 145. For the text of *Pierce the Ploughman's Crede*, see Helen Barr (ed.), *The Piers Plowman Tradition* (London, 1993), pp. 61–97; and for its anti-fraternal stance, see David Lampe, 'The Satiric Strategy of *Pierce the Ploughman's Crede*', in Bernard S. Levy and Paul E. Szarmach (eds), *The Alliterative Tradition in the Fourteenth Century* (Kent, Ohio, 1981), pp. 69–80. More generally on criticism of the friars, see Penn R. Szittya, *The Antifraternal Tradition in Medieval Literature* (Princeton, 1986); and Wendy Scase, Piers Plowman *and the New Anticlericalism* (Cambridge, 1987).

[20] See above, pp. 61–82.

[21] Fein with Raybin and Ziolkowski (eds and trans.), *Complete Harley 2253 Manuscript*, vol. 2, pp. 108–11.

and her collaborators judge it to have been chiefly comedic in tone.[22] Other critics, however, have seen it as presaging a more ominous destabilisation of the social hierarchy.[23] On the one hand, *On the Follies of Fashion* denounces as whores the women of status who adopt the new style; while on the other hand, it argues that every 'strumpet' is now inclined to follow their betters and present themselves as of superior social status:

> Uch a screwe wol hire shrude
> Thah he nabbe nout a smoke hire foule ers to hude!
> (lines 21–2)

(Every shrewish girl will dress herself up
Though she hasn't a smock to hide her foul arse!)

The poem's repeated mentions of Hell and the Devil chime well with the moralising monastic chronicles discussed in Chapter 3. More particularly, there is an obvious affinity between the sense of social instability felt in this poem and the anxieties expressed by the Commons in 1363 over the disturbing practice of dressing beyond one's status. As in *On the Follies of Fashion*, so in *W&W*, the debate resolves into a discussion of young women of lowly status who dress themselves up as their superiors and in the process make a mockery of themselves (*W&W*, lines 409–14).

Comparing *W&W* with other contemporary and near-contemporary texts inevitably involves some speculation on whether the author of one poem had read another and consciously reproduced or adapted the other's motifs, plots and ideas in his own writing. The suggested re-dating of *W&W* offered by the present study therefore requires that we confront explicitly a debate that has rumbled on for many years: namely, the relationship between this poem and the A-text of William Langland's *Piers Plowman*. The orthodoxy on *W&W*, which situates the poem in response to a sequence of specific conditions and events in 1352–3, has allowed scholars not only to celebrate the technical sophistication of this very early exemplar of the Alliterative Revival, but also to reflect on the similarities and differences between its poetics and those of *Piers Plowman*. In 1957, John Burrow argued that Langland consciously avoided the very highly developed forms of style and vocabulary evident in *W&W* in order to write a work that was more readily accessible to his bourgeois readership in London.[24] This has not stopped critics from identifying passages in the two poems that seemingly represent the influence of *W&W* upon William Langland. Ralph Hanna, for example, itemises at least six places in *Piers Plowman* where wording and/or content imply that Langland drew on *W&W*, and has suggested that Langland's original intention was to write

---

[22] *Ibid.*, vol. 2, pp. 392–3.
[23] Scattergood, 'Authority and Resistance', pp. 199–201.
[24] J. A. Burrow, 'The Audience of *Piers Plowman*', *Anglia*, 75 (1957), 373–84.

a simpler 'satire of contemporary conditions' whose scale and parameters might have stood more direct comparison with *W&W*.[25] Katharine Breen has gone further, arguing that *W&W*'s testing of genres anticipates a similar, more ambitious, and experimental poetics in *Piers Plowman*.[26]

Nearly sixty years after his initial essay, in 2014, Burrow reiterated his long-standing conviction that Langland had read *W&W*, set out the key passages that suggest the influence of the latter on *Piers Plowman*, and interpreted Langland's much starker distinction between winning (a virtue) and wasting (a vice) as a conscious reaction to the *W&W* poet's well-known equivocation between the two.[27] Such arguments have proved enduringly influential. In 2003, for example, C. David Benson described *W&W* as 'perhaps [*Piers Plowman's*] closest alliterative analogue and possibly a direct influence'; while in his 2016 survey of London literature in the later Middle Ages, Andrew Galloway refers to *W&W* as a 'direct antecedent' of *Piers Plowman*.[28]

And yet ambiguity remains.[29] From his own claim that *W&W* could be dated to the 1360s, Lawton concluded that the traditional view of the relationship between it and *Piers Plowman* could be inverted, and that *W&W*

---

[25] Ralph Hanna, *Pursuing History: Middle English Manuscripts and their Texts* (Stanford, 1996), p. 232 and p. 318 n. 40. See also Ralph Hanna, 'Alliterative Poetry', in David Wallace (ed.), *The Cambridge History of Medieval English Literature* (Cambridge, 1999), pp. 488–512, at p. 498.

[26] Katharine Breen, 'The Need for Allegory: *Wynnere and Wastoure* as an *Ars poetica*', *Yearbook of Langland Studies*, 26 (2012), 187–229, at 221–4.

[27] J. A. Burrow, 'Winning and Wasting in *Wynnere and Wastoure* and *Piers Plowman*', in Carol M. Meale and Derek Pearsall (eds), *Makers and Users of Medieval Books: Essays in Honour of A. S. G. Edwards* (Cambridge, 2014), pp. 1–12. There are numerous other points in *W&W* that bear direct comparison with *Piers Plowman*: see, for example, Myra Stokes, *Justice and Mercy in Piers Plowman: A Reading of the B Text Visio* (London, 1984), p. 22. Such cross-referencing usually conveniently leaves to one side the question of dates of composition and the possibility of direct influence in either direction.

[28] C. David Benson, *Public Piers Plowman: Modern Scholarship and Late Medieval English Culture* (University Park, Pennsylvania, 2003), p. 1; and Andrew Galloway, 'London, Southwark, Westminster', in David Wallace (ed.), *Europe: A Literary History* (2 vols, Oxford, 2016), vol. 1, pp. 322–53, at p. 339. In 2006, Galloway acknowledged Lawton's arguments but preferred to see *W&W* as a 'precedent' for *Piers Plowman*: Andrew Galloway, *The Penn Commentary on* Piers Plowman, *I: C Prologue-Passus 4; B Prologue-Passus 4; A Prologue-Passus 4* (Philadelphia, 2006), p. 10. For a selection of other works that assume the influence of *W&W* upon *Piers Plowman*, see Malcolm Godden, *The Making of Piers Plowman* (London, 1990), pp. 12, 14, 31.

[29] For example, Emily Steiner, *Reading* Piers Plowman (Cambridge, 2013), p. 5, recognises the ambiguity of the current scholarly position, stating that *W&W* 'may or may not predate the A-text [of *Piers Plowman*]'.

not only post-dated, but was also influenced by, *Piers*.[30] In her 1990 edition of *W&W*, Trigg followed the same logic by contending that the tavern scene at lines 277–82 is a conscious re-working of the episode in the A-text of *Piers Plowman* where Gluttony roisters at an inn (A-text, Passus V, 144–200).[31] For these scholars and others of their persuasion, then, there is nothing inherently illogical about arguing that *W&W* post-dates the A-text of *Piers Plowman*.

In the absence of any definitive evidence of inter-textual transmission in either direction, the present study offers a different solution to this conundrum. Suggesting that the *terminus ante quem* for the composition of *W&W* dates well into the 1360s, probably around the debate on the sumptuary laws in 1363–5, and possibly still later, around the time of the trial of Sir John atte Lee in 1368, has the effect of placing the poem full-square within the period when Langland is understood to have embarked on the writing of the A-text of *Piers Plowman*. The traditional *terminus a quo* for the composition of the latter is the great storm of 15 January 1362, known as St Maurus' Wind; this, it has always been argued, is the referent in the A-text Passus V, 14: 'the southwestryne wynd on satirday at eue' ('the south-western wind on Saturday evening').[32] In 1943, however, J. A. W. Bennett argued that the reference to 'rome renneris' (people who 'ran' to Rome in pursuit of spiritual benefits) in the A-text Passus IV, 111 necessitated a later date for the beginning of composition, in 1367–70, when Pope Urban V briefly quitted Avignon and returned to the papacy's formal place of residence in Rome.[33] This has generally been accepted as orthodoxy ever since.[34]

---

[30] David A. Lawton, 'Literary History and Scholarly Fancy: The Date of Two Middle English Alliterative Poems', *Parergon*, orig. ser., 18 (1977), 17–25, at 22.

[31] Trigg, p. 35, n. to lines 272–82. For the passage, see George Kane (ed.), *Piers Plowman: The A Version. Will's Vision of Piers Plowman and Do-Well* (London, 1960), pp. 286–92.

[32] Kane (ed.), *Piers Plowman: The A Version*, p. 271. For continued use of this in the dating of *Piers Plowman*, see, for example, Lawrence Warner, *The Myth of* Piers Plowman*: Constructing a Medieval Literary Archive* (Cambridge, 2014), p. 25. For St Maurus' Wind, see C. E. Britton, *A Meteorological Chronology to A.D. 1450* (London, 1937), pp. 144–5.

[33] J. A. W. Bennett, 'The Date of the A-Text of *Piers Plowman*', *PMLA*, 58 (1943), 566–72, at 568. For details of Urban's return to Rome, see Joëlle Rollo-Koster, *Avignon and its Papacy, 1309–1417: Popes, Institutions, and Society* (London, 2015), pp. 121–8.

[34] See, for example, George Kane, 'The Text', in John Alford (ed.), *A Companion to* Piers Plowman (Berkeley, California, 1988), pp. 175–200, at p. 184. Kane notes that 1374 marks the *terminus ante quem* for composition of the A-text. However, the scholarship that has pushed the A-text into the early 1370s does so chiefly in the belief that the figure of Lady Mede was a caricature of Alice Perrers, Edward III's mistress, who only rose to prominence after the death of Queen Philippa in 1369: see the summary by Anna P. Baldwin, 'The Historical Context', in Alford

It is by no means clear, however, that the mention of 'Rome-runners' has to be interpreted in this way. In spite of the papacy's self-imposed exile in Avignon, Rome was regarded as the natural and permanent source of papal power, so that people in England referred constantly throughout the fourteenth century to the 'pope of Rome' and the 'court of Rome', regardless of where either might actually be seated at the time.[35] *The Simonie* (line 19) repeats this idea of the 'court of Rome', and no-one has ever suggested that this can be used to date the poem to before or after the papacy's move to Avignon. Similarly, and ironically, the king's order to Wynnere at the end of *W&W* that he should take himself off to 'the pope of Rome' (line 461) has never been used as a dating device for this poem. If we followed the logic of the present analysis and the assumptions made around *Piers Plowman*'s 'Rome-runners', we might temptingly suggest that *W&W* was itself written during Urban V's return to Rome in 1367–70. But the most that can reasonably be said is that the references in both *W&W* and *Piers Plowman* are generalisations based on the fact that, no matter where the pope resided at any particular time, the spiritual and moral authority of the papacy remained in the city of Rome throughout the period of their composition.

The fact that the critical scholarship has been so reluctant to move away from a dating of 1352–3 for the writing of *W&W* has much to tell us about the wider understanding of the so-called Alliterative Revival of the fourteenth century.[36] The long-held orthodoxy is that, around 1350, there was

---

(ed.), *Companion to* Piers Plowman, pp. 67–86, at p. 80. More recent scholarship, however, emphasises that the conscious referencing of Perrers in the figure of Mede came only in the B-text, written in the later 1370s: M. Theresa Tavormina, *Kindly Similitude: Marriage and Family in "Piers Plowman"* (Cambridge, 1995), pp. 1–47; Matthew Giancarlo, 'Piers Plowman, Parliament, and the Public Voice', *Yearbook of Langland Studies*, 17 (2003), 135–74; Gwilym Dodd, 'A Parliament Full of Rats? Piers Plowman and the Good Parliament of 1376', *Historical Research*, 79 (2006), 21–49; and W. Mark Ormrod, 'The Trials of Alice Perrers', *Speculum*, 83 (2008), 366–96, at 367–8 and 394–6.

[35] See, for example, the evidence of the parliament rolls: *PROME*, vol. 4, pp. 374, 431, 451; vol. 5, pp. 14, 15, 25–7, 54, 120, 178–9, 195. Of many examples in the chronicles, we may instance a reference to the English deputation to Avignon in 1354 as going *ad Romanam curiam* ('to the court of Rome'): Charity Scott-Stokes and Chris Given-Wilson (eds and trans.), *Chronicon Anonymi Cantuariensis: The Chronicle of Anonymous of Canterbury, 1346–1365* (Oxford, 2008), p. 18. For further discussion on this point, see Míceál F. Vaughan (ed.), *Piers Plowman: The A Version* (Baltimore, 2011), p. 165.

[36] For this long-standing thesis, see the thorough historiographical survey by Ian Cornelius, *Reconstructing Alliterative Verse: The Pursuit of a Medieval Metre* (Cambridge, 2011), pp. 69–75. The classic modern statement is Thorlac Turville-Petre, *The Al-*

a sudden re-flourishing of the older alliterative forms that had characterised Anglo-Saxon poetry.[37] For Derek Pearsall, writing in 1981, reifying the Alliterative Revival was about searching for a single person, probably born and educated in the West Midlands (perhaps at Worcester), who created a template of alliteration from which other poets could work; Pearsall hazarded that the author of *W&W* may have been that very man.[38] Among the other works conventionally ascribed an early date in the Alliterative Revival is *William of Palerne*, a Middle English adaptation of an earlier Anglo-Norman romance presumed, from an internal reference, to date to some point between 1336 and 1361, and written in the English of the South-West Midlands.[39] Pearsall, however, felt that *William of Palerne* was 'not representative of the revival' either in form or in dialect, preferring *W&W* as his candidate for the foundational text of the new movement.[40] The convenience of a date in the early 1350s for *W&W* thus becomes evident, as it makes this poem precede the A-text of *Piers Plowman* by at least a decade, and can thus be seen as the first work in a movement which depended on direct inspiration from one poet to another, or rather from one text to the next.

More recently, however, scholars have been highly critical of the notion of a self-conscious and organised 'Alliterative Revival' along the lines previously charted. In 2002, Christine Chism proposed a series of 'alliterative revivals' over the fourteenth and fifteenth centuries, each one a self-contained development associated with a single major text, and none of them necessarily drawing direct inspiration from the others. In the process, interestingly, Chism demoted *W&W* to a subordinate position, no longer foundational but distinctly secondary in importance among the texts that make up the late-medieval alliterative canon.[41] In 2017, moreover, Ian Cornelius argued that the conventional notion of a 'revival' is itself suspect, given the evidence

---

literative Revival (Cambridge, 1977), reinforced by Thorlac Turville-Petre (ed.), *Alliterative Poetry of the Later Middle Ages: An Anthology* (Washington, DC, 1989).

[37] See, for example, the place accorded to *W&W* by Norman Blake, 'The Literary Language', in Norman Blake (ed.), *The Cambridge History of the English Language, II: 1066–1476* (Cambridge, 1992), pp. 500–41, at pp. 520–1.

[38] Derek Pearsall, 'The Origins of the Alliterative Revival', in Levy and Szarmach (eds), *The Alliterative Tradition*, pp. 1–24. Ralph Hanna, *Yorkshire Writers*, Sir Israel Gollancz Memorial Lecture [British Academy] (London, 2002), regards *W&W* as only 'perhaps' written in the West Midlands.

[39] G. H. V. Bunt (ed.), *William of Palerne: An Alliterative Romance* (Groningen, 1985), pp. 14–19.

[40] Pearsall, 'Origins of the Alliterative Revival', p. 17.

[41] Christine Chism, *Alliterative Revivals* (Philadelphia, 2002). Chism's only discussion of *W&W* is at p. 205. See also Christine Chism, 'Alliterative Revival', in Michael D. C. Drout (ed.), *J. R. R. Tolkien Encyclopedia: Scholarship and Critical Assessment* (Abingdon, 2007), pp. 9–10.

he adduces for 'the remains of a continuous practice of composition in a continuously evolving verse form' from the late Anglo-Saxon era to the fourteenth and fifteenth centuries.[42] The Alliterative Revival seems set, indeed, to be written out of literary history as a false dawn, a fiction now largely irrelevant to evolving understandings of the literary forms and sensibilities of late-medieval England.

By drawing the *termini a quo* for both *W&W* and *Piers Plowman* into the same decade, the 1360s, we are therefore left with a number of hypotheses: that the authors of the two poems could have been writing coterminously but entirely independently; that they had mutual knowledge of each others' texts and developed the one in the light of the other; or that they saw themselves as part of a movement, one based not necessarily on literary form but more generally in terms of commentary on the social and political ills of the times. We may speculate freely that the authors of *W&W* and *Piers Plowman* knew each other: both may have come originally from the North Midlands; both indicate in their writing that they had the essence of a formal education and were well informed of the high politics of their day; and both may have operated in the context of a great court – in the author of *W&W*'s case those of the princely or episcopal households discussed below, and in William Langland's case, perhaps that of the Lords Despenser.[43] We must be careful, however, not to be drawn by the supposition that the parallels between certain works provide incontrovertible proof of influence in one direction or the other. Burrow itemises only three very short passages in *W&W* that he is confident find direct resonance in *Piers Plowman*, and none of these actually yields direct evidence of conscious copying.[44] On the face of it, then, it seems that the safest way to characterise the relationship between the poets of *W&W* and *Piers Plowman* is that both were working in the satirical tradition and that both, in particular, were prepared to direct their criticisms against people in high places, including (at least indirectly) the king.

There remains, of course, the outside possibility that the two men could have been just one, and that both *W&W* and *Piers Plowman* fell from the quill of the same writer. Lawrence Warner's speculation on the idea that William Langland was the author-translator of *William of Palerne* has allowed him to explicate some key passages in *Piers Plowman* as reflections upon and

---

[42] Cornelius, *Reconstructing Alliterative Verse*, p. 68.

[43] For the suggestions about the author of *W&W*, see below, pp. 121–5. For the possibility of Despenser patronage of William Langland, see Kathryn Kerby-Fulton, 'Langland and the Bibliographic Ego', in Steven Justice and Kathryn Kerby-Fulton (eds), *Written Work: Langland, Labor, and Authorship* (Philadelphia, 1997), pp. 67–142, at pp. 110–22.

[44] Burrow, 'Winning and Wasting', p. 1.

reactions to earlier work on *Palerne*.⁴⁵ In the case of *W&W*, however, there is a significant impediment to seeing its author as a William Langland in training for *Piers Plowman*: namely, that there are fundamental differences in the perspectives and sensibilities of the two poems. As we have stressed throughout, the *W&W* poet has his mind set firmly on the problems of, and debates amongst, the landed elite. Unlike polemicists who came before him, such as William of Pagula, composer of the great critique of Edward III's system of household purveyance, the *Speculum regis Edwardi tertii*, or the anonymous author of the *Song against the King's Taxes*, the *W&W* poet does not take *Piers Plowman*'s 'worm's-eye' view of the political economy or seek to voice the complaint of a downtrodden peasantry.⁴⁶ Instead, his focus is firmly on the landed classes and the public debate (which we have argued as occurring in a particular controversy over the sumptuary laws in the 1360s) about whether they should pursue regimes of extravagance or of parsimony. In this respect, the author of *W&W* speaks the language not of a critical and reformist cleric but of a politically active member of the gentry.

Is it possible to extend this line of thinking and argue that the *W&W* poet was himself a layman of gentry status? There are certainly plenty of signs in the fourteenth century of laymen capable of expressing themselves in extended literary endeavours. Sir Thomas Gray of Heton wrote a notable prose chronicle in Anglo-Norman French during the late 1350s and early 1360s, and another (anonymous) layman, the Chandos Herald, wrote his *Life of the Black Prince* in Anglo-Norman verse around 1385.⁴⁷ Alongside the well-known figure of Geoffrey Chaucer, who wrote in Middle English at the end of the century, was also the trilingual John Gower, a member of the minor gentry with some expertise in the law who in the early 1390s became a retainer of Henry of Bolingbroke and thus, after 1399, an annuitant of the king.⁴⁸ The author of *W&W* would fit perfectly well with the kind of social

---

⁴⁵ Lawrence Warner, 'Langland and the Problem of *William of Palerne*', *Viator*, 37 (2006), 397–415. See also Warner, *Myth of* Piers Plowman, pp. 22–36.

⁴⁶ For the *Speculum* and its author, see J. Moisant (ed.), *De speculo regis Edwardi tertii* (Paris, 1891); Cary J. Nederman and K. L. Forhan (eds and trans.), *Medieval Political Theory – A Reader: The Quest for the Body Politic, 1100–1400* (London, 1993), pp. 200–3; Leonard E. Boyle, 'William of Pagula and the *Speculum Regis Edwardi III*', *Mediaeval Studies*, 32 (1970), 329–36.

⁴⁷ John Taylor, *English Historical Literature in the Fourteenth Century* (Oxford, 1987), pp. 167–9, 172–4; Antonia Gransden, *Historical Writing in England, II: c.1307 to the Early Sixteenth Century* (London, 1996), pp. 92–9; and John Spence, *Reimagining History in Anglo-Norman Prose Chronicles* (York, 2013), *passim*.

⁴⁸ Elisabeth Dutton with John Hines and R. F. Yeager (eds), *John Gower, Trilingual Poet: Language, Translation and Tradition* (Cambridge, 2010); David R. Carlson, *John Gower, Poetry and Propaganda in Fourteenth-Century England* (Cambridge, 2012); Stephen H. Rigby with Siân Echard (eds), *Historians on John Gower* (Cambridge, 2019).

profile offered by Gower, and the predominantly secular concerns of the poem move into sharper relief if we believe that it was indeed the product of the imagination of a member of the laity.

Most importantly and significantly, however, the very distinction between clergy and laity was beginning to become blurred in the fourteenth century as a growing number of men with training in preparation for the Church only took up minor orders and lived not from the profits of ecclesiastical benefices but from the fees and annuities they took from employers and patrons.[49] Fiona Somerset has argued that both Langland and the narrator of *Piers Plowman* inhabited this liminal space between clergy and laity, and that some of the force of Langland's writing owes itself to the tension between learned, literate clerks and the 'lewed' laity.[50] In particular, the figure of the poet Thomas Hoccleve, whose best-known work, the *Regement of Princes*, was dedicated to the future Henry V, typifies this kind of lay clerk: employed in the office of the privy seal from 1387 to 1424, Hoccleve took minor orders but gave up hope of ever having preferment in the Church, married, and spent a good deal of his time complaining about the inadequacy of the annuity owed him by the crown.[51] Hoccleve's reconstruction of the 'court of good company' hosted on May Day 1410 by Henry Somer, the chancellor of the exchequer (himself possibly the first layman to hold this role), provides a vivid glimpse of the kinds of social and literary circles that existed at least by the later fourteenth century among the lay clerks working in royal and princely government.[52] Given the content and context of *W&W*, with its general awareness of the work of parliament, the royal courts and the king's council, it does indeed seem reasonable to explore the suggestion that the poem was most likely written by someone attached to one of the great households operating in England during the 1350s and 1360s.

---

[49] Thomas Frederick Tout, 'The Household of the Chancery and its Disintegration', in H. W. C. Davis (ed.), *Essays in History Presented to Reginald Lane Poole* (Oxford, 1927), pp. 46–85; Thomas Frederick Tout, 'Literature and Learning in the English Civil Service in the Fourteenth Century', *Speculum*, 4 (1929), 365–89; and R. L. Storey, 'Gentleman-bureaucrats', in C. H. Clough (ed.), *Profession, Vocation and Culture in Later Medieval England: Essays Dedicated to the Memory of A. R. Myers* (Liverpool, 1982), pp. 90–129.

[50] Fiona Somerset, *Clerical Discourse and Lay Audience in Late Medieval England* (Cambridge, 1998), pp. 22–61.

[51] Thomas Frederick Tout, *Chapters in the Administrative History of Mediaeval England* (6 vols, Manchester, 1920–33), vol. 5, pp. 75–110, *passim*; Ethan Knapp, *The Bureaucratic Muse: Thomas Hoccleve and the Literature of Late Medieval England* (University Park, Pennsylvania, 2001).

[52] Tout, *Chapters in Administrative History*, vol. 5, p. 109 and n. 2.

In this respect there are a number of contenders for possible patrons of the *W&W* poet. The household of Edward III may seem inherently unlikely, on two grounds: that the poem contains veiled criticism of the king; and that there is no other evidence of Edward III providing direct patronage of vernacular alliterative verse. Working with the dialect evidence, however, we might well consider the courts of a number of members of the royal family who had significant authority in the North-West and/or North-East Midlands: Edward, the Black Prince (d.1376); Edward III's cousin, Henry of Grosmont, duke of Lancaster (d.1361); Edward III's third son, John of Gaunt (d.1399), who succeeded Grosmont as duke of Lancaster; and Edward III's fourth son, Edmund of Langley (d.1402), who from 1347 was lord of Conisbrough in South Yorkshire and later built up a considerable estate in that region.[53] If we wished to extend Pearsall's argument about *W&W* as the work of a Worcester-based poet, we might also relate the poem to the household of another of Edward III's cousins, Humphrey de Bohun, earl of Hereford (d.1373), who had important interests and followings in the West Midlands.[54] There are also hints in this list of possible connections that might have served the interests of the *W&W* poet and resulted in the wider circulation of his work. The Black Prince and Henry of Grosmont were both founder members of the Order of the Garter, where they were joined in 1360 by the king's three middle sons, Lionel, John and Edmund, and in 1364 by Humphrey de Bohun.[55] The fellowship of the Garter continues, then, to provide a possible – even perhaps likely – context for the initial audience and subsequent circulation of the poem.

A further possibility in the realms of patronage is that the poet of *W&W* was a clerk or layman operating in an episcopal household and circle. The growth of episcopal households in the thirteenth century meant that these functioned in many ways similarly to those of lay magnates, albeit with an inevitably larger clerical element.[56] If we were to set aside

---

[53] For previous suggestions about the links of the *W&W* poet with the courts of the Black Prince and Henry of Grosmont, see Salter, *English and International*, pp. 102–3; Bennett, *Community, Class and Careerism*, pp. 18, 231–5; Hugh E. L. Collins, *The Order of the Garter, 1348–1461: Chivalry and Politics in Late Medieval England* (Oxford, 2000), p. 257 and n. 89; and W. G. Cooke and D'A. J. D. Boulton, '*Sir Gawain and the Green Knight*: A Poem for Henry of Grosmont?', *Medium Aevum*, 68 (1999), 42–54.

[54] Gerrit H. V. Bunt, 'Localizing *William of Palerne*', in Jacek Fisiak (ed.), *Historical Linguistics and Philology* (Berlin, 1990), pp. 73–106.

[55] For details of the admissions to the Garter, see Collins, *Order of the Garter*, pp. 288–90.

[56] Philippa M. Hoskin, 'Continuing Service: The Episcopal Households of Thirteenth-Century Durham', in Philippa M. Hoskin, C. N. L. Brooke and R. Barrie Dobson (eds), *The Foundations of Medieval English Ecclesiastical History: Studies Presented to David Smith* (Woodbridge, 2005), pp. 124–38; Philippa M. Hoskin, 'Authors

the limiting factor of dialect then it might be possible, for example, to construct an argument that W&W was composed in the circle of William Edington, bishop of Winchester (1345–66), who, as treasurer of the exchequer from 1344 to 1356 and chancellor from 1356 to his death in 1366, was the co-architect (along with William Shareshull) of much of the economic and social legislation that underpinned Edward III's post-plague scheme of government.[57] The bishop of Winchester was the prelate of the Order of the Garter from the time of the fraternity's foundation, and Edington's relationship to the poem might therefore be principally defined, once again, in terms of the Garter association.[58]

Another interesting possibility that more obviously respects the dialect of the poem is that its author was a member of the household of John Thoresby, successively bishop of St Davids (1347–9) and Worcester (1349–52) and archbishop of York (1352–73). Thoresby, a long-standing royal servant, was also chancellor of England from 1349 to 1356.[59] Thoresby devoted the remainder of his career to pastoral reform within his diocese. Into this programme he incorporated the so-called *Lay Folk's Catechism*, a penitential handbook written in the vernacular by the Benedictine monk John Gaytryge and cast in basic alliterative verse to help the process of memorization. Thoresby may also have been one of the influences behind the extant York *Corpus Christi* cycle of plays, written up (in the later fourteenth century) and managed by the clergy and performed by the craft guilds of the city. This context of biblical literacy and moral didacticism suggests a ready audience in the archbishop's household for the sort of work represented by W&W. Thoresby had no particular connection with the Order of the Garter, but other elements within the poem may suggest references to him. In particular, the jibe at William Shareshull's expense at lines 317–18 fits with the politics of

---

of Bureaucracy: Developing and Creating Administrative Systems in English Episcpoal Chanceries in the Second Half of the Thirteenth Century', in Paul Binski and Elizabeth A. New (eds), *Patrons and Professionals in the Middle Ages: Proceedings of the 2010 Harlaxton Symposium* (Donington, 2012), pp. 61–78. For general patterns in the sizes of episcopal households across the fourteenth and fifteenth centuries, see C. M. Woolgar, *The Great Household in Late Medieval England* (London, 1999), p. 15.

[57] W. Mark Ormrod, *The Reign of Edward III: Crown and Political Society in England, 1327–1377* (London, 1990), pp. 86–90; R. G. Davies, 'Edington, William', in 'Oxford Dictionary of National Biography' (online): https://doi.org/10.1093/ref:odnb/8481 (accessed 20 April 2020).

[58] Martin Biddle *et al.*, *King Arthur's Round Table: An Archaeological Investigation* (Woodbridge, 2000), pp. 513–18.

[59] Jonathan Hughes, 'Thoresby, John' in 'Oxford Dictionary of National Biography' (online): https://doi.org/10.1093/ref:odnb/27333 (accessed 18 April 2020). For what follows see, more generally, Jonathan Hughes, *Pastors and Visionaries: Religion and Secular Life in Late Medieval Yorkshire* (Woodbridge, 1988).

Thoresby's relationship with the chief justice: Shareshull's excommunication and Thoresby's resignation of the chancellorship late in 1356 were both provoked by Edward III's case against Bishop Thomas de Lisle, Shareshull taking the king's side and Thoresby standing up against that position by resigning on the grounds of defending the rights of the clergy.[60] The fact that W&W is predominantly secular in its subject matter and development does not in itself preclude the possibility of its composition in the circle of John Thoresby, but perhaps reduces the likelihood of its wider reception in the context of the archbishop's pastoral programme: whereas the *Lay Folk's Catechism* survives in no fewer than twenty-six manuscripts, the Thornton version of W&W remains, as we have noted, unique.[61]

This exercise in speculation upon the authorship and patronage of W&W could no doubt be extended further: ultimately, the empirical evidence is simply not good enough to provide a definitive conclusion on the matter. The discussion also necessarily brings us back to Salter's proposition, outlined in the Introduction, that the poem was a conscious memorialisation of Sir John Wingfield.[62] Salter's argument was based on the heraldic detail of the poem. Gollancz had previously assumed that the 'three wynges … umbygon with a gold wire' ('three wings … surrounded by gold thread') (lines 117–18) worn by the knight-messenger sent by the king to call forward Wynnere and Wastoure were the three feathers of the prince of Wales, and had used this to reinforce his argument that the figure was a representation of the Black Prince. On the contrary, Salter argued, the three sets of wings were those found in the heraldic arms of the Wingfield family by the mid-fourteenth century.[63] Literary critics keen on the notion that the poem commemorates the eyre of Cheshire point to Wingfield's own prominent position in the Black Prince's administration in the North-West and his initiatives to reform the finances of the prince's administration, in which the judicial visitation of Cheshire in 1353 played a part.[64]

An argument that places W&W in the years immediately after the death of Sir John Wingfield in 1361 also serves Salter's wider purpose of releasing the poem from the dating shackles of 1352–3, since she saw W&W

---

[60] See also above, pp. 28–9
[61] Susan Powell, 'The Transmission and Circulation of *The Lay Folks' Catechism*', in Alastair J. Minnis (ed.), *Late-Medieval Religious Texts and their Transmission: Essays in Honour of A. I. Doyle* (Cambridge, 1994), pp. 67–84.
[62] See above, p. 8.
[63] Elizabeth Salter, 'The Timeliness of *Wynnere and Wastoure*', *Medium Aevum*, 47 (1978), 40–65, repr. in Elizabeth Salter, *English and International: Studies in the Literature, Art and Patronage of Medieval England*, ed. Derek Pearsall and Nicolette Zeeman (Cambridge, 1988), pp. 180–98, at pp. 195–8.
[64] See above, pp. 44–6.

primarily as a *post mortem* commemoration of the knight commissioned by members of his family. Wingfield's only child, Katherine, had married Sir Michael de la Pole, son of the merchant capitalist William de la Pole, and himself a member of the Black Prince's circle; after the resumption of the war with France in 1369, Michael performed military service in the retinue of John of Gaunt.[65] De la Pole's desire to have his father-in-law referenced in a 'courtly' poem could easily reflect his own eagerness to establish himself as a member of the chivalric elite.

Nevertheless, we have to ask why it was that the Wingfields and the de la Poles (or, indeed, any other major landed family) would have thought a debate on the political economy to be the kind of literary work appropriate to commemorating a hero of the Hundred Years War. The Chandos Herald's Anglo-Norman *Life of the Black Prince*, written in the 1380s, presents a much more obvious poem of chivalric commemoration, itemising the prince's feats of arms in a general encomium on his chivalric virtues.[66] Nor is it clear why the author of *W&W* should have marked out the knight-messenger as being 'youngeste of yeris' ('youngest in years') (line 119) when John Wingfield was an older contemporary of Edward III, and likely approaching sixty at the time of his death in 1361.[67] As things stand, then, we have to judge Salter's suggestion on the patronage of the poem as not proven.

Two alternatives may now be offered to Salter's identification of the knight-messenger. The first leads us back to the person of Edward III. It takes the alteration of only one letter in the description of the second knight's heraldry at lines 117–18 of *W&W* to provide an altogether different indication of the poet's intentions. If the 'thre wynges' ('three wings') becomes 'thre wyndes' ('three winds'), then the 'thre wyndes ... umbygon with a gold wyre' at lines 117–18 can be read very precisely as a reference to one of Edward III's own personal badges, a breath of wind bursting from clouds to reveal a golden sun. This device was a rebus for Edward's birthplace of Windsor, splitting the place name into 'winds' and 'or' (in Anglo-Norman French, 'gold').[68] This visual device is found, for example, in the decoration of the great hall of Winchester Castle carried out in 1348–9 when Edward

[65] For details of de la Pole's career, see J. S. Roskell, *The Impeachment of Michael de la Pole, Earl of Suffolk, in 1386* (Manchester, 1984).

[66] Chandos Herald, *La vie du Prince Noir*, ed. D. B. Tyson (Tübingen, 1975).

[67] Wingfield's date of birth is unknown, and most sources put it impressionistically around 1305. Mark Bailey, 'Sir John de Wingfield and the Foundation of Wingfield College', in Peter Bloore and Edward Martin (eds), *Wingfield College and its Patrons: Piety and Prestige in Medieval Suffolk* (Woodbridge, 2015), pp. 31–48, at pp. 32–4, notes that Sir John emerges in the administrative records in the mid-1320s, by which time he must have been of age.

[68] Juliet Barker, *The Tournament in England, 1100–1400* (Woodbridge, 1986), p. 183.

I's round table was first hung there.⁶⁹ It is also known to have been deployed as a verbal pun in a number of prophetic texts on the predicted achievements of Edward III.⁷⁰ If we accept that the text of *W&W* as acquired by Robert Thornton was already corrupt, and may have been corrupted further in his copying, then the change from 'wyndes' to 'wynges' could have been a relatively minor and easy mistake.

This argument about Edward III's badge of the 'winds of gold' has the effect of adding another royal referent to the series of heraldic and quasi-heraldic elements in the poem. Katharine Breen has argued that *W&W* marks the first contribution to a genre of 'heraldic literature', emphatically secular and vernacular in tone and content, and one that frames the poet's interest in matters both national and international.⁷¹ The patrons and audience of these poems were the knightly classes and, more specifically, the new profession of herald that came into being in the later Middle Ages. Such thinking leads to a second possible meaning of the 'thre wyndes ... umbygon with a gold wyre' at lines 117–18 of *W&W*: that the poem refers to Volaunt, the English royal herald whose first recorded appearances in Edward III's service come in the mid-1350s.

Heralds were normally referred to only by their professional names (hence the 'Chandos Herald' remains effectively anonymous), and these generally had some direct or indirect meaning: the office of Norroy king of arms, for example, which existed in Edward III's time, derived from the Anglo-Norman French 'nort roi', or 'north king', an allusion to a specific region of jurisdiction.⁷² In the case of Volaunt, we know the forename of the man who held the title in the middle and later years of Edward III: William. His heraldic name was normally spelled either as 'Vola[u]nt' or as 'Vaillant'. While the latter version is the Anglo-Norman for 'valiant', 'brave' or 'worthy', the former links more directly with the adverbial form derived from the verb 'voler', which means either 'to want' or 'to fly'. It is suggested here that Volaunt was used as a synonym for Vaillant because it could straightforwardly be rendered as a rebus of wings to represent flight. John Anstis, one of the first scholarly historians of the Order of the Garter, argued in the eighteenth century that the reference in the exchequer issue roll to a gift made to Volaunt for his services at the Garter feast of 1358, noted above in Chapter 1, makes it likely that William was the impresario of

---

⁶⁹ Biddle *et al.*, *King Arthur's Round Table*, pp. 393–424.
⁷⁰ Lesley A. Coote, *Prophecy and Public Affairs in Later Medieval England* (York, 2000), pp. 123–4.
⁷¹ Breen, 'Need for Allegory', pp. 203–6.
⁷² Anthony Richard Wagner, *Heralds and Heraldry in the Middle Ages* (Oxford, 1939), pp. 35–6.

this important chivalric event.[73] The references to Volaunt in the royal household accounts continue through the late 1350s and up until the end of the 1360s, after which they cease, which suggests that he either retired or died *c*.1370.[74]

The possible link between Volaunt Herald and the knight-messenger in *W&W* should not be overplayed. We have already noted in Chapter 2 that the attempts to read the second knight as a herald in the context of an emergent court of chivalry are erroneous. The specific reference at line 103 of the poem to this figure having been dubbed to knighthood also runs against historical understandings of the social status of heralds in the fourteenth century. And the elaborate description at lines 111–18 of the armour put on by the king's messenger does not reflect how heralds were dressed either on or off the field of battle in this period.[75] On the other hand, we know that, in addition to bearing the royal arms, heralds adopted personal badges, and the description of the jupon with its 'thre wynges' at lines 115–18 of *W&W* is broadly compatible with this practice. In this reading, the knight-messenger emerges as a hybrid figure representing a man of higher status than a herald, but sketched out in such a way as possibly to commemorate the conspicuous service provided by William Volaunt at the Windsor feast of 1358.

The introduction of William Volaunt into this interpretation of *W&W* does not in itself necessarily suggest that the herald was the patron of the poem, but it may have something to tell us about who precisely commissioned – or was the addressee – of this parable upon the vices of avarice and prodigality. Bringing together all that we know about the poem's content and all that has been argued about its historical context, it may now be suggested that the author of *W&W* wrote the poem not as a direct means of seeking patronage from one of the great royal, noble or episcopal households of his day, but as a conscious articulation of current political topics of debate – most obviously, the differing views on patterns of consumption argued out in the parliaments of 1363 and 1365. The poem's emphasis on the heraldry of Edward III and the Order of the Garter suggests that it may have been intended for performance at one of the Garter feasts held in or after 1358, and brought forward for consideration by a layman or clerk already in the service of one of the Garter knights. His decision to write in non-rhyming alliterative long-line verse

---

[73] John Anstis, *The Register of the Most Noble Order of the Garter* (2 vols, London, 1724), vol. 1, p. 50; vol. 2, p. 316; and see above, p. 23.

[74] TNA, E 101/393/11, fol. 76v; E 101/394/16, m. 4; E 101/395/10; and E 361/4, rot. 12d.

[75] For the dress of kings' heralds, see Anon., 'What Was a Cote Armure? A Surcoat? And a Tabard?', *The Herald and Genealogist*, 1 (1863), 235–58, at 250–1.

was a bold shift so far as royal patrons were concerned, but other versions of the alliterative form – most notably, *Sir Gawain and the Green Knight* – would apparently have considerable currency in courtly circles around the same period. While the opening stages of *W&W* represent in many ways a conventional 'praise poem' on the kingship of Edward III, the darker moments later in the text suggest that the author was capable of seriously testing the capacity of royal audiences as the butt of satire and criticism. The possibility also remains that the poem was the work of an insider: someone like Hoccleve or Gower, who worked within the existing structures of royal government and justice and wrote not simply as 'prince-pleasers' but for other literary-minded men in the royal household and other offices of central government who had varying attitudes towards the policies of the crown on current political issues.[76] *W&W* is itself set up in a divisive way, the debate beween Wynnere and Wastoure seen as resolvable either through a competition of arms or by royal intervention and arbitration. Whether the king's final judgment is seen as appropriate and effective or not, it is recognised that only he can produce a peaceful resolution of the debate. In that sense, the constitutional foundations of monarchy are upheld quite forcefully by the poem, which ends (in its extant form) on a prophetic note about Edward III's claims as the new Arthur.

---

[76] For poets in search of patronage, see esp. Richard Firth Green, *Poets and Prince-pleasers: Literature and the English Court in the Late Middle Ages* (Toronto, 1980).

6

Winner and Waster: Timeliness and Timelessness

The underlying objective of this study has been to test, re-establish and extend the argument, first developed by Hulbert and later revived and extended by Lawton and Salter, that *W&W* is likely to have been written not in the early 1350s but at some point in the 1360s (or, as Salter would have it, still later). These arguments were based on close reading of some of the crucial 'historical' passages in the poem, which under closer scrutiny need not, as supposed by others, refer solely to a cluster of events and debates around the years 1352–3; in Salter's case, the dating relied on her exploration of a heraldic motif linking the poem (as she argued) to the family circle of Sir John Wingfield, which opened up the possibility of a relatively remote composition date stretching into the 1380s and beyond. The present analysis has suggested some new frames of reference for the poem, arguing *inter alia* that an effective *terminus a quo* for the dating of the poem may now be set at the Garter feast of April 1358. As regards a *terminus ante quem*, this analysis agrees in principle with Trigg that the poem is unlikely to have been written much later than the death of Sir William Shareshull in 1370, not just because of the mention of the chief justice in the poem, but also because the whole political atmosphere of England changed so radically after the re-opening of the French war in 1369, culminating in the general state of outrage about a broken and corrupt regime expressed in the Good Parliament of 1376.

In particular, this study has demonstrated the significant number and range of possible referents within the poem to events and debates of the 1360s: the attitude of political society towards the Anglo-French diplomatic settlement of 1360; the controversies provoked by the making and unmaking of the new sumptuary laws in 1363 and 1365; the manner of funding the king's peacetime regime as determined in the parliaments of 1362, 1365 and 1368; and the scandalous dismissal of the king's steward, Sir John atte Lee, in 1368. All of this leads us to suggest that the poem's central theme, the difficulty of establishing a balance between extravagance and frugality in the domestic expenditure of the landed classes, was one man's way of making sense of wider debates about the political economy going on in the immediate aftermath of the second and third outbreaks of the Black Death in 1361–2 and 1368. In the process, the poet also drew on his memory of other events and phenomena that had occurred within his generation, including the reception of foreigners into the royal household in the first phase of the French war during the late 1330s, the founding of the Order of the Garter in 1348 and its subsequent meetings at Windsor, and the various initiatives in the enforcement of law and order particularly associated with Shareshull's time as chief justice. A closely historicised reading that emphasises the special political dynamics at work in England during the years of peace between 1360 and 1369 also serves to revise earlier interpretations of the poem as a critique of Edward III's financing of the Hundred Years War in the 1350s. Instead, this analysis has suggested that the secondary intention of the poet was to expose a very particular debate going on over who should enjoy the peace dividend arising from the 1360 settlement: a king intent on a costly campaign of royal magnificence, or a realm that had serious expectations of release from wartime fiscal burdens. In this last respect, W&W represents an important moment in the development of the late medieval political principle that 'the king should live of his own'.

A necessary final question therefore arises as to whether the depiction in W&W of the 'comliche kynge' ('handsome king') (line 86) with his 'berybrown' ('berry-brown') beard (line 91) is really a credible pen-portrait of Edward III in the 1360s. We do not, of course, rely on the poem to provide us with a life-like representation of the ruling monarch in the very moment of composition: it is important for the force of its message, rather than for strict historical accuracy, that the figure of the king be represented in the full vigour of his manhood, and thus capable, through the force of his own will, of holding together the competing factions within his household. The fact that the poem is set within the context of the Order of the Garter (founded in 1348) means that the poet may well have been indulging in his own nostalgia and reflections about a slightly earlier period in Edward III's life, when the king was at the height of his popularity following the great victories of Crécy, Calais and Neville's Cross in 1346–7. But the idea that Edward was too old by the 1360s to be represented as fit of body and mind is to ignore the clear evidence of his continued dynamism through the later stages of his middle age. In 1362 the king chose to celebrate his fiftieth birthday by mobilising the Judaeo-Christian idea of the jubilee and issuing a general pardon for all his free subjects.[1] Most politically aware people in England, including the author of W&W, were therefore reminded, in this moment of celebration, of the remarkable fact of the

---

[1] Helen Lacey, *The Royal Pardon: Access to Mercy in Fourteenth-Century England* (York, 2009), pp. 114–15; W. Mark Ormrod, 'The Use of English: Language, Law and Political Culture in Fourteenth-Century England', *Speculum*, 88 (2003), 750–87, at 762–3.

king's survival through two major plagues and a quarter-century of war. The historical record also shows that Edward III remained remarkably fit throughout his forties and fifties: apart from his taking regular medicaments for undefined complaints during his fifties, there is no evidence that he was ever seriously indisposed before the autumn of 1371 – and even then, he was still preparing to lead his army in France as he approached his sixtieth birthday in 1372.[2] In short, courtly society had every reason throughout the 1360s to think of Edward III as being in the full flowering of his years – and thus in the life-stage that medieval thought regarded as best suited to the provision of wise and just governance.[3]

Despite the resonances that the poem has with the preoccupations of the landed elite during the 1360s, *W&W* can certainly not be regarded as a bestseller of its times. While the number of extant manuscripts of any medieval poem provides only a very crude index of its contemporary circulation, the fact that the sole text of this poem left to us from the Middle Ages is that made by Robert Thornton in the fifteenth century strongly suggests that the *refrayte* between Wynnere and Wastoure turned out to have limited reach and popularity.[4] To a degree, perhaps, it was the poem's very 'timeliness' (to use Salter's term) that limited its appeal.[5] Whether one argues that it was written in the 1350s or the 1360s, *W&W* is fixed in a sequence of events and circumstances that suggests its relevance at a defined point in time. That it survived at all, and was included in Thornton's anthology, may perhaps be ascribed to the positive representation of Edward III's kingship at the outset of the poem; in this regard, the text may be seen as part of a powerful tradition of nostalgia that built up in a range of historical and literary texts around the figure of Edward III during the late fourteenth and fifteenth centuries.[6] In terms of its social or political message, by contrast, the

---

[2] W. Mark Ormrod, *Edward III* (London, 2011), pp. 462–3, 514, 529–31, 545.

[3] J. A. Burrow, *The Ages of Man: A Study in Medieval Writing and Thought* (Oxford, 1986).

[4] For modes of transmission of political texts beyond the codex in the later Middle Ages, see Wendy Scase, 'Imagining Alternatives to the Book: The Transmission of Political Poetry in Late Medieval England', in Stephen Kelly and John J. Thompson (eds), *Imagining the Book* (Turnhout, 2005), pp. 237–50.

[5] Elizabeth Salter, 'The Timeliness of *Wynnere and Wastoure*', *Medium Aevum*, 47 (1978), 40–65, repr. in Elizabeth Salter, *English and International: Studies in the Literature, Art and Patronage of Medieval England*, ed. Derek Pearsall and Nicolette Zeeman (Cambridge, 1988), pp. 180–98. Compare Derek Pearsall, 'The Timeliness of *The Simonie*', in O. S. Pickering (ed.), *Individuality and Achievement in Middle English Poetry* (Cambridge, 1997), pp. 59–72.

[6] D. A. L. Morgan, 'The Political After-life of Edward III: The Apotheosis of a Warmonger', *English Historical Review*, 112 (1997), 856–81; A. J. Pollard, *Imagining Robin Hood* (London, 2004), pp. 200–4; Ormrod, *Edward III*, pp. 587–91.

poem seems too narrow in subject matter, and perhaps too conservative and complacent in tone, to find a lasting place within the genre of complaint literature in the later fourteenth and early fifteenth centuries.

Yet it is precisely the more 'timeless' themes of the maintenance of social hierarchy and the responsibilities of wealth and power that may also have appealed to the anthologist Thornton when he happened upon the poem as part of his re-assemblage of older works. Thornton was born in the last years of the fourteenth century. On the death of his father in 1418 he became lord of the manor of East Newton in the wapentake of Ryedale within the North Riding of Yorkshire, which he held to his death in or before 1465. Well connected with other more prominent gentry families of the area, especially the Pickerings of Oswaldkirk, Robert was a regular witness to land transactions in his locale. A single royal commission hints at his occasional wider reach, when in 1453 he was appointed as a tax collector in the North Riding.[7] Thornton seems to have undertaken his collection and transcription of texts in the second quarter of the fifteenth century; Ralph Hanna believes that *W&W* was written up during the fifth phase of a ten-point chronology stretching over these years, and thus apparently in the late 1430s.[8]

Robert Thornton was a voracious compiler, and there is no need to ascribe any particular intentions to his decision to include *W&W* in his large anthology. Nevertheless, it may be suggested that Thornton's social standing as a member of the minor gentry made him and his like an integral part of the subject matter of the poem. Understanding that its major theme was the requirement upon the landed elite to establish an appropriate balance between frugality and prodigality meant that Thornton, and other readers of his status and background, could then read into the poem references that they might recognise as explicitly historical and/or potentially contemporary. Thus, for example, while the figure of the king was very likely

---

[7] For Thornton's life records, see: George R. Keiser, 'Lincoln Cathedral Library MS 91: The Life and Milieu of the Scribe', *Studies in Bibliography*, 32 (1979), 158–79; George R. Keiser, 'More Light on the Life and Milieu of Robert Thornton', *Studies in Bibliography*, 36 (1983), 111–19; Derek Brewer and A. E. B. Owen (eds), *The Thornton Manuscript (Lincoln Cathedral MS 91)*, rev. edn (London, 1977); John J. Thompson (ed.), *Robert Thornton and the London Thornton Manuscript: British Library MS Additional 31042* (Cambridge, 1987); George R. Keiser, 'Robert Thornton: Gentleman, Reader and Scribe', in Susanna Fein and Michael Johnston (eds), *Robert Thornton and his Books: Essays on the Lincoln and London Thornton Manuscripts* (York, 2014), pp. 67–108; and Michael Johnston, *Romance and the Gentry in Late Medieval England* (Oxford, 2014), pp. 160–72. For Thornton's appointment and subsequent dismissal as a collector of direct taxation in 1453–4, see *Calendar of the Fine Rolls Preserved in the Public Record Office, 1452–61* (London, 1939), pp. 47, 83–4.

[8] Ralph Hanna, 'The Growth of Robert Thornton's Books', *Studies in Bibliography*, 40 (1987), 51–61.

to be understood by informed audiences up to the middle of the fifteenth century as a depiction of Edward III, it could also be read by those with the inclination to do so as denoting that other late medieval hero and patron of chivalry, Henry V.[9] And understanding that the poem also alluded to the debate over the extent and limits of taxation allows for particular resonance in the 1430s and 1440s. In 1433, Henry VI's treasurer, Ralph, Lord Cromwell, compiled another of the 'balance sheets' akin to the ones that were drawn up for use in parliament in the 1360s.[10] This demonstrated without doubt that, as a result of a severe decline in wool exports and a consequent dramatic drop in income from the customs and subsidies, the crown could no longer fund even its ordinary expenditure without recourse to extraordinary levies in the form of direct taxation. As a result, there ensued a debate very close to that which had taken place in the 1360s over whether Henry VI might be allowed a grant of taxation solely to cover the normal costs of the state. The response of parliament in 1433, granting a single fifteenth and tenth but insisting that an overall reduction of £4,000 be made in the amounts charged on local communities, shows the extent of feeling among the polity in the 1430s, as in the 1360s, over the principle that extraordinary taxes were ultimately justified only in a state of war.[11]

More generally but also more pertinently, the agrarian economy was in a state of severe turbulence during the 1430s and 1440s.[12] There was a sequence of very poor harvests, including one of famine proportions in 1438, whose general effects were felt particularly sharply in the North. Although the resulting shortage of grain drove up market prices, it also

---

[9] For the interlocking nature of the reputations of Edward III and Henry V in the fifteenth century, see V. J. Scattergood, *Politics and Poetry in the Fifteenth Century* (London, 1971), pp. 49–50; Morgan, 'Political After-life', pp. 856–81; Ormrod, *Edward III*, pp. 587–8; Katherine Lewis, *Kingship and Masculinity in Late Medieval England* (London, 2013), *passim*.

[10] J. L. Kirby, 'The Issues of the Lancastrian Exchequer and Lord Cromwell's Estimates of 1433', *Bulletin of the Institute of Historical Research*, 24 (1951), 121–51. See also, more generally, G. L. Harriss, 'Budgeting at the Medieval Exchequer', in Chris Given-Wilson, Ann J. Kettle and Len Scales (eds), *War, Government and Aristocracy in the British Isles, c.1150–1500: Essays in Honour of Michael Prestwich* (Woodbridge, 2008), pp. 179–96.

[11] The most recent analysis, with full bibliographical apparatus, is Alex Brayson, 'The Fiscal Constitution of Later Medieval England: The Reign of Henry VI' (Unpublished Ph.D. thesis, University of York, 2013), pp. 71–101.

[12] For what follows, see A. J. Pollard, 'The North-Eastern Economy and the Agrarian Crisis of 1438–40', *Northern History*, 25 (1989), 88–105; John Hatcher, 'The Great Slump of the Mid-Fifteenth Century', in Richard Britnell and John Hatcher (eds), *Progress and Problems in Medieval England: Essays in Honour of Edward Miller* (Cambridge, 1996), pp. 237–72.

meant that most producers had less to sell and were therefore more vulnerable to making an overall loss. In the third quarter of the fourteenth century, the issue as to how landed society might best thrive in an uncertain world could still be presented to the audience of *W&W* as a matter of free choice and good judgment. By the time the poem was written out by Robert Thornton, that range of options was increasingly turning to desperate imperatives. Now, a significant number of landlords, both major and minor, found their purchasing power significantly reduced, and were forced to diversify their activities and/or make major economies in order to avoid impending financial ruin. These dire circumstances heralded the beginning of a major and prolonged economic recession through the middle years of the fifteenth century; signs of recovery only began again from the 1460s. While Robert Thornton did not select the contents of his anthologies on the basis of some kind of crude 'relevance', it remains quite striking just how prescient the theme of political economy within *W&W* was, and remained, for his own and the next generation of landholders in fifteenth-century England.

None of what has gone before means that *W&W* cannot also be read as engaging in timeless truths that are to be understood on a cultural and philosophical level, rather than simply as a commentary on the sociopolitics of a particular historical period. To some degree, the destabilising of *W&W*'s place in the so-called Alliterative Revival, discussed in Chapter 5, has itself liberated modern and post-modern literary criticism: as Breen put it in 2012, 'Belatedly, but utterly appropriately, *Wynnere and Wastoure* has ceased to be a piece of literary historical evidence and become a poem.'[13] This book is meant as a contribution to that process of liberation. It has engaged in a deeper historicising of the text of *W&W* not as a means of limiting the poem in time and space, but rather by arguing that a fuller examination of the poem's wide range of historical referents adds substantively to an understanding of its wider meanings for contemporary and near-contemporary audiences. Readings of *W&W* will continue to reveal the richness of the text and its susceptibility to a range of critical approaches, historicist and otherwise. If this book makes one contribution to those ongoing readings, then it is to show that historicism need not be a reductive device but can substantively enhance the meaning and value of a text both as history and as literature.

---

[13] Katharine Breen, 'The Need for Allegory: *Wynnere and Wastoure* as an *Ars poetica*', *Yearbook of Langland Studies*, 26 (2012), 187–229, at 190.

Appendix 1

Timeline, 1337–70

1337–1453	The Hundred Years War.
1340	Edward III of England declares himself 'king of France'.
1344	Arthurian Round Table at Windsor Castle.
1346	Edward III defeats the French at the battle of Crécy.
1346	English forces defeat the Scots at the battle of Neville's Cross and take prisoner their king, David II.
1346–7	English forces besiege the town of Calais and take it in 1347.
1348	Round of tournaments in England to celebrate the victories of 1346–7. Includes a tournament at Windsor in June 1348 at which the Order of the Garter was probably instituted.
1348–9	First outbreak of the Black Death in England; government passes the Ordinance of Labourers in spring 1349.
1349	First meeting of the Order of the Garter on St George's Day, 23 April.
1350	Sir William Shareshull becomes chief justice of the court of king's bench.
1351	First parliament since the outbreak of the plague; government passes the Statute of Labourers and Statute of Provisors.
1352	Parliament grants three years of direct taxation in return for legislation on a range of economic affairs; passage of the Statute of Treasons.
1353	Sir William Shareshull heads the eyre of Cheshire.
1353	Great council grants the crown the wool subsidy in return for legislation establishing the wool staple in England. Statute of Praemunire.
1355–7	Black Prince's campaign through France, culminating in the victory at Poitiers in 1357, with John II of France taken prisoner.

1357	Treaty of Berwick with the Scots results in release of David II on payment of large ransom.
1358	St George's Day feast at Windsor mounted on an unprecedented scale as a sign of English dominance over France and Scotland.
1358	Second eyre of Cheshire, led by Sir William Shareshull.
1360	Treaty of Brétigny, followed by Treaty of Calais, make Edward III sovereign ruler of enlarged duchy of Aquitaine but require him to give up the title to the French throne; John II to be released from captivity on payment of a large ransom.
1361	Treaty of Calais accepted in parliament.
1361–2	Second outbreak of the Black Death in England. St Maurus' Wind (1362). Sir William Shareshull retires as chief justice of king's bench (1361) but returns to service of the Black Prince in eyre of Denbigh (1362).
1362	First peacetime grant of the wool subsidy in parliament.
1363	Sumptuary laws passed in parliament. The wool staple moved to Calais, with a promise to parliament that it will remain there perpetually.
1365	Sumptuary laws withdrawn in parliament; second peacetime grant of the wool subsidy. Second Statute of Provisors and Praemunire.
1366	Formal abolition of Peter's Pence in England.
1368	Third outbreak of the Black Death in England.
1368	Trial of Sir John atte Lee in parliament; third peacetime grant of the wool subsidy.
1369	Edward III resumes title of 'king of France' and re-opens war with the French.
1370	Death of Sir William Shareshull.

Appendix 2

A Modern English Version of *Winner and Waster*

Note: The modern rendering of *W&W* offered here is based on the various editions and translations itemised above, p. ix, and on my own independent interpretations. In places where the original is defective, Turville-Petre provides important hypothetical readings, generally adopted by Trigg and Ginsberg. I draw freely on the modern English versions provided by Gollancz and Millett. The former, however, stays so close to the original that it sometimes obscures meanings, and the suggested readings are not always secure; Millett is therefore a default, though I also deviate from her understanding in a few places (see, for example, the discussion of line 387 above, p. 68 and n. 21). No attempt has been made to preserve the alliterative style of the original, though some relatively archaic forms (for example, 'laund' at lines 49, 54 and 209 and 'comely king' at lines 86 and 199) are retained for their particular technical sense (in the former case: see p. 16) or their more general literary reverberation (in the latter: see p. 10, n. 28).

Here begins a treatise and a good short debate between Winner and Waster

[Prologue]
After Britain was begun, and Brutus possessed it
Through the taking of Troy by internal treason,[1]
Marvels have been seen in various reigns,
But never so many as now, by the ninth part.
5   For all is 'Wit' and 'Will' that we have to cope with now,
Wise and sly words, each one obscuring the next.
No western man, while this world lasts, will risk
Sending his son south to see or to hear,
But he shall stay behind, while [his father] grows old.

---

[1] For the myth of the foundation of Britain by Brutus, grandson of Aeneas, see above, p. 10 n. 27.

10   For there was a saying of Solomon the wise,[2]
(It will soon come to pass, I expect nothing else):
'When waves wax wild and walls are down,
And hares shall crouch on hearth-stones as their lairs,
And mere boys of low birth, with boasting and with pride
15   Shall marry high-born ladies, and lead them at their will,
Then, the dreadful day of doom, it will draw near.'
But whoever will see with clarity and speak the truth
May say that it will come soon, and is nearly here.
Once there were lords in the land who loved in their hearts
20   To hear makers of mirth who had tales to tell;
But now there is no shared friendship, but only faintness of heart,
Wise words within, that were never spoken
Or read in any romance that anyone heard.
Now a mere child without a beard
25   Who never had the wit to put words together,
As long as he can jangle like a jay and tell japes,
Will be believed and loved, and applauded in time
Much more than the writer who makes his own works.
But when men are revealed for what they are,
30   Work will bear witness to which one knows best.

[First fitt]
But I shall tell you a tale of a time in my past
As I went in the West, wandering on my own.
By the bank of a stream (the sun was bright),
Under a fine wood by a pleasant meadow
35   Many flowers unfolded where my foot stepped.
I laid my head on a mound by a hawthorn tree;
The thrushes sang loudly, thronging together,
Woodpeckers hopped from one hazel bush to another,
Wild geese with their beaks made the trees ring out,
40   The jay jangled above, amidst the joy of the fowls,
The rivulet rushed boldly between its banks.
So rude were the rough streams that made so much noise,
That it was nearly night before I could slumber,
For the din of the deep water and the chattering of fowls.

---

[2] The Old Testament figure of King Solomon: see II Samuel, I Chronicles and I Kings.

45	But at last as I lay there, my eyelids locked,
	And swiftly I was swept into a dream.
	I thought I was in the world, but whereabouts I did not know,
	On a lovely laund of an even green
	That lay encircled by earthworks extending a mile.[3]
50	On either side were two armies in bright hauberks,
	Hard hats on their heads, and helmets with crests;
	Their banners were unfurled and lowered ready to meet;
	Rushing out of the woods, they formed up in phalanxes;
	There was only the length of a laund between these lords.
55	And all prayed for peace until the prince should come,
	For he was better fitted than anyone else
	To part them, and advise them, and to rule on the quarrel
	That each side on the field had, in hatred, towards the other.[4]
	At the crest of a cliff was set a pavilion,
60	The roof and the sides all arrayed with red,
	Adorned with English bezants embossed with gold
	Girdled about with garters of dark blue;
	And every garter glittered richly with gold.[5]
	Then there were coloured words in the weave of cloth,
65	Painted in light blue, with points in between,
	That were well designed, with well-formed letters,
	And all stating one motto, in English words,
	'Shamed be the knight who thinks ill of it'.[6]
	Now may our Lord keep safe the king of this country!

---

[3] For the significance of the 'laund' surrounded by earthworks, as an open space used for recreation and jousting, see pp. 16–17.

[4] For the expectation that the quarrel between the two parties (unnamed at this point) ought to be resolved by peaceful arbitration, see pp. 50–1.

[5] The colours noted in lines 60–2 have significance: red was the background colour of the English royal coat of arms, and blue that of the French. The use of blue in relation to the symbol of the Order of the Garter reflects Edward III's claim to the French throne.

[6] The Middle English line 'Hethyng have the hathell that any harme thynkes' is a rendering of the Anglo-Norman French motto of the Order of the Garter, *Honi soit qui mal y pense*. 'Hathell', which objectifies the unstated recipient of shame in the original, is added for alliterative effect, but by referring to the knightly class has the effect of emphasising the chivalric themes of honour and shame, on which the motto plays. See also n. to line 432.

70	High in the woods a knight stood up,
	Attired like a wild man with twisted tufts of fur,[7]
	With a helmet on his head, and a hat above that
	And over the hat, an angry beast,
	A lithe, long leopard, looking fearsome,
75	Made all in yellow gold of the best sort.[8]
	But the helmet backing behind the neck
	Was divided cleanly into four quarters,
	Two with the fleurs-de-lis of France above and below,
	And two of them embroidered with six fearsome English beasts,
80	Three leopards above, and three below;[9]
	At every corner was a stud of a splendid pearl,
	Tasselled with fine silk protruding out elegantly.
	And by the pavilion I knew the knight that I saw
	And hoped to see many wonders before I went away.
85	And as I waited within, I rapidly became aware
	Of a comely king crowned in gold,
	Sitting on a silken bench with a sceptre in his hand,
	One of the loveliest lords, to those who love him in their hearts,
	That anyone under the sun ever saw with his own eyes.
90	This king was beautifully clothed in a tunic and cloak,
	As berry-brown as his beard, embroidered with fowls,
	Falcons of fine gold flapping their wings,
	And each one bore in blue, as it seemed to me,
	A deep blue garter, beautifully adorned.[10]
95	That great lord was gaily girded about
	With a brightly coloured belt embroidered with fowls,
	With drakes and ducks, which seemed to be trembling
	For fear of the falcons' claws, lest they were caught.
	And still I said to myself, 'I would think it strange

[7] For the wild man, or *woodwose*, see p. 5 n. 10.

[8] The crest of the leopard (the heraldic symbol of England) indicates that the wild man is in the service of the king.

[9] These are the heraldic arms of England quartered with those of France, as used by Edward III from 1340. See W. Mark Ormrod, *Edward III* (London, 2011), pp. 604–8.

[10] The royal household accounts indicate that the garter emblem was only used at the celebration of the feast of the Order of the Garter, held each year at Windsor on 23 April. See p. 18.

100	If this lord did not ride some time to the river.'
	The king bade a man who was standing beside him,
	One of the finest knights, who never failed him,[11]
	'Remember I dubbed you knight, to deal out blows;
	Go quickly on your way to declare my will,
105	Go, tell the fierce warriors over there who wait on the field
	That they should not come any nearer together,
	For if they strike one stroke, they will never stint.'
	'Yes, lord,' said the knight, 'while my life endures.'
	He climbed down the bank and stayed for a while
110	Until he was equipped and bound in the best array.
	He clapped his legs in iron to the lower bones,
	With chest- and lower-armour polished brightly,
	With arm-braces of burnished steel linked very thickly,
	With plates buckled at the back to protect the body,
115	With a well-fitting jupon fastened at the sides,
	A broad escutcheon behind, and another on the breastplate,
	With three life-like wings worked on it
	Surrounded by gold thread.[12] Wherewith I recognised that man:
	Why! He was the youngest in years, but the quickest in wit
120	That any man in the world knew at his age.
	He broke a branch in his hand and boldly brandished it,
	And set out at a brisk trot, and took his way
	Where the soldiers of both sides stood in the field.
	He said, 'Lo! The king of this land, may the Lord keep him,
125	Sends his errand by me, as it most pleased him,
	That no man should be so bold, on pain of both his eyes,
	To strike a single stroke, or to stir up others
	To raise a rout in his realm, so royal it is,
	Using your powers openly to disturb his peace.
130	For this is the custom here, and will ever stand:
	If any man is so bold as to ride forth with a banner
	Within this noble kingdom, except the king alone,
	Then he shall lose his land, and his life thereafter.
	But since you do not know this people, or the kingdom,[13]

---

[11] For attempts to construct this character as Edward of Woodstock (the Black Prince), eldest son of Edward III, see pp. 6, 9, 44–5.

[12] For the interpretation of the arms or badge of golden-edged 'wings', see pp. 20, 125–6.

[13] For the re-interpretation of the end of line 134, see pp. 48–50.

135	He will forgive this offence, of his own prerogative.
	I have travelled far and wide through foreign lands,
	But never saw I such a sight, I tell you;
	For here are all the men of France in fighting array,
	Of Lorraine, of Lombardy, and of lowland Spain,
140	Men from Westphalia, that live in a state of war,
	From England and Ireland, and many Easterlings,[14]
	All armed in steel, ready to deal strokes.
	And yonder a black banner stands on the battlefield,[15]
	With three papal bulls of white embroidered in it,
145	And each one has a cord of hemp hanging down from it
	Sealed with a heavy lead, so it seems to me;
	The head of Holy Church, I believe he is here,
	As fierce for the fight as the people he leads.
	Another banner is raised with a bend of green,
150	With three white-haired heads, with hoods aloft,
	Skilfully curled and combed to the neck.
	These are the men of this land who should protect our laws,
	But are ready to fight today with many strokes.
	I hold him but a fool who prefers to fight while he can dispute instead,
155	When he has found his friend that failed him never.
	The third banner on the battlefield is of bleached white,
	With six sandals, I see, in sable black,
	And each one has a brown strap with two buckles;
	These are St Francis's men,[16] who say that all flesh shall soon pass.
160	They are so fierce and eager, though they fight only seldom.
	I know it was for profit they went from their homes;
	He who lured them here must have a full purse.
	The fourth banner on the battlefield is borne up aloft
	With both borders of black, and a ball in the middle
165	Just as the sun is in the summertime
	When it has most strength, on Midsummer's Eve.
	That was Dominic who has come to deal blows;
	His banner is borne up by many bold men.[17]
	And since the pope is so prompt to give these preachers help,

---

[14] For the meaning of 'Easterlings', see p. 26, n. 34.
[15] For the scholarly discussion of the six banners identified at lines 143–87, see pp. 27–8.
[16] The oldest of the mendicant orders of friars, the order of St Francis.
[17] The mendicant order of St Dominic, otherwise known as the friars preachers (see line 171).

170	And Francis with his people is also reinforced,
	And they lead all the lords of the land with their wit,
	No man in the world can be matched against them,
	Or gain any grace upon Earth, under God himself.
	And yet the fifth [banner] on the field is the finest of all,
175	A bright banner of white, with three boars' heads.
	By any knowledge that I have, they seemed to be Carmelites,[18]
	For they are the people who love to serve Our Lady.
	If I should speak the truth, it seems nothing less
	But that the friars, with other people, will win the field.
180	The sixth [banner] is of silk (and so are they all),
	White as whalebone, if the truth be told,
	With belts of black buckled together,
	The ends tapered and tucked away,
	And all of the leather aloft that hangs down
185	Shines by the sharpening of the shaving-blade.
	They are the order of Augustinians,[19] for that I know
	From the glint of the belts on their banner.
	And other signs I saw set upon high,
	Some showing wool, and some wine-barrels,
190	Some merchants' marks, so many and so thronged
	That I have no idea in all the world
	What man under the sun could reckon them all up.
	And strong, over there, are simple men at arms,
	Bold well-born squires and many bowmen
195	Who, if they strike one stroke, will not think of stopping
	Till either army is hewn to death upon the heath.
	Therefore I bid the two who brought them here
	That you wend with me, before any woe should befall,
	To our comely king, who rules this country,
200	And when he discovers where the fault lies,
	Let neither man be angry to act according to his judgment.'
	From either side there rode out a man, as it seemed to me,
	Knights full comely, on caparisoned steeds,
	And said, 'Sir messenger, bless you betides!

---

[18] The mendicant order of the Carmelites.

[19] The fourth and final of the mendicant orders to be mentioned by *W&W*, the order of the Augustinians or Austin friars.

205 We know the king well; he clothes us both,
   And has fostered and fed us these twenty-five winters;[20]
   Now you go on before, and we shall follow after.'
   And now, their bridles ready, they set out upon their ways;
   They dismounted at the laund and left their horses,
210 And climbed up the cliff and fell upon their knees.
   The king took them by the hands and ordered them both to rise,
   And said, 'Welcome, both, as members of our household.'
   The king glanced to one side and asked for wine;
   His men brought it at once, in silver bowls.
215 It seemed I supped so deeply that it blurred both my eyes:
   And he that wishes to listen to any more of this work,
   Fill me up freshly and fast, for here a fitt ends.

[Second Fitt]
   But then the king spoke up, and said, 'Make known your names,
   And why the hostility is so hot between your two hearts;
220 If I must judge you today, let me hear the facts.'
   'Now certainly, lord,' said the first, 'The truth to tell:
   My name is Winner, a man that helps all the world,
   For people learn from me, with my wit:
   Those who will save wisely, and not spend too much,
225 And live upon little, I like them better.
   Wit goes with me, and guides me well;
   When I gather my goods together, that gladdens my heart.
   But this wicked, false thief who stands before you
   Thinks to strike me down and destroy me forever.
230 All that I win by my wits, he wastes through pride,
   I gather, I glean, and he lets it all go,
   I pinch and I save, and he opens the purse.
   Why does this scoundrel have no care how corn sells?
   His lands all lie fallow, his looms are sold,

---

[20] See also line 212. For the significance of the (at this point still otherwise unidentified) characters of Wynnere and Wastoure as members of the royal household, see pp. 49–60.

235	His dovecots are ruined, his fishponds are dry.
	The Devil may wonder at the wealth he enjoys at home:
	Only hunger and big houses and eager hounds.
	Except for a halberd and a spear stored in a corner,
	A sword at his bed-head, he commands nothing else
240	Than a good gelding to ride out to his friends.
	Then he will boast often, brandishing his sword –
	This wicked, accursed thief that people call Waster –
	That he will destroy the land if he lives long enough.
	Therefore judge us today, for the love of God in Heaven,
245	To fight on with our people till one of us falls.'
	'Yes, Winner,' said Waster, 'Your words are arrogant,
	But I shall tell you a tale that will annoy you more.
	When you have tossed and turned, and lain awake all night,
	And disturbed everyone who lives around you,
250	And have crammed your broad houses full of woolsacks,
	The roof-beams bending, such are the bacons hanging there,
	Silver pennies stuffed into steel-bound chests:
	What would become of that wealth if no waste were to happen?
	Some would rot, some would rust, some the rats would feed on.
255	Give up cramming your chests, for the love of Christ in Heaven!
	Let the people and the poor have part of your silver;
	For if you would walk abroad, and pay attention,
	You would weep for pity, so rife are the poor.
	For if you live any longer in this manner, to be sure,
260	You will be hanged in Hell for what you hoard here.
	For such a sin you have sold your soul into Hell,
	Where pain is everlasting, world without end.'[21]
	'Stop talking, Waster,' said the rich man Winner,
	'You're complaining of a grievance that you yourself caused.
265	With your violence and strife you destroy my goods,
	With feasting and waking on winter nights,
	In excess, in unthrift, in the arrogance of pride.
	There is no source of wealth flowing through your hands
	That is not given and granted before you have got it.

---

[21] The reference at lines 260–2 to the sin of avarice, one of the seven deadly sins in the medieval Church, accounts for the belief that Winner will go to Hell.

270	You lead men in your retinue very richly attired;
	Some have girdles of gold that have cost more
	Than all the good free land that you had before.
	You do not follow your fathers, who fostered you all,
	In collecting a good harvest and gathering the corn
275	Before the cold winter with its glittering frosts[22]
	After rainless drought in the dead month[23]
	And you will go to the tavern, with the wine-casks,
	And everyone serves you with a bowl to blur your eyes.
	You order your drinks, and what your heart desires,
280	Wife, widow or wench, whatever may be had.
	Then there is nothing but "Fill it up!" and "Fetch forth" to get your money,
	"Wee-hee!" and "Climb up!" and not a word more.[24]
	But when this pleasure has passed, the wine must be paid for.
	Then you must lay pledges or sell your land:
285	May our Lord damn you for such wicked deeds![25]
	And since God chose the one he loved and left out the other,
	Every man ought to be inspired by fear to work in the fields.[26]
	Teach your men to till and to fence in your fields,
	Increase your rentals, clear up your enclosures,
290	Or keep on living as you have, and take the consequences:
	That is, first the food fails, and then [Hell-]fire comes
	To burn you up with a single blast for your baleful deeds,
	And yet a greater cold is to come, as a clerk told me.'
	'Yea, Winner,' said Waster, 'your words are in vain;
295	With our feasts and our fare we feed the poor.
	It pleases the Prince who created Paradise
	When Christ's people have a share, and pleases him all the better
	Than if it is held on to and hidden, and hoarded in coffers
	So that the sun does not see it once in seven winters,

---

[22] For attempts to read this as a reference to specific meteorological events, see p. 9.

[23] A comment on habitually low rainfall in the month of March, referenced in the 'General Prologue' to Chaucer's *Canterbury Tales* and more widely in medieval literature.

[24] Turville-Petre points out the sexual connotations of the calls in this line.

[25] Wynnere returns to the issue of the seven deadly sins, and in return for Wastoure's comments accuses the latter of gluttony.

[26] The allusion at lines 286–7 is apparently to Christ (the 'chosen one') and Adam (the one 'left out'), and to the biblical story of God's condemnation of Adam to hard labour for his livelihood: Genesis 3.

300	Or the friars take it when you die
	To paint their pillars or plaster their walls.
	Your son and your executors ruin each other,
	Give a dole when you are dead, because you never dared,
	And never cared for feasts or mind-ales.[27]
305	But doles after your death do you no more good
	Than a bright lantern late in the night
	When it is borne at your back, man, in truth.
	Now would God that it might be as I could devise
	That you, Winner, you wretch, and Wanhope,[28] your brother,
310	And also ember-days and the vigils of saints
	The Friday and its friend on the far side,[29]
	Were drowned in the deep sea, where never drought would occur,[30]
	And judged guilty of their sins by a jury of twelve;
	And these men on the benches with their lawyers' caps,
315	Known far and wide as the best of learned men,
	As good as Aristotle or Augustine the wise,
	So all of them should be ruined, and Shareshull too,
	Who said that I pricked with armed power to disturb his peace![31]
	Therefore, comely king, having heard our case,
320	Let us swiftly with swords strike now together;
	For what was said long ago, I now see is true,
	"The richer a man is, the more will he fear;
	The more he has of his own, the feebler his heart becomes."'
	But then this wretched Winner looked angry,
325	And said, 'It is pointless speech, to say such words!
	Lo: this wretched Waster, who is known far and wide.
	There is no emperor or king or knight that will follow you,
	No baron or knight-bachelor, or any man that you love
	Save four or five fellows who owe you their loyalty.

---

[27] A dole was a sum of money or goods given to the poor; 'mind-ales' refers to the practice of holding commemorative events at which the deceased was honoured by the distribution of doles.

[28] The character of Wanhope does not otherwise appear in the poem. The name carries the meaning of 'Despair'.

[29] The references at lines 310–11 are to days in the ecclesiastical calendar when fasting was required. Friday's 'friend on the far side' is Saturday.

[30] For attempts to read this as a reference to a specific meteorological event, see p. 9.

[31] The reference is to Sir William Shareshull, chief justice of the court of king's bench. For discussion, see pp. 5–6, 40–8, 124–5.

330	And these he summons to dine on so many dainties
	That every man in this world may weep for sorrow.
	The boar's head will be brought in on high, with vegetables,
	Broad bucks' haunches, covered in sauce,
	Venison with frumenty, and rich pheasants,
335	Baked meat nearby, set on the board,
	Pies of chopped meat, grilled fowls,
	And each man I see has six men's portions.
	And if this were not enough, another [course] follows,
	A roast with rich stews and royal spices,
340	Kids carved down the back, quartered swans,
	Ten-inch tarts; it vexes my heart
	To see the board so overly spread with splendid dishes
	As if it were a cross, adorned with rings and precious stones.
	The third course would be a marvel to tell,
345	For all is Martinmas salt-meat that I know of,[32]
	Nothing but herbs with the meat, without wild fowl
	Except for a hen for him that heads the household.
	And he will have birds prepared on a fine spit,
	Geese, bitterns, and snipe with their bills,
350	Larks and linnets dusted with sugar,
	Woodcock and woodpeckers, all warm and hot,
	Teals and titmice, to take whatever they please;
	Rabbit stews, and sweet custards,[33]
	Pastries and pies that cost a great deal,
355	Diced meat that men steep to fill their gullets,
	Every dish costing a mark for two people:[34]
	That surely burns your bowels with pain.
	I am vexed by your trumpeters; they blast so loudly
	That every man in the street can hear them blaring.

---

[32] A reference to the feast of St Martin (11 November), which was the season for laying up salted meats.

[33] This and the next six lines are defective in the manuscript; the reconstruction used here is that of Ginsberg, in turn following Turville-Petre and Trigg.

[34] It was conventional for food to be served (and accounted for) in small groups called messes, which often numbered four people but could be less (or more). See C. M. Woolgar, *The Great Household in Late Medieval England* (London, 1999), p. 11, and compare the 'six men's portions' at line 337.

360	Then they will say to themselves, as they ride together,
	"You have no hope of the help of the King of Heaven."
	So you are scorned with reason, and disgraced thereafter,
	For paying a ransom of silver for a single repast.[35]
	But once in a hall I heard from the tongue of a herdsman,
365	"Better to have many meals than one merry night."
	And he that wishes to listen to any more of this work,
	Fill me up freshly and fast, for here a fitt ends.

[Third Fitt]

	'Yea, Winner,' said Waster, 'I know well myself
	What will become of you within a few years.
370	Through the plenty of corn that the people sow,
	Which God will grant of His grace to grow on the Earth
	To prevent the price from rising too high,
	You will go mad and in wild despair,
	Hoping for a hard year, and thus hang yourself.
375	Would you have lords live as lads on foot,
	Prelates like the priests who keep the parishes,
	Proud merchants of standing like pedlars in the towns?
	Let lords live as they please, lads as befits them,
	The one on bacon and beef, the other on bitterns and swans,
380	They on husks of rye, they on fine wheat,
	They on thin gruel, they on good stews;
	Then the people may have a share, who stand in poverty,
	With a good morsel of meat to cheer them.
	If birds were to fly out and never be caught,
385	And wild beasts were to spend all their lives in woods,
	And fish were to swim in the stream, and eat each other,
	A hen would cost just a halfpenny in less than half a year
	And there wouldn't be a lad in the land to serve a lord.
	This surely you see for yourself:
390	He who wants to win wealth must find a waster,
	For what saddens one man, gladdens another.'
	'Now,' Winner said to Waster, 'I wonder in my heart
	At these poor penniless men who want to buy furs,
	Silken saddles with rich circlets.

---

[35] For the possible historical resonance of the 'ransom of silver' in this line, see pp. 94–5.

395	Lest you anger your wives, you follow their wishes,
	You sell wood after wood within a short time,
	Both the oak and the ash, and all that grows there.
	The seedlings and the saplings you keep for your children,
	And say God will grant his grace to grow them in the end
400	To save your sons; but the shame is your own.
	It is profitless to save the soil if you mean to sell it.
	Your forefathers were inclined, when a friend came to them,
	To go into the woods and show him the covers,
	In each holt they had, to hunt for a hare,
405	And bring into the broad laund bucks aplenty
	To catch and to release, to lighten their hearts.
	Now it is leased and sold, my sorrow is greater,
	Wasted wilfully, to please your wives.
	Those who would be lords in the land and fine ladies
410	Are now foolish girls of the new fashion, so excessively dressed
	With broad trailing sleeves that sweep to the ground,
	The borders all edged around with ermine –
	That is as hard, I think, to handle in the dark
	As a poor, simple girl who never worked silk.
415	But whoever looks on the face of our Lady of Heaven,[36]
	How she fled for fear far out of her homeland
	On an ambling ass, without any more pride
	Than a child on her breast, and a broken halter
	That Joseph held in his hand to protect her.
420	Although she ruled all of this world, her clothing was poor
	To set an example, and to show others
	How to leave pomp and pride, as poverty often teaches.'
	Then Waster angrily cast up his eyes,
	And said, 'Winner, you wretch, I wonder in my heart
425	What our garments have cost you, wretch, to buy,
	That you should upbraid ladies for their bright clothes,
	Since we guarantee to pay in silver.
	It is proper for a man to provide for his loved one,
	To follow her wishes and thus win her favour.

---

[36] The biblical reference at lines 415–19 is to the flight into Egypt undertaken by the Virgin and St Joseph after the birth of Christ (Matthew 2).

430	Then she will love him truly like her own life,
	Make him bold and eager with swords to smite,
	To avoid ignominy and shame where men are gathered.[37]
	And if my people are finely arrayed, it pleases me all the better
	To see them with my own eyes looking fair and free.
435	And you niggards sleep so soundly at night,
	Snoring as you stretch, raising your buttocks.
	You give orders to wait on the weather, and then curse the time
	That you failed to fit out your buildings and organise your servants.
	Wherefore, Winner, you wrongfully waste your time,
440	Because you will never get a good or happy day.
	At the time of your death the Devil will give away your goods;
	Those you wish to inherit will never have them,
	Your wicked executors will scatter them about,
	And you will have the heat of Hell for what you saved here.[38]
445	You take no heed of a tale that was told long ago.
	I think that man is crazy who worries about winning a mate;
	Have her whom you shall have, and hold her for a while,
	Take the cup as it comes, the chance as it falls,
	For whoever's life is longest is left to fetch
450	Wood that he shall waste to warm his heels
	From further than his father did by fifteen miles.
	Now I can go on no longer; but Sir King, by your troth,
	Tell us where we should be; I think the day is flying.
	My heart is still sore, and it does me harm
455	Ever having in my sight the one that I hate.'
	The king looked kindly at the two men,
	And said, 'Sirs, cease your brawls and your bold speech,
	And I shall decide today where you should be,
	Each man in the land where he is loved most.
460	Winner, wend your way far overseas,
	Pass forth by Paris to the pope of Rome;[39]
	The cardinals know you well, and will keep you in fair estate,
	Making your sides to lie in silken sheets;
	They will feed you and foster you and further your desire,

---

[37] The emphasis on dishonour or shame in aristocratic culture suggests that this line may also refer back to the motto of the Order of the Garter at line 68.

[38] Another reference, as at lines 260–2, to the penalties suffered by the soul as a result of the sin of avarice.

[39] For the significance of the 'pope of Rome', see pp. 117–18.

465 Willing to go mad rather than to anger you at all.
    But look, Sir, by your life, when I send you letters
    That you should hurry home to me by horse or on foot,
    And when I know you intend to come, he shall go away[40]
    And stay with another lord until you take your leave;
470 For though you stay in this town until the day of your death,
    You will never have to walk a single foot with him.
    And you, Waster, I order that you stay
    Where wealth is wasted most, so wing your way there;
    Go forth to Cheapside,[41] and set up a room there,
475 Take care that your window is open wide, and wait there
    Until anyone with a purse passes through the town.
    Take him to the tavern, until he gets drunk,
    Make him drink all night, so that he is dry the next day,
    Then offer him some Cretan wine to comfort him.
480 Bring him to Bread Street,[42] beckon with your finger,
    Show him fat shoulders of mutton,
    "Hot for the hungry", a hen or two.
    Set him softly on a seat, and then send out;
    Bring out of the town the best you may find,
485 And see your servant gets a slap unless he spreads the cloth properly.
    But let him pay before he is allowed to go, and then pick him so clean
    That anyone who finds a penny in his purse be damned.
    When all is drunk and done with, do not tarry,
    But send him out of town, to chase after more.
490 Then pass on to Poultry,[43] where the people know you,
    And direct your buyer to recognise the food you like:
    The herons, the roast meats, the well-served chicken,
    The partridges, the plovers, the other pulled game,
    Bullfinches, ducks, expensive egrets:

---

[40] This and the following five lines are defective in the manuscript; Turville-Petre's edition provides the best hypothetical reconstruction, and his suggestions are generally followed in subsequent editions.

[41] A prominent street in the commercial heartland of medieval London.

[42] Like Cheapside, a major commercial street in the capital.

[43] A third street in the centre of London, named (as the author of *W&W* clearly understands) for its markets selling game birds.

495   The more you waste your money, the better Winner likes it.
       And look to me, Winner, if you want to gain wealth,
       When I go to the wars to lead my men;
       For at the proud walls of great Paris[44]
       I plan to have it done, and dub you to knight,[45]
500   And give great gifts, of gold and of silver,
       To those of my allegiance who love me in their hearts.
       And afterwards, with the knights in my train, follow me
       To the church of Cologne, where the Kings lie ...'[46]

---

[44] Turville-Petre interprets 'pales of Parys' as the Palais de la Cité in the heart of Paris; but the possible reference to the siege of Paris in 1360 (see pp. 32–4) makes the 'pales' more likely an allusion to the city walls.

[45] The poet appears to have forgotten that he had earlier represented both Wynnere and Wastoure as knights: see line 203 and further discussion above, pp. 86–7.

[46] A reference to the shrine of the Magi (the Three Kings) at Cologne Cathedral, for the historical significance of which see above, pp. 32–3. The manuscript breaks off at this point and the extant text is incomplete.

Bibliography

Unpublished primary sources

Kew, The National Archives

E 101   Exchequer, King's Remembrancer: Various Accounts

E 361   Exchequer, Pipe Office: Enrolled Wardrobe and Household Accounts

E 403   Exchequer of Receipt: Issue Rolls

SC 8   Special Collections: Ancient Petitions

London, British Library

Additional MS 31042   Robert Thornton Miscellany

Harley MS 2253   'The Harley Lyrics'

Published primary sources

Barr, Helen (ed.), *The Piers Plowman Tradition* (London, 1993).

Brand, Paul, Seymour Phillips, W. Mark Ormrod, Geoffrey Martin, Chris Given-Wilson, Anne Curry and Rosemary Horrox (eds and trans), *The Parliament Rolls of Medieval England* (16 vols, Woodbridge, 2005).

Brewer, Derek and A. E. B. Owen (eds), *The Thornton Manuscript (Lincoln Cathedral MS 91)* (London, 1977).

Brie, F. W. D. (ed.), *The Brut, or, The Chronicles of England*, EETS, OS 131, 136 (2 vols, London, 1906–8).

Broome, Dorothy M. (ed.), 'The Ransom of John II, King of France, 1360–1370', *Camden Miscellany XIV*, Camden Society, 3rd ser., 37 (London, 1926).

Bunt, G. H. V. (ed.), *William of Palerne: An Alliterative Romance* (Groningen, 1985).

Calendar of the Fine Rolls Preserved in the Public Record Office, 1452–61 (London, 1939).

Calendar of the Patent Rolls Preserved in the Public Record Office, 1350–4 (London, 1907).

Chandos Herald, *La vie du Prince Noir*, ed. D. B. Tyson (Tübingen, 1975).

Chaplais, Pierre, 'Some Documents Regarding the Fulfilment of the Treaty of Brétigny, 1361–1369', in *Camden Miscellany XIX*, Camden Society, 3rd ser., 80 (London, 1952).

Cheney, C. R., *A Handbook of Dates for Students of British History*, new edn, rev. M. Jones (Cambridge, 2000).

Coss, Peter (ed.), *Thomas Wright's Political Songs of England* (Cambridge, 1996).

Dean, James (ed.), *The Simonie* (Kalamazoo, 1996).

Duncan, A. A. M. (ed.), 'A Question about the Succession, 1364', in *Miscellany of the Scottish History Society XII*, Scottish History Society, 5th ser., 7 (Edinburgh, 1994), 1–57.

Fein, Susanna with David Raybin and Jan Ziolkowski (eds and trans.), *The Complete Harley 2253 Manuscript* (3 vols, Kalamazoo, 2015).

Froissart, Jean, *Chroniques*, ed. S. Luce *et al.*, 15 vols (Paris, 1859–1975).

Ginsberg, Warren (ed.), *Wynnere and Wastoure and The Parlement of the Thre Ages* (Kalamazoo, 1992).

Gollancz, Sir Israel (ed. and trans.), *A Good Short Debate between Winner and Waster: An Alliterative Poem on Social and Economic Problems in England in the Year 1352, with Modern English Rendering* (London, 1920; repr. Cambridge, 1974).

Gray, Sir Thomas, *Scalacronica*, ed. and trans. Andy King, Surtees Society 209 (Durham, 2005).

Hall, P. and P. Booth (eds), *The Chester County Court Indictment Roll, 1354–1377: Dealing with Serious Crime in Late Medieval Cheshire*, Chetham Society 3rd series, 53 (2019).

Haydon, Frank S. (ed.), *Eulogium historiarum*, Rolls Series, 9 (3 vols, London, 1858–63).

Horrox, Rosemary (ed. and trans.), *The Black Death* (Manchester, 1994).

Kane, George (ed.), *Piers Plowman: The A Version. Will's Vision of Piers Plowman and Do-Well* (London, 1960).

Knight, Stephen and Thomas Ohlgren (eds), *Robin Hood and Other Outlaw Tales* (Kalamazoo, 1997).

Lancaster, Henry of Grosmont, First Duke of, *The Book of Holy Medicines*, trans. C. J. Batt, The French of England Translation Series, 8 (Tempe, Arizona, 2014).

—— *Le livre de seyntz medicines*, ed. E. J. Arnould, Anglo-Norman Texts, 2 (Oxford, 1940).

Luders, A., *et al.* (eds), *Statutes of the Realm* (11 vols, London, 1810–28).

Lyon, Mary, Bryce Lyon, Henry S. Lucas and Jean de Sturler (eds), *The Wardrobe Book of William de Norwell: 12 July 1338 to 27 May 1340* (Brussels, 1983).

Mandeville, Jean de, *Le livre des merveilles*, ed. Christine Deluz (Paris, 2000).

Martin, Geoffrey (ed. and trans.), *Knighton's Chronicle, 1337–1396* (Oxford, 1995).

Moisant, J. (ed.), *De speculo Regis Edwardi Tertii* (Paris, 1891).

Myers, A. R. (ed.), *The Household of Edward IV: The Black Book and the Ordinance of 1478* (Manchester, 1959).

Nederman, Cary J. and K. L. Forhan (eds and trans.), *Medieval Political Theory – A Reader: The Quest for the Body Politic, 1100–1400* (London, 1993).

Ormrod, W. Mark, Helen Killick and Phil Bradford (eds), *Early Common Petitions in the English Parliament, c.1290–c.1420*, Camden Society, 5th ser., 52 (Cambridge, 2017).

Preest, David (trans.), *The Chronicle of Geoffrey le Baker of Swinbrook* (Woodbridge, 2012).

Register of Edward the Black Prince (4 vols, London, 1930–3).

Rymer, Thomas (ed.), *Foedera, conventiones, literae et cujuscunque generi acta publica* (3 vols in 6 parts, London, 1816–30).

Sayles, G. O. (ed. and trans.), *Select Cases in the Court of King's Bench, Edward I–Richard III*, ed. G. O. Sayles, Selden Society 55, 57, 58, 74, 76, 82, 88 (7 vols, London, 1936–71).

Scott-Stokes, Charity and Chris Given-Wilson (eds and trans.), *Chronicon Anonymi Cantuariensis: The Chronicle of Anonymous of Canterbury, 1346–1365* (Oxford, 2008).

Tait, James (ed.), *Chronica Johannis de Reading et Anonymi Cantuariensis* (Manchester, 1914).

Thompson, Edmund Maunde (ed.), *Adae Murimuth, Continuatio chronicarum. Robertus de Avesbury, De gestis mirabilibus Regis Edwardi Tertii*, ed. Edmund Maunde Thompson, Rolls Series, 93 (London, 1889).

—— (ed.), *Chronicon Galfridi le Baker de Swynebroke* (Oxford, 1889).

Thompson, John J. (ed.), *Robert Thornton and the London Thornton Manuscript: British Library MS Additional 31042* (Cambridge, 1987).

Tolkien, J. R. R. and E. V. Gordon (eds), *Sir Gawain and the Green Knight* (Oxford, 1967).

Trigg, Stephanie (ed.), *Wynnere and Wastoure*, EETS OS 297 (Oxford, 1990).

Turville-Petre, Thorlac (ed.), *Alliterative Poetry of the Later Middle Ages: An Anthology* (Washington, DC, 1989).

—— (ed.), 'An Anthology of Medieval Poems and Drama', in *Medieval Literature: Chaucer and the Alliterative Tradition*, ed. Brian Ford, rev. ed. (Harmondsworth, 1982), pp. 387–602.

Tyrrell, Edward and Nicholas Harris Nicolas (eds), *A Chronicle of London from 1089 to 1483* (London, 1827).

Vaughan, Míceál F. (ed.), *Piers Plowman: The A Version* (Baltimore, 2011).

Viard, J. and E. Déprez (eds), *Chronique de Jean le Bel* (2 vols, Paris, 1904–5).

Walsingham, Thomas, *Chronicon Angliae*, ed. Edward Maunde Thompson, Rolls Series, 64 (London, 1874).

—— *Historia Anglicana*, ed. Henry T. Riley, Rolls Series, 28 (2 vols, London, 1863–4).

Wright, Thomas (ed.), *Political Poems and Songs Relating to English History*, Rolls Series, 14 (2 vols, London, 1859–61).

Published secondary sources

Aberth, John, *Criminal Churchmen in the Reign of Edward III: The Case of Bishop Thomas de Lisle* (University Park, Pennsylvania, 1996).

Anderson, Jesse May, 'A Note on the Date of *Winnere and Wastere*', *Modern Language Notes*, 43 (1928), 47–9.

Andre, Elsbeth, *Ein Königshof auf Reisen: Der Kontinentaufenthalt Eduards III von England, 1338–40* (Cologne, 1996).

Anon., 'What Was a Cote Armure? A Surcoat? And a Tabard?', *The Herald and Genealogist*, 1 (1863), 235–58.

Anstis, John, *The Register of the Most Noble Order of the Garter* (2 vols, London, 1724).

Astell, Ann W., *Political Allegory in Late Medieval England* (London, 1999).

Astill, Grenville, 'Windsor in the Context of Medieval Berkshire', in Laurence Keen and Eileen Scarff (eds), *Windsor: Medieval Archaeology, Art and Architecture of the Thames Valley*, British Archaeological Association Conference Transactions, 25 (Leeds, 2002), pp. 1–14.

Autrand, Françoise, 'The Peacemakers and the State: Pontifical Diplomacy and the Anglo-French Conflict in the Fourteenth Century', in *War and Competition between States*, ed. Philippe Contamine (Oxford, 2000), pp. 249–77.

Ayton, Andrew, 'Armies and Military Communities in Fourteenth-Century England', in Peter R. Coss and Christopher Tyerman (eds), *Soldiers, Nobles and Gentlemen: Essays in Honour of Maurice Keen* (Woodbridge, 2009), pp. 215–39.

—— 'Edward III and the English Aristocracy at the Beginning of the Hundred Years War', in Matthew Strickland (ed.), *Armies, Chivalry and Warfare in Medieval Britain and France* (Stamford, 1998), pp. 173–206.

—— 'English Armies in the Fourteenth Century', in Anne Curry and Michael Hughes (eds), *Arms, Armies and Fortifications in the Hundred Years War* (Woodbridge, 1994), pp. 21–38.

—— *Knights and Warhorses: Military Service and the English Aristocracy under Edward III* (Woodbridge, 1994).

Bailey, Mark, *The Decline of Serfdom in Late Medieval England: From Bondage to Freedom* (Woodbridge, 2014).

—— 'Historiographical Essay: The Commercialisation of the English Economy, 1086–1500', *Journal of Medieval History*, 24 (1998), 297–311.

—— 'Introduction: England in the Age of the Black Death', in Mark Bailey (ed.), *Town and Countryside in the Age of the Black Death: Essays in Honour of John Hatcher* (Turnhout, 2012), pp. xix–xxxvii.

—— 'Sir John de Wingfield and the Foundation of Wingfield College', in Peter Bloore and Edward Martin (eds), *Wingfield College and its Patrons: Piety and Prestige in Medieval Suffolk* (Woodbridge, 2015), pp. 31–48.

Baker, Denise M., 'Meed and the Economics of Chivalry in *Piers Plowman*', in Denise M. Baker (ed.), *Inscribing the Hundred Years' War in French and English Cultures* (Albany, New York, 2000), pp. 55–72.

Baker, John H., *An Introduction to English Legal History*, 4th edn (Oxford, 2007).

Baker, R. L., *The English Customs Service, 1307–43: A Study of Medieval Administration* (Philadelphia, 1961).

—— 'The Government of Calais in 1363', in William Chester Jordan, Bruce McNab and Teofilio F. Ruiz (eds), *Order and Innovation in the Middle Ages: Essays in Honor of Joseph R. Strayer* (Princeton, 1976), pp. 207–14.

Baldwin, Anna P., 'The Historical Context', in John Alford (ed.), *A Companion to* Piers Plowman (Berkeley, California, 1988), pp. 67–86.

Baldwin, Frances Elizabeth, *Sumptuary Legislation and Personal Regulation in England* (Baltimore, 1926).

Barber, Richard, *Edward III and the Triumph of England: The Battle of Crécy and the Company of the Garter* (London, 2013).

—— *Magnificence and Princely Splendour in the Middle Ages* (Woodbridge, 2020).

Barker, Juliet, *The Tournament in England, 1100–1400* (Woodbridge, 1986).

Barnie, John, *War in Medieval English Society: Social Values and the Hundred Years War* (London, 1974).

Barr, Helen, *Socioliterary Practice in Late Medieval England* (Oxford, 2001).

Barrell, A. D. M., 'The Ordinance of Provisors of 1343', *Historical Research*, 63 (1991), 264–77.

Barron, Caroline, 'Chivalry, Pageantry and Merchant Culture in Medieval London', in Peter R. Coss and Maurice Keen (eds), *Heraldry, Pageantry and Social Display in Medieval England* (Woodbridge, 2002), pp. 219–41.

Bellamy, J. G., *Crime and Public Order in England in the Later Middle Ages* (London, 1973).

—— *The Law of Treason in England in the Later Middle Ages* (Cambridge, 1970).

—— 'Sir John de Annesley and the Chandos Inheritance', *Nottingham Mediaeval Studies*, 10 (1966), 94–106.

Bellis, Joanna, *The Hundred Years War in Literature, 1337–1600* (Cambridge, 2016).

Beltz, George Frederick, *Memorials of the Most Noble Order of the Garter* (London, 1841).

Bennett, J. A. W., 'The Date of the A-Text of *Piers Plowman*', *PMLA*, 58 (1943), 566–72.

Bennett, Michael J., 'Careerism in Late Medieval England', in Joel Rosenthal and Colin Richmond (eds), *People, Politics and Community in the Later Middle Ages* (Gloucester, 1987), pp. 19–39.

—— *Community, Class and Careerism: Cheshire and Lancashire Society in the Age of* Sir Gawain and the Green Knight (Cambridge, 1983).

—— 'The Court of Richard II and the Promotion of Literature', in Barbara A. Hanawalt (ed.), *Chaucer's England: Literature in Historical Context* (Minneapolis, 1992), pp. 3–20.

—— '*Sir Gawain and the Green Knight* and the Literary Achievement of the North-West Midlands: The Historical Background', *Journal of Medieval History*, 5 (1979), 63–88.

—— 'Mandeville's *Travels* and the Anglo-French Moment', *Medium Aevum*, 75 (2006), 273–92.

Benson, C. David, *Public Piers Plowman: Modern Scholarship and Late Medieval English Culture* (University Park, Pennsylvania, 2003).

Berard, Christopher, 'Edward III's Abandoned Order of the Round Table', in Elizabeth Archibald and David F. Johnson (eds), *Arthurian Literature XXIX* (Cambridge, 2012), pp. 1–40.

Bernheimer, Richard, *Wild Men in the Middle Ages* (Cambridge, Massachusetts, 1952).

Bestul, Thomas H., *Satire and Allegory in* Wynnere and Wastoure (Lincoln, Nebraska, 1974).

Biddle, Martin *et al.*, *King Arthur's Round Table: An Archaeological Investigation* (Woodbridge, 2000).

Blandeau, Agnès, 'Wynnere and Wastoure, a 14th-Century Alliterative Poem at the Crossroads of Fact and Fiction', *Caliban: French Journal of English Studies*, 33 (2013), 133–52.

Bolton, J. L., '"The World Upside Down": Plague as an Agent of Economic and Social Change', in W. Mark Ormrod and Phillip G. Lindley (eds), *The Black Death in England, 1348–1500* (Stamford, 1996), pp. 17–78.

Bombi, Barbara, *Anglo-Papal Relations in the Early Fourteenth Century: A Study in Medieval Diplomacy* (Oxford, 2019).

Bonney, Richard and W. Mark Ormrod, 'Introduction. Crises, Revolutions and Self-Sustained Growth: Towards a Conceptual Model of Change in Fiscal History', in W. Mark Ormrod, Margaret Bonney and Richard Bonney (eds), *Crises, Revolutions and Self-Sustained Growth: Essays in European Fiscal History, 1130–1830* (Stamford, 1999), pp. 1–21.

Booth, P. H. W., *The Financial Administration of the Lordship and County of Chester, 1272–1377*, Chetham Society, 3rd ser., 28 (Manchester, 1981).

—— 'Taxation and Public Order: Cheshire in 1353', *Northern History*, 12 (1976), 16–31.

Boulton, D'Arcy Jonathan Dacre, *The Knights of the Crown: The Monarchical Orders of Knighthood in Later Medieval Europe, 1325–1520* (Woodbridge, 1987).

Boyle, Leonard E., 'William of Pagula and the *Speculum Regis Edwardi III*', *Mediaeval Studies*, 32 (1970), 329–36.

Bradley, Henry, 'Wynnere and Wastoure', *The Athenaeum*, 120, no. 3943 (23 May 1903), 657–8.

—— '"Wynnere and Wastoure"', *The Athenaeum*, 120, no. 3948 (27 June 1903), 816–17.

Braid, Robert, 'Behind the Ordinance of Labourers: Economic Regulation and Market Control in London before the Black Death', *Journal of Legal History*, 34 (2013), 3–30.

Breen, Katharine, 'The Need for Allegory: *Wynnere and Wastoure* as an *Ars poetica*', *Yearbook of Langland Studies*, 26 (2012), 187–229.

Britnell, R. H., *The Commercialisation of English Society, 1000–1500*, 2nd edn (Manchester, 1997).

—— 'English Agricultural Output and Prices, 1350–1450: National Trends and Regional Divergences', in Ben Dodds and Richard H. Britnell (eds), *Agriculture and Rural Society after the Black Death: Common Themes and Regional Variations* (Hatfield, 2008), pp. 20–39.

—— 'Price-Setting in English Borough Markets, 1349–1500', *Canadian Journal of History*, 31 (1996), 1–15.

Britton, C. E., *A Meteorological Chronology to A.D. 1450* (London, 1937).

Broadberry, Stephen, Bruce M. S. Campbell, Alexander Klein, Mark Overton and Bas van Leeuwen, *British Economic Growth, 1270–1870* (Cambridge, 2015).

Brown, Warren C., *Violence in Medieval Europe* (London, 2011).

Brumble, H. David, *Classical Myths and Legends in the Middle Ages and Renaissance: A Dictionary of Allegorical Meanings* (London, 1998).

Bryant, Brantley L., 'Talking with the Taxman about Poetry: England's Economy in "Against the King's Taxes" and *Wynnere and Wastoure*', *Studies in Medieval and Renaissance History*, 3rd ser., 5 (2008), 219–48.

Bunt, Gerrit H. V., 'Localizing *William of Palerne*', in Jacek Fisiak (ed.), *Historical Linguistics and Philology* (Berlin, 1990), pp. 73–106.

Burrow, J. A., *The Ages of Man: A Study in Medieval Writing and Thought* (Oxford, 1986).

—— 'The Audience of *Piers Plowman*', *Anglia*, 75 (1957), 373–84.

—— 'Winning and Wasting in *Wynnere and Wastoure* and *Piers Plowman*', in Carol M. Meale and Derek Pearsall (eds), *Makers and Users of Medieval Books: Essays in Honour of A. S. G. Edwards* (Cambridge, 2014), pp. 1–12.

Butterfield, Ardis, *The Familiar Enemy: Chaucer, Language, and Nation in the Hundred Years War* (Oxford, 2009).

Campbell, Bruce M. S., *The Great Transition: Climate, Disease and Society in the Late Medieval World* (Cambridge, 2016).

—— and Cormac Ó Gráda, 'Harvest Shortfalls, Grain Prices, and Famines in Preindustrial England', *Journal of Economic History*, 71 (2011), 859–86.

—— 'The Land', in Rosemary Horrox and W. Mark Ormrod (eds), *A Social History of England, 1200–1500* (Cambridge, 2006), pp. 179–237.

Candy, Christopher A., 'A Growing Trust: Edward III and his Household Knights, 1330–1340', in L. J. Andrew Villalon and Donald J. Kagay (eds), *The Hundred Years War, III: Further Considerations* (Leiden, 2013), pp. 49–62.

Carlson, David R., *John Gower, Poetry and Propaganda in Fourteenth-Century England* (Cambridge, 2012).

Carpenter, Christine, 'Bastard Feudalism in England in the Fourteenth Century', in Steve Boardman and Julian Goodare (eds), *Kings, Lords and Men in Scotland and Britain, 1300–1625: Essays in Honour of Jenny Wormald* (Edinburgh, 2014), pp. 59–92.

Carus-Wilson, Eleanor and Olive Coleman, *England's Export Trade, 1275–1547* (Oxford, 1963).

Catto, Jeremy, 'Religion and the English Nobility in the Later Fourteenth Century', in Hugh Lloyd-Jones, Valerie Pearl and Blair Worden (eds),

History and Imagination: Essays in Honour of H. R. Trevor-Roper (London, 1981), pp. 43–55.

Cheyette, F., 'Kings, Courts, Cures, and Sinecures: The Statute of Provisors and the Common Law', *Traditio*, 19 (1963), 295–349.

Childs, Wendy R., 'Government and Market in the Early Fourteenth Century', in Rémy Ambühl, James Bothwell and Laura Tompkins (eds), *Ruling Fourteenth-Century England: Essays in Honour of Christopher Given-Wilson* (Woodbridge, 2019), pp. 37–57.

Chism, Christine, 'Alliterative Revival', in Michael D. C. Drout (ed.), *J. R. R. Tolkien Encyclopedia: Scholarship and Critical Assessment* (Abingdon, 2007), pp. 9–10.

—— *Alliterative Revivals* (Philadelphia, 2002).

Clanchy, M. T., 'Law and Love in the Middle Ages', in J. A. Bossy (ed.), *Disputes and Settlements: Law and Human Relations in the West* (Cambridge, 1983), pp. 47–67.

Coleman, Janet, *English Literature in History, 1350–1400: Medieval Readers and Writers* (London, 1981).

Coleman, Joyce, 'The Complaint of the Makers: *Wynnere and Wastoure* and the "Misperformance Topos" in Medieval England', in Evelyn Birge Vitz, Nancy Freeman Regalado and Marilyn Lawrence (eds), *Performing Medieval Narrative* (Cambridge, 2005), pp. 27–40.

Collins, Hugh E. L., *The Order of the Garter, 1348–1461: Chivalry and Politics in Late Medieval England* (Oxford, 2000).

Conlee, John W., *Middle English Debate Poetry: A Critical Anthology* (East Lansing, Michigan, 1991).

Cooke, W. G., '*Sir Gawain and the Green Knight*: A Restored Dating', *Medium Aevum*, 58 (1989), 34–48.

—— and D'A. J. D. Boulton, '*Sir Gawain and the Green Knight*: A Poem for Henry of Grosmont?', *Medium Aevum*, 68 (1999), 42–54.

Coote, Lesley A., *Prophecy and Public Affairs in Later Medieval England* (York, 2000).

Cornelius, Ian, *Reconstructing Alliterative Verse: The Pursuit of a Medieval Metre* (Cambridge, 2011).

Coss, Peter R., *The Origins of the English Gentry* (Cambridge, 2003).

Davies, R. G., 'Edington, William', in 'Oxford Dictionary of National Biography' (online): https://doi-org/10.1093/ref:odnb/8481 (accessed 20 April 2020).

Davis, James, *Medieval Market Morality: Life, Law and Ethics in the English Marketplace, 1200–1500* (Cambridge, 2012).

Dawson, James Doyne, 'Richard FitzRalph and the Fourteenth-Century Poverty Controversies', *Journal of Ecclesiastical History*, 34 (1983), 315–44.

Delachenal, R., *Histoire de Charles V* (5 vols, Paris, 1909–31).

Denny-Brown, Andrea, *Fashioning Change: The Trope of Clothing in High- and Late-Medieval England* (Columbus, Ohio, 2012).

Déprez, E., 'La conference d'Avignon, 1344: L'arbitrage pontifical entre la France et l'Angleterre', in A. G. Little and F. M. Powicke (eds), *Essays in Medieval History Presented to Thomas Frederick Tout* (Manchester, 1925), pp. 301–20.

Dodd, Gwilym, 'A Parliament Full of Rats? *Piers Plowman* and the Good Parliament of 1376', *Historical Research*, 79 (2006), 21–49.

—— 'Was Thomas Favent a Political Pamphleteer? Faction and Politics in Later Fourteenth-Century London', *Journal of Medieval History*, 37 (2011), 397–418.

Du Boulay, F. R. H., *An Age of Ambition: English Society in the Late Middle Ages* (New York, 1970).

Dutton, Elisabeth, with John Hines and R. F. Yeager (eds), *John Gower, Trilingual Poet: Language, Translation and Tradition* (Cambridge, 2010).

Dyer, Christopher, 'Changes in Diet in the Late Middle Ages: The Case of the Harvest Workers', *Agricultural History Review*, 36 (1988), 22–37.

—— *Standards of Living in the Later Middle Ages: Social Change in England, c.1200–1520* (Cambridge, 1989).

—— 'Work Ethics in the Fourteenth Century', in James S. Bothwell, P. J. P. Goldberg and W. Mark Ormrod (eds), *The Problem of Labour in Fourteenth-Century England* (York, 2000), pp. 21–41.

Edwards, J. G., *The Second Century of the English Parliament* (Oxford, 1979).

Elliott, Ralph W. V., 'The Topography of *Wynnere and Wastoure*', *English Studies*, 48 (1967), 134–40.

Emden, Alfred B., *A Survey of Dominicans in England* (Rome, 1967).

Faith, R. J., 'The "Great Rumour" of 1377 and Peasant Ideology', in R. H. Hilton and T. H. Aston (eds), *The English Rising of 1381* (Cambridge, 1981), pp. 43–73.

Farmer, David L., 'Prices and Wages, 1350–1500', in Edward Miller (ed.), *The Agrarian History of England and Wales III: 1348–1500* (Cambridge, 1991), pp. 431–525.

Fletcher, Christopher D., 'Corruption at Court: Crisis and the Theme of *luxuria* in England and France, c.1340–1422', in Stephen Gunn and Antheun Janse (eds), *The Court as a Stage: England and the Low Countries in the Late Middle Ages* (Woodbridge, 2006), pp. 28–38.

Flood, Victoria, *Prophecy, Politics and Place in Medieval England: From Geoffrey of Monmouth to Thomas of Erceldoune* (Cambridge, 2016).

—— '*Wynnere and Wastoure* and the Influence of Political Prophecy', *Chaucer Review*, 49 (2015), 427–48.

Fowler, Kenneth, *The King's Lieutenant: Henry of Grosmont, First Duke of Lancaster, 1310–1361* (New York, 1969).

Fryde, E. B., *Studies in Medieval Trade and Finance* (London, 1983).

—— *William de la Pole, Merchant and King's Banker* (London, 1988).

—— and Natalie M. Fryde, 'Peasant Rebellion and Peasant Discontents', in Edward Miller (ed.), *The Agrarian History of England and Wales III: 1348–1500* (Cambridge, 1991), pp. 744–819.

Fryde, Natalie M., 'Edward III's Removal of his Ministers and Judges, 1340–1', *Bulletin of the Institute of Historical Research*, 48 (1975), 149–61.

—— 'A Medieval Robber Baron: Sir John Molyns of Stoke Poges, Buckinghamshire', in R. F. Hunnisett and J. B. Post (eds), *Medieval Legal Records Edited in Memory of C. A. F. Meekings* (London, 1978), pp. 197–221.

Galloway, Andrew, 'London, Southwark, Westminster', in David Wallace (ed.), *Europe: A Literary History* (2 vols, Oxford, 2016).

—— *The Penn Commentary on* Piers Plowman, *I: C Prologue-Passus 4; B Prologue-Passus 4; A Prologue-Passus 4* (Philadelphia, 2006).

Giancarlo, Matthew, '*Piers Plowman*, Parliament, and the Public Voice', *Yearbook of Langland Studies*, 17 (2003), 135–74.

Given-Wilson, Chris, 'The Merger of Edward III and Queen Philippa's Households, 1360–9', *Bulletin of the Institute of Historical Research*, 51 (1978), 183–7.

—— 'Purveyance for the Royal Household, 1362–1413', *Bulletin of the Institute of Historical Research*, 56 (1983), 145–63.

—— *The Royal Household and the King's Affinity: Service, Politics and Finance in England, 1360–1413* (London, 1986).

—— and Françoise Bériac, 'Edward III's Prisoners of War: The Battle of Poitiers and its Context', *English Historical Review*, 116 (2001), 802–33.

Goddard, Richard, 'The Merchant', in Stephen H. Rigby, with the assistance of Alastair J. Minnis (eds), *Historians on Chaucer: The 'General Prologue' to the* Canterbury Tales (Oxford, 2014), pp. 170–86.

Godden, Malcolm, *The Making of Piers Plowman* (London, 1990).

Goldberg, P. J. P., *Medieval England: A Social History, 1250–1550* (London, 2004).

Gollancz, Israel, 'A Note on "Wynnere and Wastoure"', *The Athenaeum*, 118, no. 3852 (24 August 1901), 254–5.

—— 'A Note on "Wynnere and Wastoure"', *The Athenaeum*, 118, no. 3855 (14 September 1901), 351.

Goodall, John A., 'Some Aspects of Heraldry and the Role of Heralds in Relation to the Ceremonies of the Late Medieval and Early Tudor Court', *Antiquaries Journal*, 82 (2002), 69–91.

Gransden, Antonia, *Historical Writing in England, II: c.1307 to the Early Sixteenth Century* (London, 1996).

Gras, N. S. B., *The Early English Customs System*, Harvard Economic Studies, 18 (Cambridge, Massachusetts, 1918).

Grassi, J. L., 'Royal Clerks from the Archdiocese of York in the Fourteenth Century', *Northern History*, 5 (1970), 12–33.

Graves, E. B., 'The Legal Significance of the Statute of Praemunire', in Charles H. Taylor (ed.), *Anniversary Essays Presented to C. H. Haskins* (New York, 1929), pp. 57–80.

Green, David, 'The Military Personnel of Edward the Black Prince', *Medieval Prosopography*, 21 (2000), 133–52.

Green, Richard Firth, *A Crisis of Truth: Literature and Law in Ricardian England* (Philadelphia, 1999).

—— 'John Ball's Letters: Literary History and Historical Literature', in Barbara A. Hanawalt (ed.), *Chaucer's England: Literature in Historical Context* (Minneapolis, 1992), pp. 176–200.

—— *Poets and Princepleasers: Literature and the English Court in the Late Middle Ages* (Toronto, 1980).

Grummitt, David and Jean-Françoise Lassalmonie, 'Royal Public Finance (*c.*1290–1523)', in Christopher Fletcher, Jean-Philippe Genet and John Watts (eds), *Government and Political Life in England and France, c.1300–c.1500* (Cambridge, 2015), pp. 116–49.

Hamilton, J. S., 'A Reassessment of the Loyalty of the Household Knights of Edward II', in W. Mark Ormrod (ed.), *Fourteenth Century England VII* (Woodbridge, 2012), pp. 47–72.

Hanna, Ralph, 'Alliterative Poetry', in David Wallace (ed.), *The Cambridge History of Medieval English Literature* (Cambridge, 1999), pp. 488–512.

—— 'The Growth of Robert Thornton's Books', *Studies in Bibliography*, 40 (1987), 51–61.

—— *London Literature, 1300–1380* (Cambridge, 2005).

—— *Pursuing History: Middle English Manuscripts and their Texts* (Stanford, 1996).

—— *Yorkshire Writers*, Sir Israel Gollancz Memorial Lecture [British Academy] (London, 2002).

Harrington, David V., 'Indeterminacy in *Winner and Waster* and *The Parliament of the Three Ages*', *Chaucer Review*, 20 (1986), 246–57.

Harriss, G. L., 'Budgeting at the Medieval Exchequer', in Chris Given-Wilson, Ann J. Kettle and Len Scales (eds), *War, Government and Aristocracy in the British Isles, c.1150–1500: Essays in Honour of Michael Prestwich* (Woodbridge, 2008), pp. 179–96.

—— *King, Parliament and Public Finance in Medieval England to 1369* (Oxford, 1975).

—— *Shaping the Nation: England, 1360–1461* (Oxford, 2005).

Harvey, Barbara F., 'Introduction: The Crisis of the Early Fourteenth Century', in Bruce M. S. Campbell (ed.), *Before the Black Death: Studies in the 'Crisis' of the Early Fourteenth Century* (Manchester, 1991), pp. 1–24.

Harvey, Katherine, *Episcopal Appointments in England, c.1214–1344: From Episcopal Election to Papal Provision* (Abingdon, 2016).

Harwood, Britton J., 'Anxious over Peasants: Textual Disorder in *Winner and Waster*', *Journal of Medieval and Early Modern Studies*, 36 (2006), 291–319.

—— 'The Displacement of Labor in *Winner and Waster*', in Kellie Robertson and Michael Uebel (eds), *The Middle Ages at Work: Practicing Labor in Late Medieval England* (New York, 2004), pp. 157–77.

Hatcher, John, 'England in the Aftermath of the Black Death', *Past & Present*, 144 (1994), 3–35.

—— 'The Great Slump of the Mid-Fifteenth Century', in Richard Britnell and John Hatcher (eds), *Progress and Problems in Medieval England: Essays in Honour of Edward Miller* (Cambridge, 1996), pp. 237–72.

—— and Mark Bailey, *Modelling the Middle Ages: The History and Theory of England's Economic Development* (Oxford, 2001).

Havely, N. R., 'The Dominicans and their Banner in *Wynnere and Wastoure*', *Notes & Queries*, 30:3 (June 1983), 207–9.

Hazell, Dinah, *Poverty in Late Medieval English Literature: The Meene and the Riche* (Dublin, 2009).

Hefferan, Matthew, 'Edward III's Household Knights and the Crécy Campaign of 1346', *Historical Research*, 92 (2019), 24–49.

—— 'Family, Loyalty and the Royal Household in the Fourteenth Century', in David Green and Chris Given-Wilson (eds), *Fourteenth Century England XI* (Woodbridge, 2019), pp. 129–54.

Hersh, Cara, '"Wyse wordes withinn": Private Property and Public Knowledge in *Wynnere and Wastoure*', *Modern Philology*, 107 (2010), 507–27.

Hexter, J. H., *Reappraisals in History*, 2nd edn (London, 1979).

Hicks, Michael A., *Bastard Feudalism* (London, 1995).

Hilton, R. H., 'Peasant Movements in England before 1381', *Economic History Review*, 2nd ser., 2 (1949), 117–36.

Holmes, George, *The Good Parliament* (Oxford, 1975).

Horobin, Simon, '"In London and *opeland*": The Dialect and Circulation of the C Version of *Piers Plowman*', *Medium Aevum*, 74 (2005), 248–69.

Horrox, Rosemary, *The de la Poles of Hull*, East Yorkshire Local History Series, 38 (Beverley, 1983).

—— 'The Urban Gentry in the Fifteenth Century', in John A. F. Thomson (ed.), *Towns and Townspeople in the Fifteenth Century* (Gloucester, 1988), pp. 22–44.

Hoskin, Philippa M., 'Authors of Bureaucracy: Developing and Creating Administrative Systems in English Episcpoal Chanceries in the Second Half of the Thirteenth Century', in Paul Binski and Elizabeth A. New (eds), *Patrons and Professionals in the Middle Ages: Proceedings of the 2010 Harlaxton Symposium* (Donington, 2012), pp. 61–78.

—— 'Continuing Service: The Episcopal Households of Thirteenth-Century Durham', in Philippa M. Hoskin, C. N. L. Brooke and R. Barrie Dobson (eds), *The Foundations of Medieval English Ecclesiastical History: Studies Presented to David Smith* (Woodbridge, 2005), pp. 124–38.

Hulbert, J. R., 'The Problems of Authorship and the Date of *Wynnere and Wastoure*', *Modern Philology*, 18 (1920), 31–40.

Hunt, Alan, *Governance of the Consuming Passions: A History of Sumptuary Law* (Basingstoke, 1996).

Huppé, B. F., 'The A-Text of *Piers Plowman* and the Norman Wars', *PMLA*, 54 (1939), 37–55.

Husband, Timothy, *The Wild Man: Medieval Myth and Symbolism* (New York, 1980).

Ingledew, Francis, Sir Gawain and the Green Knight *and the Order of the Garter* (Notre Dame, 2006).

Jacobs, Nicolas, 'The Typology of Debate and the Interpretation of *Wynnere and Wastoure*', *Review of English Studies*, new ser., 36 (1985), 481–500.

James, Jerry D., 'The Undercutting of Conventions in *Wynnere and Wastoure*', *Modern Language Quarterly*, 25 (1964), 243–58.

Johnson, Eleanor, 'The Poetics of Waste: Medieval English Ecocriticism', *PMLA*, 127 (2012), 460–76.

Johnston, Michael, *Romance and the Gentry in Late Medieval England* (Oxford, 2014).

—— 'Thornton Manuscripts', in Siân Echard and Robert Rouse (eds), *The Encyclopaedia of Medieval Literature in Britain* (4 vols, Chichester, 2017), vol. 4, pp. 1785–9.

Jones, W. R., 'Relations of the Two Jurisdictions: Conflict and Cooperation in England during the Thirteenth and Fourteenth Centuries', *Studies in Medieval and Renaissance History*, orig. ser., 7 (1979), 102–32.

Justice, Steven, *Writing and Rebellion: England in 1381* (Berkeley, California, 1994).

Kaeuper, Richard W., *Chivalry and Violence in Medieval Europe* (Woodbridge, 2001).

—— 'An Historian's Reading of the *Tale of Gamelyn*', *Medium Aevum*, 52 (1983), 51–62.

—— 'Private War', in William W. Kibler, Grover A. Zinn, Lawrence Earp and John Bell Henneman, Jr. (eds), *Medieval France: An Encyclopedia* (New York, 1995), p. 760.

—— *War, Justice, and Public Order: England and France in the Later Middle Ages* (Oxford, 1988).

Kane, George, 'The Text', in John Alford (ed.), *A Companion to* Piers Plowman (Berkeley, California, 1988), pp. 175–200.

Keen, Maurice H., *English Society in the Later Middle Ages, 1348–1500* (London, 1990).

—— 'The Jurisdiction and Origins of the Constable's Court', in J. Gillingham and J. C. Holt (eds), *War and Government in the Middle Ages: Essays in Honour of J. O. Prestwich* (Woodbridge, 1984), pp. 159–69.

—— *The Laws of War in the Late Middle Ages* (London, 1965).

—— 'Treason Trials under the Law of Arms', *Transactions of the Royal Historical Society*, 5th ser., 12 (1962), 85–103.

Keiser, George R., 'Lincoln Cathedral Library MS 91: The Life and Milieu of the Scribe', *Studies in Bibliography*, 32 (1979), 158–79.

—— 'More Light on the Life and Milieu of Robert Thornton', *Studies in Bibliography*, 36 (1983), 111–19.

—— 'Robert Thornton: Gentleman, Reader and Scribe', in Susanna Fein and Michael Johnston (eds), *Robert Thornton and his Books: Essays on the Lincoln and London Thornton Manuscripts* (York, 2014), pp. 67–108.

Kerby-Fulton, Kathryn, 'Langland and the Bibliographic Ego', in Steven Justice and Kathryn Kerby-Fulton (eds), *Written Work: Langland, Labor, and Authorship* (Philadelphia, 1997), pp. 67–142.

King, Andy, 'False Traitors or Worthy Knights? Treason and Rebellion against Edward II in the *Scalacronica* and the Anglo-Norman Prose *Brut* Chronicles', *Historical Research*, 88 (2015), 34–47.

—— 'War and Peace: A Knight's Tale. The Ethics of War in Sir Thomas Gray's *Scalacronica*', in Chris Given-Wilson, Ann J. Kettle and Len Scales (eds), *War, Government and Aristocracy in the British Isles, c.1150–1500: Essays in Honour of Michael Prestwich* (Woodbridge, 2008), pp. 148–62.

—— '"War", "Rebellion" or "Perilous Times"? Political Taxonomy and the Conflict in England, 1321–2', in Rémy Ambühl, James Bothwell and Laura Tompkins (eds), *Ruling Fourteenth-Century England: Essays in Honour of Christopher Given-Wilson* (Woodbridge, 2019), pp. 113–32.

Kirby, J. L., 'The Issues of the Lancastrian Exchequer and Lord Cromwell's Estimates of 1433', *Bulletin of the Institute of Historical Research*, 24 (1951), 121–51.

Knapp, Ethan, *The Bureaucratic Muse: Thomas Hoccleve and the Literature of Late Medieval England* (University Park, Pennsylvania, 2001).

Kowaleski, Maryanne, 'A Consumer Economy', in Rosemary Horrox and W. Mark Ormrod (eds), *A Social History of England, 1200–1500* (Cambridge, 2006), pp. 238–59.

Lacey, Helen, *The Royal Pardon: Access to Mercy in Fourteenth-Century England* (York, 2009).

Lachaud, Frédérique, 'Dress and Social Status in England before the Sumptuary Laws', in Peter R. Coss and Maurice Keen (eds), *Heraldry, Pageantry and Social Display in Medieval England* (Woodbridge, 2002), pp. 105–23.

Lampe, David, 'The Satiric Strategy of *Pierce the Ploughman's Crede*', in Bernard S. Levy and Paul E. Szarmach (eds), *The Alliterative Tradition in the Fourteenth Century* (Kent, Ohio, 1981), pp. 69–80.

Lawton, David, A., 'Literary History and Scholarly Fancy: The Date of Two Middle English Alliterative Poems', *Parergon*, orig. ser., 18 (1977), 17–25.

—— 'The Unity of Middle English Alliterative Poetry', *Speculum*, 58 (1983), 72–94.

Le Patourel, John, *Feudal Empires: Norman and Plantagenet* (London, 1984).

Lewis, Katherine, *Kingship and Masculinity in Late Medieval England* (London, 2013).

Little, A. G., 'A Royal Inquiry into Property Held by the Mendicant Friars in England in 1349 and 1350', in J. G. Edwards, V. H. Galbraith and E. F. Jacobs (eds), *Historical Essays in Honour of James Tait* (Manchester, 1933), pp. 179–88.

Lloyd, T. H., *The English Wool Trade in the Middle Ages* (Cambridge, 1977).

Lowe, Ben, *Imagining Peace: A History of Early English Pacifist Ideas, 1340–1560* (Philadelphia, 1997).

Lyon, Bryce D., *From Fief to Indenture: The Transition to Non-Feudal Contracts in Western Europe* (Cambridge, Massachusetts, 1956).

McFarlane, Kenneth Bruce, *The Nobility of Late Medieval England* (Oxford, 1973).

McIntosh, Angus, 'The Textual Transmission of the Alliterative *Morte Arthure*', in Norman Davies and C. L. Wrenn (eds), *English and Medieval Studies Presented to J. R. R. Tolkien on his Seventieth Birthday* (London, 1962), pp. 231–40.

——, M. L. Samuels and Michael Benskin (eds), *A Linguistic Atlas of Late Medieval English* (4 vols, Aberdeen, 1986).

McKelvie, Gordon, *Bastard Feudalism, English Society and the Law: The Statutes of Livery, 1390–1520* (Woodbridge, 2020).

McLean, Will, 'Outrance and Plaisance', *Journal of Medieval Military History*, 8 (2010), 155–70.

Maddern, Philippa C., 'Social Mobility', in Rosemary Horrox and W. Mark Ormrod (eds), *A Social History of England, 1200–1500* (Cambridge, 2006), pp. 113–33.

Maddicott, J. R., *The English Peasantry and the Demands of the Crown, 1294–1341*, Past & Present Supplement, 1 (Cambridge, 1975).

—— 'Poems of Social Protest in Early Fourteenth-Century England', in W. Mark Ormrod (ed.), *England in the Fourteenth Century: Proceedings of the 1985 Harlaxton Symposium* (Woodbridge, 1986), pp. 130–44.

Mann, Jill, *Chaucer and Medieval Estates Satire: The Literature of Social Classes and the* General Prologue *to the* Canterbury Tales (Cambridge, 1973).

Martin, Diane, 'Prosecutions of the Statutes of Provisors and Praemunire in the King's Bench, 1377–1394', in Jeffrey Hamilton (ed.), *Fourteenth Century England VI* (Woodbridge, 2006), pp. 109–23.

Mate, Mavis E., 'The Agrarian Economy of South-East England before the Black Death: Depressed or Buoyant?', in Bruce M. S. Campbell (ed.), *Before the Black Death: Studies in the 'Crisis' of the Early Fourteenth Century* (Manchester, 1991), pp. 79–109.

—— 'Work and Leisure,' in Rosemary Horrox and W. Mark Ormrod (eds), *A Social History of England, 1200–1500* (Cambridge, 2006), pp. 276–92.

Mathews, Jana, 'The Case for Misprision in *Wynnere and Wastoure*', *Notes & Queries*, 46 (1999), 317–21.

Matthews, David, *Writing to the King: Nation, Kingship and Literature in England, 1250–1350* (Cambridge, 2010).

Mertes, Kate, 'The *Liber niger* of Edward IV: A New Version', *Bulletin of the Institute of Historical Research*, 54 (1981), 29–39.

Middleton, Anne, 'The Idea of Public Poetry in the Reign of Richard II', *Speculum*, 53 (1978), 94–114.

Mileson, S. A., *Parks in Medieval England* (Oxford, 2009).

Mills, Mabel H., 'The Collectors of the Customs', in J. F. Willard, W. A. Morris, J. R. Strayer and W. H. Dunham (eds), *The English Government at Work, 1327–1336* (3 vols, Cambridge, Massachusetts, 1940–50), vol. 2, pp. 168–200.

Mollat, Guy, 'Innocent VI et les tentatives de paix entre la France et l'Angleterre (1353–1355)', *Revue d'histoire ecclésiastique*, 10 (1909), 729–43.

Moorhouse, Stephen, 'The Medieval Parks of Yorkshire: Function, Contents and Chronology', in Robert Liddiard (ed.), *The Medieval Park: New Perspectives* (Macclesfield, 2007), pp. 99–127.

Moran, D. V., '*Wynnere and Wastoure*: An Extended Footnote', *Neuphilologische Mitteilungen*, 73 (1972), 683–5.

Moreton, C. E., 'A Social Gulf? The Upper and Lower Gentry of Later Medieval England', *Journal of Medieval History*, 17 (1991), 255–62.

Morgan, D. A. L., 'The Political After-life of Edward III: The Apotheosis of a Warmonger', *English Historical Review*, 112 (1997), 856–81.

Müller, Miriam, 'Food, Hierarchy and Class Conflict', in Richard Goddard, John Langdon and Miriam Müller (eds), *Survival and Discord in Medieval Society: Essays in Honour of Christopher Dyer* (Turnhout, 2010), pp. 231–48.

Munby, Julian, Richard Barber and Richard Brown, *Edward III's Round Table at Windsor: The House of the Round Table and the Windsor Festival of 1344* (Woodbridge, 2007).

Munro, John H. A., 'The Late Medieval Decline of English Demesne Agriculture: Demographic, Monetary, and Political-Fiscal Factors', in Mark Bailey (ed.), *Town and Countryside in the Age of the Black Death: Essays in Honour of John Hatcher* (Turnhout, 2012), pp. 299–348.

Murphy, Neil, *The Captivity of John II, 1356–60: The Royal Image in Later Medieval England and France* (Basingstoke, 2016).

Musson, Anthony, *Medieval Law in Context: The Growth of Legal Consciousness from Magna Carta to the Peasants' Revolt* (Manchester, 2001).

—— *Public Order and Law Enforcement: The Local Administration of Criminal Justice, 1294–1350* (Woodbridge, 1996).

—— 'Reconstructing English Labor Laws: A Medieval Perspective', in Kellie Robertson and Michael Uebel (eds), *The Middle Ages and Work: Practicing Labor in Late Medieval England* (New York, 2004), pp. 113–32.

—— and W. Mark Ormrod, *The Evolution of English Justice: Law, Politics and Society in the Fourteenth Century* (Basingstoke, 1999).

—— and Nigel Ramsay, 'Introduction', in Anthony Musson and Nigel Ramsay (eds), *Courts of Chivalry and Admiralty in Late Medieval Europe* (Woodbridge, 2018), pp. 1–13.

Neilson, George, 'A Note on *Wynnere and Wastoure*', *The Athenaeum*, 118, no. 3853 (7 September 1901), 319.

—— 'A Note on "Wynnere and Wastoure"', *The Athenaeum*, 118, no. 3849 (3 August 1901), 157.

—— 'A Note on "Wynnere and Wastoure"', *The Athenaeum*, 118, no. 3854 (7 September 1901), 319.

—— '"Wynnere and Wastoure"', *The Athenaeum*, 120, no. 3955 (15 August 1903), 221.

—— '"Wynnere and Wastoure" and the "Awntyres"', *The Athenaeum*, 120, no. 3946 (13 June 1903), 754–5.

Newton, Stella Mary, *Fashion in the Age of the Black Prince: A Study of the Years 1340–1365* (Woodbridge, 1980).

Nightingale, Pamela, *A Medieval Mercantile Community: The Grocers' Company and the Politics of Trade in London, 1000–1485* (London, 1995).

Nolan, Maura B., '"With tresone within": *Wynnere and Wastoure*, Chivalric Self-Representation, and the Law', *Journal of Medieval and Early Modern Studies*, 26 (1996), 1–28.

Offler, H. S., 'England and Germany at the Beginning of the Hundred Years' War', *English Historical Review*, 54 (1939), 608–31.

Ohlgren, Thomas, '*Edwardus redivivus* in *A Gest of Robyn Hode*', *Journal of English and Germanic Philology*, 15 (2000), 1–28.

Oliver, Clementine, *Political Pamphleteering in Fourteenth-Century England* (York, 2010).

Ormrod, W. Mark, 'Competing Capitals? York and London in the Fourteenth Century', in Sarah Rees Jones, Richard Marks and A. J. Minnis (eds), *Courts and Regions in Medieval Europe* (York, 2000), pp. 75–98.

—— 'The Crown and the English Economy, 1290–1348', in Bruce M. S. Campbell (ed.), *Before the Black Death: Studies in the 'Crisis' of the Early Fourteenth Century* (Manchester, 1991), pp. 149–83.

—— *Edward III* (London, 2011).

—— 'England in the Middle Ages', in Richard Bonney (ed.), *The Rise of the Fiscal State in Europe, c.1200–1815* (Oxford, 1999), pp. 19–52.

—— 'The English Crown and the Customs, 1349–63', *Economic History Review*, 2nd ser., 40 (1987), 27–40.

—— 'For Arthur and St George: Edward III, Windsor Castle and the Order of the Garter', in Nigel Saul (ed.), *St George's Chapel, Windsor, in the Fourteenth Century* (Woodbridge, 2005), pp. 13–34.

—— 'The Foundation and Early Development of the Order of the Garter in England, 1348–1399', *Frühmittelalterliche Studien*, 50 (2016), 361–92.

—— 'Parliament, Political Economy and State Formation in Later Medieval England', in Peter Hoppenbrouwers, Antheun Jansen and Robert Stein (eds), *Power and Persuasion: Essays on the Art of State Building in Honour of W. P. Blockmans* (Turnhout, 2010), pp. 123–39.

—— 'Parliamentary Scrutiny of Royal Ministers and Courtiers in Fourteenth-Century England: The Disgrace of Sir John Atte Lee (1368)', in Richard W. Kaeuper (ed.), *Law, Governance and Justice: New Views on Medieval Constitutionalism* (Leiden, 2013), pp. 161–88.

—— 'The Personal Religion of Edward III', *Speculum*, 64 (1989), 849–77.

—— *Political Life in Medieval England, 1300–1450* (Basingstoke, 1995).

—— 'A Problem of Precedence: Edward III, the Double Monarchy and the Royal Style', in James Bothwell (ed.), *The Age of Edward III* (York, 2000), pp. 133–54.

—— *The Reign of Edward III: Crown and Political Society in England, 1327–1377* (London, 1990).

—— 'The Royal Nursery: A Household for the Younger Children of Edward III', *English Historical Review*, 120 (2005), 398–415.

—— 'The Trials of Alice Perrers', *Speculum*, 83 (2008), 366–96.

—— 'The Use of English: Language, Law and Political Culture in Fourteenth-Century England', *Speculum*, 88 (2003), 750–87.

Palmer, J. J. N., 'England, France, the Papacy and the Flemish Succession, 1361–69', *Journal of Medieval History*, 2 (1976), 339–64.

—— and A. P. Wells, 'Ecclesiastical Reform and the Politics of the Hundred Years War during the Pontificate of Urban V (1362–70)', in C. T. Allmand (ed.), *War, Literature and Politics in the Late Middle Ages* (Liverpool, 1976), pp. 169–89.

Palmer, Robert C., *English Law in the Age of the Black Death, 1348–1381: A Transformation of Governance and Law* (London, 1993).

Payling, Simon J., 'Social Mobility, Demographic Change, and Landed Society in Late Medieval England', *Economic History Review*, 2nd ser., 45 (1992), 51–73.

Pearsall, Derek, 'The Origins of the Alliterative Revival', in Bernard S. Levy and Paul E. Szarmach (eds), *The Alliterative Tradition in the Fourteenth Century* (Kent, Ohio, 1981), pp. 1–24.

—— 'The Timeliness of *The Simonie*', in O. S. Pickering (ed.), *Individuality and Achievement in Middle English Poetry* (Cambridge, 1997), pp. 59–72.

Penn, S. A. C. and Christopher Dyer, 'Wages and Earnings in Late Medieval England: Evidence from the Enforcement of the Labour Laws', *Economic History Review*, 2nd ser., 43 (1990), 356–76.

Phillips, Kim, 'Masculinities and the Medieval English Sumptuary Laws', *Gender & History*, 19 (2007), 22–42.

Plöger, Karsten, *England and the Avignon Popes: The Practice of Diplomacy in Late Medieval Europe* (London, 2005).

Pollard, A. J., *Imagining Robin Hood* (London, 2004).

—— 'The North-Eastern Economy and the Agrarian Crisis of 1438–40', *Northern History*, 25 (1989), 88–105.

Postan, M. M., *Essays on Medieval Agriculture and General Problems of the Medieval Economy* (Cambridge, 1973).

—— *The Medieval Economy and Society* (Harmondsworth, 1970).

Powell, Edward, 'Arbitration and the Law in England in the Later Middle Ages', *Transactions of the Royal Historical Society*, 5th ser., 33 (1983), 49–67.

—— 'Settlement of Disputes by Arbitration in Fifteenth-Century England', *Law and History Review*, 2 (1984), 21–43.

Powell, J. Enoch and K. Wallis, *The House of Lords in the Middle Ages: A History of the English House of Lords to 1540* (London, 1967).

Powell, Susan, 'The Transmission and Circulation of *The Lay Folks' Catechism*', in Alastair J. Minnis (ed.), *Late-Medieval Religious Texts and their Transmission: Essays in Honour of A. I. Doyle* (Cambridge, 1994), pp. 67–84.

Prescott, Andrew, '"Great and horrible rumour": Shaping the English Revolt of 1381', in Justine Firnhaber-Baker and Dirk Schoenaers (eds), *The Routledge History Handbook of Medieval Revolt* (London, 2017), pp. 76–103.

Putnam, Bertha H., 'Chief Justice Shareshull and the Economic and Legal Codes of 1351–1352', *University of Toronto Law Journal*, 5 (1943–4), 251–81.

—— *The Place in Legal History of Sir William Shareshull, Chief Justice of the King's Bench* (Cambridge, 1950).

―― 'The Transformation of the Keepers of the Peace into the Justices of the Peace, 1327–1380', *Transactions of the Royal Historical Society*, 4th ser., 12 (1929), 19–48.

Rackham, Oliver, *Ancient Woodland: Its History, Vegetation and Uses in England* (London, 1980).

Rayborn, Tim, *Against the Friars: Antifraternalism in Medieval France and England* (Jefferson, North Carolina, 2014).

Reed, Thomas L., Jr, *Middle English Debate Poetry and the Aesthetics of Irresolution* (Columbia, Missouri, 1990).

Revard, Carter, 'The Outlaw's Song of Trailbaston', in Thomas H. Ohlgren (ed.), *Medieval Outlaws: Ten Tales in Modern English* (Stroud, 1998), pp. 99–105, 302–4, 329–31.

―― 'The Papelard Priest and the Black Prince's Men: Audiences of an Alliterative Poem, ca. 1350–1370', *Studies in the Age of Chaucer*, 23 (2001), 359–406.

―― 'Scribe and Provenance', in Susanna Fein (ed.), *Studies in the Harley Manuscript: The Scribes, Contents, and Social Contexts of British Library MS Harley 2253* (Kalamazoo, 2000), pp. 21–109.

Richardson, Amanda, *The Forest, Park and Palace of Clarendon, c.1200–c.1650*, British Archaeological Reports British Series, 387 (Oxford, 2005).

Rigby, Stephen H., 'English Society in the Later Middle Ages: Deference, Ambition and Conflict', in Peter Brown (ed.), *A Companion to Medieval English Literature and Culture, c.1350–c.1500* (Oxford, 2007), pp. 25–39.

―― 'Introduction', in Rosemary Horrox and W. Mark Ormrod (eds), *A Social History of England, 1200–1500* (Cambridge, 2006), pp. 1–30.

―― *English Society in the Later Middle Ages: Class, Status and Gender* (Basingstoke, 1995).

―― with Siân Echard (eds), *Historians on John Gower* (Cambridge, 2019).

Rigg, A. G., 'John of Bridlington's Prophecy: A New Look', *Speculum*, 63 (1988), 596–613.

Robbins, Rossell Hope, 'Poems Dealing with Contemporary Conditions', in E. Burke Severs and Albert E. Hartung (eds), *A Manual of the Writings in Middle English, 1050–1500* (8 vols, New Haven, 1967–89), vol. 5, pp. 1385–6.

Roebuck, Derek and Arthur L. Marriott, *Mediation and Arbitration in the Middle Ages: England, 1154–1558* (Oxford, 2013).

Rogers, Clifford, *War Cruel and Sharp: English Strategy under Edward III, 1327–1360* (Woodbridge, 2000).

Rollo-Koster, Joëlle, *Avignon and its Papacy, 1309–1417: Popes, Institutions, and Society* (London, 2015).

Roney, Lois, '*Winner and Waster*'s "Wyse Wordes": Teaching Economics and Nationalism in Fourteenth-Century England', *Speculum*, 69 (1994), 1070–1100.

Roskell, J. S., *The Impeachment of Michael de la Pole, Earl of Suffolk, in 1386* (Manchester, 1984).

Ruddick, Andrea, *English Identity and Political Culture in the Fourteenth Century* (Cambridge, 2013).

Russell, M. J., 'Trial by Battle in the Court of Chivalry', *Journal of Legal History*, 29 (2008), 335–57.

Salter, Elizabeth, *Fourteenth-Century English Poetry: Contexts and Readings* (Oxford, 1983).

—— 'The Timeliness of *Wynnere and Wastoure*', *Medium Aevum*, 47 (1978), 40–65, repr. in Elizabeth Salter, *English and International: Studies in the Literature, Art and Patronage of Medieval England*, ed. Derek Pearsall and Nicolette Zeeman (Cambridge, 1988), pp. 180–98.

Saul, Nigel, *Knights and Esquires: The Gloucestershire Gentry in the Fourteenth Century* (Oxford, 1981).

Scase, Wendy, 'Imagining Alternatives to the Book: The Transmission of Political Poetry in Late Medieval England', in Stephen Kelly and John J. Thompson (eds), *Imagining the Book* (Turnhout, 2005), pp. 237–50.

—— *Literature and Complaint in England, 1272–1553* (Oxford, 2007).

—— Piers Plowman *and the New Anticlericalism* (Cambridge, 1987).

—— 'Satire on the Retinues of the Great (MS Harley 2253): Unpaid Bills and the Politics of Purveyance', in Anne Marie D'Arcy and Alan John Fletcher (eds), *Studies in Late Medieval and Early Renaissance Texts in Honour of John Scattergood* (Dublin, 2005), pp. 305–20.

Scattergood, John, 'Authority and Resistance: The Political Verse', in Susanna Fein (ed.), *Studies in the Harley Manuscript: The Scribes, Contents, and Social Contexts of British Library MS Harley 2253* (Kalamazoo, 2000), pp. 163–201.

—— *Politics and Poetry in the Fifteenth Century* (London, 1971).

—— '*The Tale of Gamelyn*: The Noble Robber as Provincial Hero', in Carole M. Meale (ed.), *Readings in Medieval English Romance* (Cambridge, 1994), pp. 159–94.

—— '*Winner and Waster* and the Mid-Fourteenth-Century Economy', in Tom Dunne (ed.), *The Writer as Witness: Literature as Historical Evidence*, Historical Studies, 16 (Cork, 1987), pp. 39–57.

Schmidt, Karl-Heinz, 'Schumpeter and the Crisis of the Tax State', in Jürgen G. Backhaus (ed.), *Joseph Alois Schumpeter: Entrepreneurship, Style and Vision* (Boston, Massachusetts, 2003), pp. 337–51.

Schneider, Eric B., 'Prices and Production: Agricultural Supply Response in Fourteenth-Century England', *Economic History Review*, 2nd ser., 67 (2014), 66–91.

Schumpeter, J. A., 'The Crisis of the Tax State', *International Economic Papers*, 4 (1954), 5–38.

Seabourne, Gwen, *Royal Regulation of Loans and Sales in Medieval England: 'Monkish Superstition and Civil Tyranny'* (Woodbridge, 2003).

Shepherd, Geoffrey, 'The Nature of Alliterative Poetry in Late Medieval England', in J. A. Burrow (ed.), *Middle English Literature: British Academy Gollancz Lectures* (Oxford, 1989), 141–60.

Smallwood, T. M., 'The Prophecy of the Six Kings', *Speculum*, 60 (1985), 571–92.

Smith, D. Vance, *Arts of Possession: The Middle English Household Imaginary* (Minneapolis, 2003).

Somerset, Fiona, *Clerical Discourse and Lay Audience in Late Medieval England* (Cambridge, 1998).

Spearing, A. C., *Medieval Dream-Poetry* (Cambridge, 1976).

Speirs, John, *Medieval English Poetry: The Non-Chaucerian Tradition*, 2nd edn (London, 1971).

Spence, John, *Reimagining History in Anglo-Norman Prose Chronicles* (York, 2013).

Starkey, David, 'The Age of the Household: Politics, Society and the Arts, *c*.1350–*c*.1550', in Stephen Medcalf (ed.), *The Context of English Literature: The Later Middle Ages* (London, 1981), pp. 225–90.

Steadman, J. M., 'The Date of *Winnere and Wastoure*', *Modern Philology*, 19 (1921), 211–19.

Steel, Anthony, *The Receipt of the Exchequer, 1377–1485* (Cambridge, 1954).

Steiner, Emily, *Reading* Piers Plowman (Cambridge, 2013).

Stern, Karen, 'The London Thornton Miscellany: A New Description of BM Addit. MS. 31042', *Scriptorium*, 30 (1976), 26–37, 210–18.

Stillwell, Gardiner, '*Wynnere and Wastoure* and the Hundred Years' War', *ELH*, 8 (1941), 241–7.

Stokes, Myra, *Justice and Mercy in Piers Plowman: A Reading of the B Text Visio* (London, 1984).

Storey, R. L., 'Gentleman-bureaucrats', in C. H. Clough (ed.), *Profession, Vocation and Culture in Later Medieval England: Essays Dedicated to the Memory of A. R. Myers* (Liverpool, 1982), pp. 90–129.

Stubbs, William, *The Constitutional History of England*, 4th edn (3 vols, Oxford, 1906).

Summerson, Henry, 'Grey, John, First Lord Grey of Rotherfield (1300–1359)' 'Oxford Dictionary of National Biography' (online): https://doi-org/10.1093/ref:odnb/11544 (accessed 23 January 2019).

Sumption, Jonathan, *The Hundred Years War* (4 vols, London, 1990–2015).

Sutton, Anne F., *The Mercery of London: Trade, Goods and People, 1130–1578* (Aldershot, 2005).

Sweeten, David, '"Whoso wele schal wyn, a wastour moste he fynde": Intereliant Economies and Social Capital', in Craig E. Bertolet and Robert Epstein (eds), *Money, Commerce, and Economics in Late Medieval English Literature* (Basingstoke, 2018), pp. 31–46.

Szittya, Penn R., *The Antifraternal Tradition in Medieval Literature* (Princeton, 1986).

Tavormina, M. Theresa, *Kindly Similitude: Marriage and Family in* Piers Plowman (Cambridge, 1995).

Taylor, John, *English Historical Literature in the Fourteenth Century* (Oxford, 1987).

Tebbit, Alistair, 'Household Knights and Military Service under the Direction of Edward II', in Gwilym Dodd and Anthony Musson (eds), *The Reign of Edward II: New Perspectives* (York, 2006), pp. 76–96.

—— 'Royal Patronage and Political Allegiance: The Household Knights of Edward II', in Michael Prestwich, Richard Britnell and Robin Frame (eds), *Thirteenth Century England X* (Woodbridge, 2005), pp. 197–208.

Tompkins, Laura, 'Alice Perrers and the Goldsmiths' Mistery: New Evidence Concerning the Identity of Edward III's Mistress', *English Historical Review*, 130 (2015), 1361–91.

Tout, Thomas Frederick, *Chapters in the Administrative History of Mediaeval England* (6 vols, Manchester, 1920–33).

—— 'The Household of the Chancery and its Disintegration', in H. W. C. Davis (ed.), *Essays in History Presented to Reginald Lane Poole* (Oxford, 1927), pp. 46–85.

—— 'Literature and Learning in the English Civil Service in the Fourteenth Century', *Speculum*, 4 (1929), 365–89.

—— and Dorothy M. Broome, 'A National Balance Sheet for 1362–3', *English Historical Review*, 39 (1924), 404–19.

Trautz, Fritz, *Die Könige von England und das Reich, 1272–1377* (Heidelberg, 1961).

Trigg, Stephanie, 'Israel Gollancz's "Wynnere and Wastoure": Political Satire or Editorial Politics?', in Gregory Krutzmann and James Simpson (eds), *Medieval English Religious and Ethical Literature: Essays in Honour of G. H. Russell* (Cambridge, 1986), pp. 115–27.

—— 'The Rhetoric of Excess in *Winner and Waster*', *Yearbook of Langland Studies*, 3 (1989), 91–108, repr. in Stephanie Trigg (ed.), *Medieval English Poetry* (London, 1993), pp. 186–202.

—— *Shame and Honor: A Vulgar History of the Order of the Garter* (Philadelphia, 2012).

Turner, Marion, *Chaucer: A European Life* (Princeton, 2019).

Turville-Petre, Thorlac, *The Alliterative Revival* (Cambridge, 1977).

—— *England the Nation: Language, Literature, and National Identity, 1290–1340* (Oxford, 1996).

—— 'Humphrey de Bohun and *William of Palerne*', *Neuphilologische Mitteilungen*, 75 (1974), 250–2.

—— 'The Prologue of *Wynnere and Wastoure*', *Leeds Studies in English*, new ser., 18 (1987), 19–29.

—— '*Wynnere and Wastoure*: When and Where?', in L. A. J. R. Houwen and A. A. McDonald (eds), *Loyal Letters: Studies on Medieval Alliterative Poetry & Prose* (Groningen, 1994), pp. 155–66.

Unwin, George, 'The Estate of Merchants, 1336–1365', in George Unwin (ed.), *Finance and Trade under Edward III* (Manchester, 1918), pp. 179–255.

Vale, Juliet, *Edward III and Chivalry: Chivalric Society and Its Contexts, 1270–1350* (Woodbridge, 1982).

—— 'Violence and the Tournament', in Richard W. Kaeuper (ed.), *Violence in Medieval Society* (Woodbridge, 2000), pp. 143–58.

Vale, Malcolm, 'England, France and the Origins of the Hundred Years War', in Michael Jones and Malcolm Vale (eds), *England and her Neighbours, 1066–1453: Essays in Honour of Pierre Chaplais* (London, 1989), pp. 199–216.

Wagner, Anthony Richard, *Heralds and Heraldry in the Middle Ages* (Oxford, 1939).

—— *Heralds of England: A History of the Office and College of Arms* (London, 1967).

Walker, Simon, *The Lancastrian Affinity, 1361–1399* (Oxford, 1990).

Walsh, Katherine, *A Fourteenth-Century Scholar and Primate: Richard FitzRalph in Oxford, Avignon and Armagh* (Oxford, 1981).

Warner, Lawrence, 'Langland and the Problem of *William of Palerne*', *Viator*, 37 (2006), 397–415.

—— *The Myth of* Piers Plowman: *Constructing a Medieval Literary Archive* (Cambridge, 2014).

Watts, John, *The Making of Polities: Europe, 1300–1500* (Cambridge, 2009).

Weiskott, Eric, *English Alliterative Verse: Poetic Tradition and Literary History* (Cambridge, 2016).

Wilks, Michael, *Wyclif: Political Ideas and Practice* (Oxford, 2000).

Wilson, Christopher, 'The Royal Lodgings of Edward III at Windsor Castle: Form, Function, Representation', in Laurence Keen and Eileen Scarff (eds), *Windsor: Medieval Archaeology, Art and Architecture of the Thames Valley*, British Archaeological Association Conference Transactions, 25 (Leeds, 2002), pp. 15–94.

Wood, Diana, *Clement VI: The Pontificate and Ideas of an Avignon Pope* (Cambridge, 1989).

Woolgar, Christopher M., *The Culture of Food in England, 1200–1500* (London, 2016).

—— *The Great Household in Late Medieval England* (London, 1999).

Yunck, John A., *The Lineage of Lady Meed: The Development of Mediaeval Venality Satire* (South Bend, 1963).

Online resources

'The Anglo-Norman Online Hub: Anglo-Norman Dictionary', http://www.anglo-norman.net (accessed 10 March 2020).

'The Digital Index of Middle English Verse', https://www.dimev.net (accessed 10 March 2020).

'Middle English Dictionary', quod.lib.umich.edu (accessed 10 March 2020).

'Winner and Waster: Translation' in 'Wessex Parallel WebTexts', www.soton.ac.uk/~wpwt/trans/winner/wintrans.htm (accessed 10 March 2020).

Unpublished Dissertations and Theses

Brayson, Alex, 'The Fiscal Constitution of Later Medieval England: The Reign of Henry VI' (Unpublished Ph.D. thesis, University of York, 2013).

Elema, Ariella, 'Trial by Battle in France and England' (Unpublished Ph.D. dissertation, University of Toronto, 2012).

Hefferan, Matthew, 'Edward III's Household Knights in War and Peace, 1327–1377' (Unpublished Ph.D. thesis, University of Nottingham, 2018).

Lutkin, Jessica, 'Goldsmiths and the English Court, 1360–1413' (Unpublished Ph.D. thesis, University of London, 2008).

Martin, Emma, 'The Performance of Idleness in Late Medieval English Society: Work, Leisure and the Sin of Sloth' (Unpublished Ph. D. thesis, University of York, 2017).

Ormrod, W. Mark, 'Edward III's Government of England, *c.*1346–*c.*1356' (Unpublished D.Phil. thesis, University of Oxford, 1984).

Shenton, Caroline, 'The English Court and the Restoration of Royal Prestige, 1327–1345' (Unpublished D.Phil. thesis, University of Oxford, 1995).

Verduyn, A. J., 'The Attitude of the Parliamentary Commons to Law and Order under Edward III' (Unpublished D.Phil. thesis, University of Oxford, 1991).

Index

Alliterative Morte Arthure 3
Alliterative Revival 118–20, 136
Aristotle 12, 48, 111
Aubrichecourt, Eustace d' 50
Augustine, saint 12, 111
Avignon 29, 31, 117–18

Black Book of the Household 89
Black Death 65, 75, 131–2
Bohun, Humphrey de (d. 1373), earl of Hereford 123
Boulogne, Guy de, bishop of Porto 31
Bradestone, Thomas 58
Brampton, John 59
Brétigny, treaty of (1360) 34
Brutus of Troy 10

Calais 10, 34, 132
   treaty of (1360) 34–5, 91, 103
Capocci, Nicola, cardinal 32
Chandos Herald, *Life of the Black Prince* 121, 126, 127
Chaucer, Geoffrey 3, 12–13, 121
   Canterbury Tales 110, 113
Chester, palatinate of 6, 45–6
   eyre of Cheshire (1353) 11, 39, 44–6, 60, 71, 125
chivalry, court of 51–2, 128
Clarendon (Wilts) 17
Clement VI, pope 30–31
Cologne 2, 32–3
Conisburgh (Yorks) 123
Cornwall 45
Coucy, Enguerrand de (d. 1397), earl of Bedford 24
Crécy, battle of (1346) 10, 132

Cromwell, Ralph (d. 1456), treasurer 135
Darnhall (Cheshire) 71
David II, king of Scotland 14, 23–4
Denbigh, lordship of 45
Despenser family 120
   Eleanor (née Clare), wife Hugh Despenser the Younger 54
Devil 2, 20, 115
Devon 45

Eam, Henry 50
East Newton (Yorks) 1, 134
Edington, William, bishop of Winchester 124
Edmund of Langley (d. 1402), earl of Cambridge 36, 123
Edward I, king of England 16
Edward III, king of England 33–7
   as arbiter 39, 51–7
   and the Church 28–9, 31–2
   depiction in *W&W* 10–11, 89, 92–3, 99, 129, 132–5
   expenditure of 92–3, 95, 100–2, 132
   finances of 76–7, 82–95, 98–9, 100–3
   heraldry and badges of 1, 5, 126–7, 128
   household of 14, 49–50, 57–60, 83–9, 92, 97–8, 101, 103, 123, 132
   and Order of the Garter 14, 15, 18–20, 22–4
Edward of Woodstock, prince of Wales *alias* Black Prince (d. 1376) 6, 8, 9, 11, 16, 19, 23, 24, 37, 39, 44–6, 123, 125–6
Erghome, John 99–100, 102

FitzRalph, Richard, archbishop of Armagh 28, 29, 30

Garter, Order of the 1, 5, 12, 15, 18–19, 21–2, 123–4, 131
  foundation of 10, 11, 18
  Garter feasts 18–19, 21, 24, 128
    feast of 1358 11, 14, 15, 22–5, 27, 37, 95, 128, 131
  heraldry and insignia of 17, 18, 21–2
Gaytryge, John, *Lay Folk's Catechism* 124–5
Gower, John 102, 121–2, 129
Gray, Thomas (d. 1369), of Heton 35, 37, 121
Green, Henry, chief justice of king's bench 46–7, 48
Grey, John (d. 1359), of Rotherfield 54–5, 58
Grosmont, Henry of (d. 1361), duke of Lancaster 20, 23, 53, 123
Guînes, peace conference at (1353–4) 31

Henry IV, king of England 121
Henry V, king of England 122, 135
Henry VI, king of England 135
heralds 23, 24, 51–2, 127–8
Hoccleve, Thomas 122, 129
Hundred Years War 11, 15, 29, 32, 34, 36, 83–4, 99, 132

Innocent III, pope 32, 36
Innocent VI, pope 29, 32
Isabella of Woodstock, daughter of Edward III 24

Joan of Kent, princess of Wales and Aquitaine 24
John, king of England 32, 36
John II, king of France 14, 22, 23–4, 31–2, 34–5, 37, 53, 91, 95, 103
John of Gaunt (d. 1399), duke of Lancaster 123, 126

Kings Langley (Herts) 92

Lancaster, duke of *see* Grosmont; John of Gaunt

Langland, William, *Piers Plowman* 3, 11, 35, 37, 70, 103, 106, 109–10, 114, 115–17, 119, 120, 122
Latimer, William (d. 1381), steward of the king's household 102
Lee, John atte (d. 1370), steward of the king's household 59–60, 101, 117, 131
Lincoln 46
Lionel of Antwerp (d. 1368), duke of Clarence 123
Lisle, Thomas de, bishop of Ely 28–9, 30, 32, 125
London 2, 4, 31, 76, 96–8
  Tower of 91, 98, 103
  treaty of (1358) 32
Louis IX, king of France 44
Ludwig IV, holy roman emperor 33

Marche, Thomas de la 52, 57
Mauny, Walter (d. 1372) 50
mendicants 25–30, 37, 112–14
merchants 86, 98, 105–6
Molyns, John (d. 1360) 58, 59
Montague, William (d. 1344), earl of Salisbury 8
Morton, John, archbishop of Canterbury, chancellor 99

Neville, John (d. 1388), steward of the king's household 102
Neville's Cross, battle of (1346) 10, 132

On the Follies of Fashion 114–15
ordinances
  Labourers (1349) 65, 72
  Provisors (1343) 31
  Staple (1353) 98 & n. 40
Otto III, duke of Brunswick–Lüneburg 53
Outlaw's Song of Trailbaston 109–11

Pagula, William of 121
papacy 29–32, 36, 114, 117–18
Paris 32–4, 36, 53, 95–6
parliament 51, 77, 99, 100–1, 103
  sessions of
    1332 41

1343   30
1351   41
1352   6, 9, 40–2, 83–4
1355   28
1358   32
1361   35
1362   11, 41, 90, 131
1363   11, 73–6, 78, 81, 128
1365   11, 36, 41, 80–1, 90, 128, 131
1366   36, 41
1368   41, 69, 90, 101, 131
1376 (Good Parliament)   102, 103, 131
1386 (Wonderful Parliament)   103
1388 (Merciless Parliament)   103
Pearl (Gawain) Poet   3, 46
  Sir Gawain and the Green Knight   3, 10, 22, 129
Peasants' Revolt (1381)   71, 106–7, 109
Perrers, Alice   100, 102, 117 n. 34
Philippa of Hainault, queen of England, wife of Edward III   23, 92
Pickering family   134
Pierce the Ploughman's Crede   114
Poitiers, battle of (1356)   10, 22, 32, 37
Pole, Michael de la (d. 1389), earl of Suffolk   77, 126
Pole, William de la (d. 1366)   77, 84, 126
Prophecy of John of Bridlington   99
Prophecy of the Six Kings   33

Rheims   34
Richard II, king of England   46
Rome   2, 32, 95–6, 112, 117–18

Satire on the Consistory Courts   109
Scrope, Geoffrey, chief justice of king's bench   41
Shareshull, William, chief justice of king's bench   5–6, 7, 10, 29, 40–8, 60, 72, 111, 124–5, 131, 132
Sheppey, Isle of (Kent)   92
The Simonie   109, 112–13, 118
Song against the Friars   110, 113
Song against the King's Taxes   86, 106, 107–9, 121

Song of the Husbandman   86, 106
Song on the Venality of the Judges   109, 110
statutes
  Forestalling (1351)   72
  Labourers (1351)   9, 65, 69, 71–2
  Praemunire (1353)   28–9, 31
  Provisors (1351)   31
  Purveyors (1362)   93–4, 101
  Sumptuary Laws (1363)   14, 73–81, 114–15, 117, 121, 131
  Treasons (1352)   6, 11, 14, 39, 42–4, 60
  Weights and Measures (1352)   72
Sumner, Henry, chancellor of the exchequer   122

Tale of Gamelyn   110
Talleyrand, Hélie, cardinal of Périgord   30–2
taxation, papal   32, 36
taxation, royal   11, 83–5, 88, 89–91, 100–3, 135
Thoresby, John, archbishop of York   29, 124–5
Thornton, Robert   1, 4, 14, 127, 133–6
Thorpe, Robert, chief justice of common pleas   29
Thorpe, William, chief justice of king's bench   46–7, 48
tournaments   6, 15–27, 31, 37

Urban V, pope   36, 117–18

Vale Royal Abbey (Cheshire)   16, 71
Viscount, John   52, 57
Volaunt, William   23, 127–8

Wake, Lady Blanche   28
Wenceslaus I, duke of Luxembourg and Brabant   23
Westminster Palace   52, 92
William of Palerne   21, 119, 120–1
Winchester Castle (Hants)   126–7
Windsor (Berks)   17–20, 126
  castle   17, 24, 92
  Garter Feasts at   *see* Garter, Order of

Round Table at (1344)   19–20
Great Park   4, 17, 20, 37
Wingfield, John (d. 1361)   8, 125–6, 131
Winner and Waster
  audience of   12, 21, 81, 109, 110, 128–9, 133–6
  author of   12–13, 15, 46–7, 102–3, 109, 110, 115, 120–5, 128–9
  characters in
    first knight *alias* wild man/ *wodewyse*   1, 5
    king   1–2, 16–17, 32–3, 36, 43, 84, 86–7, 102, 132–3
      as arbiter   39–40, 50, 53–60, 95–7, 99, 112, 129
    lawyers   25–7, 44, 47–8, 63, 110–12
    men–at–arms   25–7, 37, 63
    mendicants   25–30, 37, 112–14
    merchants   25–6, 63, 84
    pope   26–7, 29–30, 113–14, 118
    Scharshull *see* Shareshull, William
    second knight *alias* herald/ knight–messenger   1–2, 6, 8–9, 25, 40, 42–5, 48–9, 50–1, 57–8, 113, 125–8
    Wastoure   2, 8, 10–11, 21, 42, 43–4, 47–8, 53–4, 56, 66–7, 70, 71–2, 74, 78–80, 81, 83, 89, 93–7, 98, 110–11, 112
      character of   2
      followers of   25–7, 79
      as member of the royal household   49–60, 86–7
      as personification of Edward III   89, 92–3, 99
      as representation of landed elite   61–5
    Wynnere   2, 8, 10–11, 21, 32, 36, 43–4, 53–4, 56, 66–7, 72, 78–80, 83–4, 89, 93–7, 98, 99, 112, 118
      character of   2
      followers of   25–7, 63, 84, 110–11
      as member of the royal household   49–60, 86–7
      as personification of Edward III   89, 92–3, 99
      as representation of merchant class   61–5, 84
  date of composition   3, 5–13, 15, 21, 37, 39, 60, 81–2, 83, 98–9, 115–20, 131, 133
  dialect   4, 6, 13, 45–6, 123
  editions of   ix, 139
  heraldry in   5, 8, 27, 126–8
  manuscript of   1–2, 133
  metre   3, 48
  patronage of   123–5
  performance of   p. 6 n.16, 54, 128
  popularity of   133
  setting of   16–19
Wyclif, John   102

York   46, 47, 124

Zouche, William de la (d. 1337), of Ashby   54–5, 58

Publisher's Note

Sadly, Mark Ormrod died shortly after delivering the manuscript to us – which was, despite everything, typically meticulously prepared. We are honoured to publish his final book.

We would like to acknowledge, with tremendous gratitude, the invaluable assistance of Sebastian Sobecki, for reading through the text, and Robert Kinsey, one of Mark's former PhD students, for preparing the index. The volume could not have appeared without them.

Caroline Palmer
Editorial Director: Medieval Studies
December 2020

www.ingramcontent.com/pod-product-compliance
Lightning Source LLC
Chambersburg PA
CBHW080837230426
43665CB00021B/2869